COMPETITIVE

COMMUNICATION

A Rhetoric for Modern Business

BARRY ECKHOUSE

New York • Oxford

OXFORD UNIVERSITY PRESS

1999

Oxford University Press

Oxford New York
Athens Auckland Bangkok Bogotá Buenos Aires Calcutta
Cape Town Chennai Dar es Salaam Delhi Florence Hong Kong Istanbul
Karachi Kuala Lumpur Madrid Melbourne Mexico City Mumbai
Nairobi Paris São Paulo Singapore Taipei Tokyo Toronto Warsaw

and associated companies in
Berlin Ibadan

Published by Oxford University Press, Inc.
198 Madison Avenue, New York, New York 10016
http://www.oup-usa.org

Oxford is a registered trademark of Oxford University Press

Library of Congress Cataloging-in-Publication Data
Eckhouse, Barry Edward.
    Competitive communication : a rhetoric for modern business / Barry
Eckhouse.
        p. cm.
    Includes bibliographical references and index.
    ISBN 978-0-19-511590-1
    1. Business communication.   2. English language—Business English.
3. English language—Rhetoric.   4. Competition.   I. Title.
HF5718.E25   1999
808'.06665—DC21   98-14425
                                                                  CIP

Printed in the United States of America
on acid-free paper.

CONTENTS

■ Chapter 7   **Managing Ethos: Argument and Credibility 119**

■ Chapter 8   **Managing Ethos: Conciseness   131**

PREFACE

This book is about *competitive communication*, the kind of communication that seeks and competes for an audience's attention, agreement, or action. Although such communication is not limited to the world of business, I will suggest that it is a particularly intelligent way to think about the important exchanges that take place there. This book is also an *example* of competitive communication, since it is an attempt to present my readers with something that is different in the field of business communication and something that I hope will be of value to them as practitioners.

This book differs from others in several respects. First, it emphasizes the competitive dimension of communication in a way that should be familiar to anyone who is aware of contemporary business trends and practice. *Competition* is a term frequently used in discussions of modern business, though it has yet to be used to describe the kind of communication that takes place there. By using it as an organizing concept for this book, I hope to provide my readers with a way of understanding communication that is already familiar to them through their practice in business.

This book differs from others in another, more significant respect. It emphasizes the construction of arguments, an intellectual activity that blurs the distinction between communication and thought (not that it was ever that clear to begin with). Such emphasis is almost absent from the current market of books on business communication. Although some have discussed persuasion, and others have given attention to the parts of an argument, few have said anything about how argument, as a specific form of persuasion, is constructed or presented. This is especially unfortunate because argument, as a useful form of reasoned persuasion, is indispensable to working professionals who must convince others of their point of view. It is also indispensable if one is to be clear about one's point of view in the first place.

A unique feature of this book is its reliance on the discipline of rhetoric and its use of classical and contemporary models to provide the practitioner with a systematic approach to constructing an argument, from the initial stages of the plan to the final steps of the presentation. Although I do not continually refer to Aristotle's *enthymeme* by its Greek name, this logical device nevertheless serves as the foundation of discussion and practice in Chapters 3 through 6. This book offers the first extensive application of this classical device in business communication and extends its usefulness in composition by integrating it with the proofline, a diagram for representing reasoning, developed by the English philosopher Stephen Toulmin.

This book also differs from others in its discussion of the rhetorical concept of ethos and Aristotle's three qualities of intelligence, character, and goodwill. I discuss ethos at chapter length, and I attempt to use it as a unifying concept for a string of concerns that others have treated as relatively isolated and unconnected. Among these concerns are goodwill letters, the "you attitude," sexism in language, and other matters that I hope will be better understood if an underlying principle is offered. To do this, I offer ethos as part of a systematic approach to managing language in the process of revision. I offer five categories that constitute an ordered procedure for learning techniques of revision and thus managing ethos. Each category is distinct, yet each is related to the next in a way that should provide comprehensiveness without confusion. These chapters on revising for ethos draw on recent studies of business communication or authoritative studies of usage to avoid longstanding but groundless advice on matters that affect readability. Where research is unavailable, I have provided reasons for the reader to consider.

If this book differs from others because of what it covers, it also differs because of what it does not cover. For example, I do not say much about the importance of effective communication or about its role in the business organization. Almost every major survey of working professionals shows that the ability to communicate effectively ranks at the very top of contributors to job effectiveness, satisfaction, and success. Other surveys indicate that writing and speaking are the major forms of transmission in the business organization. For that very reason, I have omitted coverage of it in this book. I am assuming that my readers appreciate the critical importance of communicating effectively in business, know how it figures into their organization, and are interested primarily in improving their understanding and ability.

Nor do I discuss at any length how changes in the shape of modern business appear to be increasing the premium that managers have long placed on an ability to communicate effectively. I decided not to bring this into the discussion even though one of my reviewers made several excellent points about how the well-documented movement from manufacturing to service industries has in turn moved communication from an ancillary role to a central one, so much so that one can now say "talk is work." Although I believe this is true, I also believe that it argues less for its inclusion in the discussion of this book and more for being mindful of the increased value argument acquires as a consequence of it.

I have also not said much about formats or technology, the containers and conductors of messages in business, though both are commonly covered at length in other major texts. Whether one writes in the format of a memo or letter or leaves a voice message is important in several respects, but I believe matters of format and medium are separable from the critical considerations in communicating competitively. Thus, readers will not find material in this book classified by formats such as "memo," or document types such as "bad-news letters" or "sales reports" unless this material serves as examples. These formats and types contain messages that have more in common with each other than their cosmetic differences might suggest. Therefore, I have resisted discussing formats and types. I have instead emphasized messages by concentrating on similarities in structure and strategy.

As a topic for discussion, technology is more difficult to resist. The growth in this area in general and its influence on business messages in particular make it an excellent candidate for discussion in a book on communication in business. Hypertext, multimedia presentation, workgroup writing, and Internet-based exchange are all areas that might make a book on business communication appear incomplete if they were omitted. However, I have not covered them here because I wish to direct specific attention to the business communicator's message, not so much to the way it is entered, stored, or transmitted. The one exception is my treatment of computer-assisted text analysis, which I have covered in a final chapter on ethos. I have included this because my business students, who are also working professionals, are relying on this form of analysis with increasing frequency and because impressive improvements in parsing technology show it can contribute to text revision in ways not possible at the time the second edition of this book was written.

I have also not tried to cover many other matters that are covered in other books, particularly if they have been covered well. As Macon Leary says in Anne Tyler's *Accidental Tourist,* "In travel, as in life, less is invariably more." I believe this, to a degree, and I have tried to keep it in mind while writing this book. I have looked for ways to limit the material here to concerns that I believe are relevant to my readers and to limit even those concerns to controlled discussions. In those discussions, I have tried to follow my own advice on conciseness. In these matters, I hope my readers also find that this book differs from others.

Finally, this book differs in the most important way, in its prospective audience. It is intended primarily for graduate students of business, particularly those in traditional executive MBA programs, or for serious undergraduates with a strong interest in argument, persuasion, and the world of business. This appears to me only fitting because these are the kinds of students who most helped to create it. They are graduate business students at Saint Mary's College of California, graduates and undergraduates at the Haas School of Business at the University of California, Berkeley, and working professionals in a variety of businesses and industries. The work they produce is the best test of the material covered in this book, and I am delighted to feature some of their work in the three appendices.

About This Edition

First published in 1993 as *Competitive Writing*, this book has undergone extensive revision as a consequence of review by my academic colleagues and use by my graduate students and other working professionals. However, the most apparent change is probably the least substantial: the emphasis on communication, both writing and speaking, as opposed to writing only. This change, suggested by several of my academic colleagues, simply recognizes that most of what I have said about writing in the first edition applies equally to oral messages. Although the two media are certainly different in important ways, and communicators will do well to respect this, I believe that any difference in the media will have little to do with processes I discuss. Constructing a claim, discovering its support, and determining opposition are among the more important events of developing an argument, and they are relatively unaffected by the choice of oral or written presentation.

Nevertheless, several changes are substantial and worth comment. The first is the increased attention to rhetoric and argument. All of the reviewers, including students and other working professionals, had hoped for more on this, and I hope in turn they will be happy with the additions. An original second chapter on argument has been expanded to four chapters, including an entirely new one on the ethics of argument and fallacies of reasoning. To prepare the reader for these chapters, I provided another new chapter, a case study that introduces the foundation concepts of rhetoric and competition as part of an actual firm's efforts at gaining advantage in an increasingly competitive marketplace.

Another major change is worth additional comment here, in part because it represents a way of resolving several apparently conflicting views. A number of my academic reviewers felt strongly that the five sections on editing and readability, while important, were finally too basic and that they distracted from the more intellectually engaging material on argumentation. They felt that a better connection was needed between these sections and the emphasis on rhetoric that characterized the rest of the book. Although I agree that the sections on argument are more engaging, my own students have persuaded me (not always an easy task) that these chapters are both important and appropriate for a book that concentrates on argument. They felt that the presentation of readability in the context of competition made good sense. They also felt that the probability of success in argument would be greatly influenced by readable prose. I agree with them, and I agree with my colleagues. As a consequence, I have tried to respond to students and colleagues alike by recasting these sections into an extended discussion of rhetorical ethos, which strikes me as a good solution, and one that I hope will not run the risk of displeasing both groups. However, having said that, I will add that the next edition of this book may well appear in two volumes: one will be devoted to invention and composition; the other to analysis and editorial review. Should that happen, the work would follow the more classical division of invention and judgment, or rhetoric and dialectic. Until then, I hope the present work will be well received both by those who study communication in the world of business and by those who practice it.

Competitive Communication on the Web: www.rhetor.com

This edition features a web site that contains selected material in searchable form, as well as additions or revisions that may be made after publication. Students, teachers, trainers, and others are invited to visit this site for updates and exercises that may be used to supplement the text in teaching or independent learning. Located at www.rhetor.com, this site also offers a threaded discussion board and a response form for readers who want to exchange comments on the book and contribute to its development and improvement.

Questions or comments to the author may be made at the web site, through the discussion boards, feedback sections, or directly by e-mail to barry@rhetor.com.

Acknowledgments

Generous people from both academic and corporate communities have reviewed parts of the manuscript for this book, contributed important examples to the presentation, or promoted in other ways the overall effort of this literary production. I want to thank them now.

My colleagues at colleges and universities across the United States include Victoria Aarons, Trinity University; Paul Argenti, Dartmouth College; William Baker, Brigham Young University; Stephanie Bobo, University of California, Berkeley; Marvin Brown, University of San Francisco; William Crisman, Pennsylvania State University; John Gage, University of Oregon; Janice McCormick, Harvard University; Thomas McCullough, University of California, Berkeley; Claudia McIsaac, Santa Clara University; Arthur Quinn, University of California, Berkeley; Amelia Van Vleck, University of Texas, Austin; Joan Vesper, University of Washington; Alistair Williamson, Harvard Business School Press; and Michele Zak, Stanford University. To my special colleague and fellow rhetorician, Rebecca Carroll, I am grateful beyond words, for her invaluable review of my work and for the light she has brought into my life.

I also wish to thank those who have helped to complement the contributions of my academic colleagues by "insisting" that the principles of this book have a place in the practice of working professionals. Valued contributors here include Bert Armijo, Mobius Technologies; Ken Donnelly, Bay Area Rapid Transit; Richard Dorfman, General Electric; Chuck Drake, Clorox Company; Crystal Elledge, Pacific Bell; Pam Harris, Kaiser Permanente; Michael Hassel, Kalok Corporation; Jon Jardine, Bank of America; Marian Kinblad, Harris & Associates; Rod Maslowski, Pacific Gas and Electric; John Miller, Tosco Oil; Dick Robinson, Frito Lay; Bette Smith, Pacific Bell; Teresa Supnet-Rosa, McCormick & Company; and Tom Teel, John Wagner Associates.

Oxford University Press joins me in expressing strong appreciation to the following reviewers: Michele Zak, Stanford University; William Sonnenschein, University of California, Berkeley; Jeanette W. Gilsdorf, California State University, Long Beach; David Morand, Penn State University, Harrisburg; Marshall Scott Poole, Texas A&M University; Russell W. Driver, University of Oklahoma; and James Suchan, Naval Postgraduate School. Their examination of the manuscript during the early stages of this project has helped to insure that the audience for this book will be well served.

I am especially grateful to the architects and management of MBT Associates and David Lindemulder, their Vice President of Marketing, for their willingness to let me discuss them in the first chapter of this book. I believe they are taking the right rhetorical steps to gain advantage as communicators in a very competitive industry, and I hope the good example they have set will be followed by others.

I wish in addition to thank Kenneth MacLeod, Senior Editor at Oxford University Press, for supporting this effort to link two disciplines not often connected in the publishing world. In an early letter of review, he wrote: "I was initially interested in your project because of the linkage you provide between rhetoric, an area with a long-standing tradition at Oxford, and business strategy, a new and important area of concentration. Unfortunately, too few books, trade or text, link the liberal arts and business." He has certainly maintained that interest, and I very much appreciate his professionalism and commitment to this project.

A very special thanks to the Saint Mary's College Alumni Association for their generous funding of my recent research on argument. Their support enabled me to continue my discussions and an exchange of ideas and materials with members of the Communications Program at the Harvard Business School, where William Ellet was my collegial and gracious host. There I have twice had the pleasure of working with a team of writing instructors who possess an extraordinary level of talent and dedication. I would like to thank them for their interest in my work and for their contributions to it: Janice Blake, Shelley Fishman, Peter Segal, John Sturtevant, and Patti Toland.

Finally, I am very grateful to my good friends and colleagues who encouraged me to reconstruct this project after completed portions of the original manuscript were destroyed in the Oakland Hills fire.

Orinda, California   B.E.
January 1998

INTRODUCTION

▓ Competition and Communication

This book argues that communication in modern business is essentially a *competitive* activity, a rhetorical venture in which writers and speakers attempt to gain advantage over other forces that contend for their audience's attention. Of course, nothing is new about the concept of competition, particularly in contemporary studies of business and especially in discussions of strategy, industry analysis, and marketing.[1] However, this concept has yet to be used much in studies outside of these more traditional areas of business. This is unfortunate. Competition can provide a familiar and illuminating way of understanding activities that are not in the mainstream of business studies but are nevertheless essential to its successful practice. One of these activities is business communication.[2] This book presents modern business communication as significantly competitive and offers competition as a conceptually useful way of thinking about it.[3]

"Competition" is used in this book in a combination of general and specialized senses. In its general sense, competition follows a typically abstract dictionary definition: "an effort made by two or more parties acting independently to secure the business of a third party by offering the most favorable terms."[4] In this sense, writers in business are realistically viewed as agents who compete to secure the "business" of the reader, the third party. "Business," of course, may be any number of things but routinely includes attention to the message, cooperation, approval, agreement, or action as a consequence of it. The "most favorable terms" may also refer to many things—ease of understanding and quality of reasoning among them—but they take on more specific meaning when competition is discussed in its more specialized sense.

In its more specialized sense, competition may be further understood as it is used in contemporary discussions of industry analysis and strategy. There it is viewed as a way of gaining advantage along two lines: low cost or differentiation.[5] A firm may gain advantage by offering a product or service that is lower in cost than a competitor's or by offering a product or service that is different in a way that is valuable to its customers. Similarly, writers and speakers in business may gain competitive advantage through messages—the literary equivalent of products or services—if they are differentiated in the sense that they offer the audience something different that is of value. These messages also compete if they offer "reduced cost," in the sense that they require from the audience the least amount of rhetorical investment or effort for what would otherwise be an equivalent return in meaning.

Writers and speakers thus communicate competitively when they attempt to gain advantage over other forces that contend for their audience's attention by *producing messages that are differentiated or reduced in cost.* Differentiation and reduction may be achieved in many ways, and this book attempts to cover some of the more significant options that are available to those who communicate in business. In particular, we will be concerned with messages like the following:

> In effect, it was hypothesized that certain physical data categories including housing types and densities, land use characteristics, and ecological location constitute a scalable content area. This could be called a continuum of residential desirability. Likewise, it was hypothesized that several social data categories, describing the same census tracts, and referring generally to the social stratification system of the city, would also be scalable. This scale would be called a continuum of socio-economic status. Thirdly, it was hypothesized that there would be a high positive correlation between the scale types on each continuum.[6]

Probably the best way to appreciate the competitive (or noncompetitive) character of this passage is by considering another version, or revision, of it. Here is a "translation":

> Rich people live in big houses set further apart than those of poor people. By looking at an aerial photograph of any American city, we can distinguish the richer from the poorer neighborhoods.

A number of comments might be made about the original passage and the translation. For example, one might sidestep analysis entirely and offer an evaluation. Here is one possibility: "The first passage is terrible. The second is much better."[7] At the other end of the spectrum, one might withhold all value judgments, and simply draw attention to the factual differences between the two passages by pointing out the difference in the number of words used to express essentially the same ideas, the kinds of words used, the way they are ordered, how they are punctuated, and how they are formed. In an even more clinical approach, we might run each passage through a computer-assisted text analysis and compare the different scores on available scales of readability.

While each of the approaches above would have its merits (all but the first will be applied in later chapters of this book), the predominant concern of this book is to consider the *competitive* character of each passage, and that necessarily involves a consideration of the reader. Here we ask whether such a message is differentiated from others that may be competing for the reader's attention and whether the time required for the reader to understand either passage is significantly reduced. We also ask the practical question: how can the more competitive message be achieved? Considering competition in this way—as a linguistic and literary matter as opposed to a financial and physical concern—extends the common use of competition to include communicating in business. This extended concept of competition informs the content of this book and directs both the selection of chapter subjects and the methods and techniques they cover.

■ Communication and Rhetoric

Similarly influential in determining the subject matter of this book is the concept of rhetoric, which is treated both as a discipline that studies effective communication in oral and written media and as a linguistic practice that places the audience at the center of communicative activity. Because this book argues that communication in modern business is essentially a competitive activity—a rhetorical venture in which writers and speakers attempt to gain advantage over other forces that contend for their audience's attention—it relies heavily on a well-established academic field, rhetoric, for guidance on matters that involve word and thought. The art of effective written and oral communication is in general a rhetorical concern, and classical rhetoric is generally regarded as an audience-centered enterprise. One modern scholar of classical rhetoric, Edward P. J. Corbett, puts the matter concisely:

> The basic notion underlying classical rhetoric is that any act of verbal communication between human beings comprises four components: (1) a speaker or writer, (2) listeners or readers, (3) a message or text, and (4) a reality or universe that the message or text is talking about. All four of those components play a part in business and professional communications; but of those four, the one that gets primary consideration is audience—that is, the listeners or readers.[8]

This book shares Corbett's view of classical rhetoric and narrows it only slightly to speak specifically to the interests of working professionals in the world of competitive business. It also narrows it more significantly to consider a specific but central concern of both classical and modern rhetoric: the use of argument in effective communication. This book thus takes a rhetorical approach to producing competitive messages in the world of business.

■ Rhetoric and Business

Taking a rhetorical approach to business communication is not without considerable historical precedent, as several historical examples of rhetoric's intersection with business might show. For the ancient Greeks, an understanding of rhetoric offered an opportunity to do well in life through one's acquired ability to argue well. One might employ rhetoric, for example, to improve the chances of success in litigation over property confiscated through the greater political power of another. Others would use rhetoric to gain political advantage in the first place, to overcome the arguments made by their opponents. Still others might use it in less formal channels, as people do today, to further their positions in business or social arenas.

Since rhetoric was so critical for practical success, a market for it would soon become apparent. And into this market stepped instructors prepared to teach the skills of rhetoric, the ability to argue and persuade, to those who were prepared to pay for their tutorial service. Those who offered these tutorial services were known as *sophists*. They were a combination of modern-day freelance trainer and professor. Many enjoyed their reputations for offering sound instruction and for being ethical in their practice. Probably the best among them, a Greek by the name of Isocrates, epitomized the good sophist.

Other sophists did not enjoy such reputations. Like the proponents of contemporary get-rich schemes—everything from chain letters to the late-night nothing-down real estate programs—some sophists became known for their lack of scruples as they offered to teach the ways of persuasion. Were they practicing today, and of course their modern counterparts are, they might be invited for an interview on *60 Minutes*. The Greek sophist Gorgias is often the one that comes to the minds of most students of rhetoric when they think of the less principled sophists, the kind who today might serve as media consultant to an oil company attempting by any means to avoid accepting blame for a toxic spill.[9]

Regardless of their inclinations toward ethical practice, the Greek sophists enjoyed considerable financial success as extracurricular teachers of rhetoric, as others offering similar instruction have throughout the history of the western world. However, the Middle Ages witnessed a shift away from sophists and the individual freelance teacher as rhetoric became an institutionalized part of formal education and the early liberal arts. The discipline of Rhetoric was in fact one of the seven liberal arts, which informed medieval education. The arts were divided into the trivium of Rhetoric, Grammar, and Logic; and the quadrivium of Music, Arithmetic, Geometry, and Astronomy.

Business, in the form of the discipline we know today, was not taught as a subject in the Middle Ages, but that does not mean that rhetoric has nothing to offer the practitioner in the world of exchange outside the academy. A number of rhetorical works were available to those intending to write in forms appropriate to commercial exchange. One in particular, the *Ars Dictaminis*, or art of letter writing, offered instruction in effective communication within the world of commerce and politics, and it was organized around patterns of arrangement found in the Roman rhetorics of Cicero and Quintilian. It has both modern and ultramodern counterparts today, both in the form of manuals for writing business letters and in computer-based templates that the modern manager can adapt to the particular task at hand.

During the English Renaissance, rhetoric was rediscovered as part of a larger rediscovery of classical works, and it continued to occupy an important place in the formal system of education, at least in England. Popular handbooks were also plentiful as writers continued to adapt rhetorics to the needs of their audiences. The Renaissance also witnessed an important development in the medium of expression: the production of the first rhetorics in the vernacular. Prior to the sixteenth century, rhetorics were written in Greek or Latin, and the exercises produced by students were in Latin. In the sixteenth century, the first English-language rhetorics emerged, as schoolmasters and students alike began to write in the vernacular. This offered an unprecedented access to the art of rhetoric. No longer confined solely to a program of study within the academy, these materials would now be more widely available to practitioners in the professions.

Along with the emergence of rhetorics in the vernacular, the sixteenth century witnessed a dramatic change in the way the art of rhetoric was conceived, one that would influence the future of the discipline and the way rhetoric would be received in both academic and business communities. This change was initiated by the tremendously influential French scholar Peter Ramus.[10] Ramus revised the subjects of the trivium in a way that withdrew from rhetoric the traditional elements of discovery (*inventio*) and arrangement (*dispositio*) of material. These he placed in the domain of logic and left rhetoric with style (*elecutio*) and delivery (*pronuntiatio*).[11] Thus truncated, rhetoric now appeared "insubstantial," a condition that persists today, as evidenced by the expressions "mere rhetoric," "just rhetoric," or "empty rhetoric" when used to signify style without substance.

Although other centuries contributed in their own way to the intellectual history of rhetoric, we live today with the legacies of the two sixteenth-century developments of vernacular rhetorics and a dramatically revised academic conception of the art. As one writer referring to the sixteenth century has said: "Many vernacular rhetorics appeared in England from this point on, but the most popular were not necessarily the soundest rhetorics or the most venturesome."[12] This is certainly true today, though probably less in Europe than in the United States, as the more popular treatments of traditional topics exist in a severely abbreviated form for modern managers, even though they might well appreciate a greater depth and length of treatment. At the same time, rhetoric as a comprehensive discipline of language study and practice exists in only a few of our colleges and universities, which suggests the appropriateness of place for a discipline that has lost its "substance."[13]

In spite of this current state of affairs, and perhaps even because of it, some are once again "discovering" the art of rhetoric, and several are attempting to connect the discipline to the world of work and traditional subject areas within business and economics.[14] Still, the connections between rhetoric in general, classical rhetoric in particular, and the profession of business are relatively unexamined in contemporary treatments of either discipline, despite the historical precedent for their interaction. In the chapters that follow, I hope to examine those connections more closely, and contribute something of currency to a historically well-established and important art.

▨ Overview of This Book

This Introduction is intended to lay out the book's major concepts and terms, allowing the rest of the book to be presented in a way that is relatively free of classical terminology. Readers will benefit from becoming familiar with the Greek and Roman sources of key concepts, even if they have no intention of mastering the vocabulary, and such familiarity is not possible without at least mentioning the terms.[15] Nevertheless, using these terms throughout the book would impede understanding, distract from the practical tasks at hand, and even contradict some of the advice given in other chapters.[16] Hence, terms such as *enthymeme*, *brevitas*, and *dispositio* will be mentioned in this introduction, acknowledged for their status as sources of important ideas, and then put quietly away so the concepts to which they refer may receive full attention from contemporary readers.

Chapter 1 introduces the book's principal concepts of competition and rhetoric, and it demonstrates the importance of classical rhetoric's emphasis on audience by offering a case study of a firm that found itself in a newly competitive environment and decided to assess its key communications with clients. MBT Associates, an award-winning architectural firm based in San Francisco, made this assessment of its interview presentation, its primary means of communicating its service and identity to its clients. As a consequence of this assessment, MBT discovered the classical priority of placing primary emphasis on audience, which it then positioned at the center of its rhetorical and competitive efforts. As a result, it was able not only to redesign its interview for greater success with clients in the marketplace, but also to reveal several defining and distinctive features of its own business.

Chapter 2 introduces the informative message and the world of information. In this chapter, the contrary forces of increased information and reduced time are introduced as some of the important forces that contend for the audience's attention. The communicator is presented with the rhetorical concept of *dispositio*, a form of principled organization as a means of gaining advantage over these competing forces. By producing this kind of organized message, the communicator—in this case the writer—is able to *differentiate* the quality of the literary product. Interestingly enough, this form of differentiation also leads to reduced cost to the reader in the form of increased readability and facilitated comprehension. Because of this, the application of *dispositio*, or principled organization, will make documents more persuasive even if they are not argumentative. Five sample documents written according to the kind of principled organization this chapter covers may be found in Appendix A.

Chapter 3 considers the competitive character of business writing most openly, in the form of logical argument, the epitome of Aristotelian *logos*, a means of persuasion that relies on managing reasons as opposed to influencing emotions (*pathos*) or constructing character (*ethos*). Here, the forces that contend for the receiver's attention are the opposing party's own favored beliefs or convictions about issues or problems in debate. For the writer to gain advantage here requires competing directly with the reader or another opposing party. This means providing an argument that is *differentiated* by virtue of its ability to overcome the opposing point of view. The approach taken to argument in this chapter combines a classical use of enthymeme-based argumentation with a more contemporary method of planning and presenting arguments.

Chapter 4 extends the previous chapter's treatment of argument to reflect contemporary studies of argument and the emphasis that is being placed on the function of argument as a form of inquiry as well as a means of persuasion. However, it does this by emphasizing a classical concept, *refutatio,* or the refutation of opposing views.

In this chapter, argument is presented not simply as a way of convincing others of a point of view but as a way of determining one's own point of view in the first place. Perhaps paradoxically, this involves understanding the multiple points of view that are usually present in the analysis of issues as well as the opposition that will always be brought against a line of reasoning. Introduced, explained, and extended in this chapter is Stephen Toulmin's model of argument, a diagram that may be used to understand and develop multiple points of view.

In Chapter 5, the argumentative plan becomes a full presentation of the case as the rhetorical concept of *dispositio* is considered once again, but now with a view toward arranging the parts of an argument. In this chapter, the audience is placed at the center of argumentative activity as the writer considers how the argument, now discovered, may be made in the "presence" of one who can be expected to resist. The Toulmin model introduced in Chapter 4 is reintroduced and used as a logical guideline for generating the presentation. Five sample documents written according to the method of argument discussed in this chapter may be found in Appendix B.

In Chapter 6, ethical argument is considered at length with the goal of defining ethics so that it has a particularly relevant meaning for those who study management communication as well as those who practice it. Here ethics is considered not simply as the study of moral behavior but as a process that helps us determine what moral behavior is in the first place. Discussions of right and wrong behavior cannot take place without conflicting points of view and advocates prepared to debate them. Since these discussions are characterized by controversy, the use of argument, even poor argument, is unavoidable. This chapter examines argument as a form of behavior and the fallacies of reasoning as indicators of argumentation that is ethically suspect. In categorizing the fallacies, this chapter draws heavily on classical sources, especially Aristotle's discussion of *topoi* in his *Rhetoric*, and his companion discussion in *Sophistical Refutations*.

Chapter 7 introduces the rhetorical concept of *ethos*, also drawn primarily from Aristotelian rhetoric, and considers how the Aristotelian trinity of intelligence, character, and goodwill can arise from the communicator's use of language. Unlike reputation, which precedes the act of communication and may be seen as distinct from it, ethos is inseparable from the use of language, and it exists as the distinctive impression created by the communicator's use of the written or spoken word. Because ethos is heavily influenced by the choices one makes about major structural elements of argument, such as the management of opposition, this chapter reviews several of those elements and their implications for the ethos of the arguer. However, ethos is also significantly the product of sentence-level elements, where other kinds of opportunities exist for increasing the competitiveness of a message. Hence, this chapter offers an introduction to managing ethos at the sentence level.

After introducing the concept of ethos in Chapter 7, where several messages are analyzed for the ethos they contain, Chapters 8 through 12 offer a thorough-going approach to managing ethos by analyzing the kind of language that produces it, language that has been revised for conciseness, word choice, word order, grammar, and punctuation. In each case, discussion draws on the appropriate principles or concepts of classical rhetoric. For example, the discussion of conciseness recognizes the rhetorical principle of *brevitas* whereas word order, or syntax, considers *dispositio* once again, but this time at the sentence level. Although the editorial guidelines proposed in these chapters will produce neither argument nor principled organization, they will enhance both by increasing the clarity of the writer's prose. They will also assist in strengthening the persuasive appeal of such communication since they help to create an impression of credibility, give evidence of clear thought, and promote desirable features of character and personality.

Chapter 13 provides a technological capstone to the previous six chapters since it considers the role of computer technology in business composition, revision, and the management of ethos. The programs covered in this chapter emphasize many of the principles of language revision applied in preceding chapters. Because text analyzers have now become an essential element in workplace revision, and because the technology is rapidly improving, this chapter reviews current programs and their claims to help writers achieve an effective prose style, and thus an appealing ethos.

In addition to this book's division into chapters are three appendices of workplace application. These appendices show how the principles the book covers have been applied by real businesspeople in the real world of work. For example, Appendix A presents five examples of writings that demonstrate *dispositio*, the form of organization covered in Chapter 2 and discussed elsewhere in this book. Appendix B provides five examples of enthymeme-based argumentative writing, which is covered in Chapters 3 through 6. And finally, five examples of revising for ethos are offered in Appendix C. These revisions represent the application of principles covered in Chapters 7 through 12. In each of the appendices above, the writers' names and corporate affiliations have been included, so the reader may view the document as a realistic communication within a recognized organization.

At the end of each chapter is a list of related readings, a brief and often annotated bibliography of works related to that chapter's discussion. These bibliographies are intended to serve those who are interested in going into the discussion in greater depth or in becoming more familiar with the writings that have helped to shape the fields or disciplines in which such discussions occur.

NOTES

1. See, for example, Michael Porter, *Competitive Strategy* (New York: Macmillan, 1980); Michael Porter, *Competitive Advantage* (New York: Macmillan, 1985). For a recent discussion of cost and differentiation, one that reviews some of the previous thinking about these terms, see Andrew C. Boynton, "Achieving Dynamic Stability through Information Technology," *California Management Review* 35, no. 2 (Winter 1993): 58–77.

2. On the importance of writing in business, many studies exist. One that is infrequently cited but is both recent and comprehensive is Dan B. Curtis, Jerry L. Winsor, and Ronald D. Stephens, "National Preferences in Business and Communication Education," *Communication Education* 38, no. 1 (January 1989): 6–13. See also James A. Belohov, Paul O. Popp, and Michael S. Porte, "Communication: A View from the Inside of Business," *The Journal of Busi-*

ness Communication 11 (1979): 53–59; Garda W. Bowman, "What Helps or Harms Promotability?" *Harvard Business Review* 42 (January–February 1964): 6–26; Francis J. Connelly, ed., "Accreditation Research Project Report of Phase 1," *AACSB Bulletin* 14 (Winter 1980): 2–15; S. Divita, "The Business School Graduate—Does the Product Fit the Need?" L. Preston, ed., *Business Environment/Public Policy 1979 Conference Papers.* AACSB, St. Louis (1979): 167–68; Alfred G. Edge and Ronald Greenwood, "How Managers Rank Knowledge, Skills and Attributes Possessed by Business Administration Graduates," *AACSB Bulletin* 11 (October 1974): 30–34; J. W. Hildebrandt, F. A. Bond, E. L. Miller, and W. W. Swinyard, "An Executive Appraisal of Courses Which Best Prepare One for General Management," *The Journal of Business Communication* 19 (Winter 1982): 5–15.

3. This is perhaps best seen as an argument *from* analogy as opposed to an argument *to* analogy. My claim here is not that writing and competition, as it is used in its specialized sense, have significant features in common. My claim is that one, competition, can be used to provide a particularly useful explanation of the other, writing, when the audience consists of people in the business profession.

4. This one is typical. It is the third definition in the "competition" entry in *Webster's Ninth New Collegiate Dictionary.* Primary and secondary entries here simply note act and process, and describe the contest of competition.

5. This is the traditional *division,* and it is sufficient for the analogy I am drawing. However, recent writers on competition argue that a choice no longer exists between the two. Strategy thus involves considering differentiation *and* cost or cost alone as one necessary form of differentiation. They are treated as "mutually dependent requirements" in Andrew C. Boynton, "Achieving Dynamic Stability through Information Technology," *California Management Review* 35, no. 2 (Winter 1993): 58–77.

6. Sample collected by Malcom Cowley, "Sociological Habit Patterns in Linguistic Transmogrification," *The Reporter,* September 20, 1956, and quoted in Richard A. Lanham, *Revising Business Prose* (New York: Scribner, 1981).

7. Of course, this is just one view, and it is one I hope to argue for in this book. Other views certainly exist. For example, Richard Lanham (*Revising Business Prose,* 64–65) writes of this passage: " Such prose seems to aim at being scientific but actually wants to be priestly, to cast a witch doctor's spell. To translate the prose into a plain style—that is, to revise it into ordinary English—breaks the spell and defeats the purpose." From his point of view, one might just as easily argue that the translation is noncompetitive, since it reduces the persuasive force provided by the "spell."

8. Edward P. J. Corbett, "What Classical Rhetoric Has to Offer the Teacher and the Student of Business and Professional Writing" in *Writing in the Business Professions,* ed. Myra Kogen (Urbana: National Council of Teachers of English and The Association for Business Communication, 1989), 66.

9. I will be the first to admit that my sketch, if one can even call it that, of classical rhetoric is offered without any sensitivity to a rich period. The history of classical rhetoric, as Corbett has pointed out, "covers more than two thousand years, from the fifth century B.C. until the first quarter of the nineteenth century." Edward P. J. Corbett, *Classical Rhetoric for the Modern Student* (New York: Oxford, 1971), 594. He then goes on to say how presumptuous one would be to think of presenting a satisfactory survey in a few dozen pages! Of course, I do not intend even that; rather, I wish simply to point out that the intersection of rhetoric and business, which this book encourages, is not without prior instance.

10. Ramus was certainly influential, but he was not, by any means, solely responsible for the "fall" of rhetoric. By mentioning him, I intend only to point out one major influence. For a general account of rhetoric's decline in the West, see David Kaufer, *Rhetoric and the Arts of Design* (Matiwah, NJ: Lawrence Erlbaum, 1996). For a more specific and celebrated ac-

count, see Walter Ong, *Rhetoric, Romance, and Technology: Studies in the Interaction of Expression and Culture* (Ithaca, NY: Cornell University Press, 1971).

11. These four elements are drawn from Roman rhetoric, which traditionally named five offices. As a number of writers have pointed out, the fifth office, memory (*memoria*) is one that Ramus apparently ignored.

12. Corbett, *Classical Rhetoric for the Modern Student*, 610.

13. For more on the place of the discipline of rhetoric in modern education, see Albert R. Kitzhaber, *A Bibliography on Rhetoric in American Colleges, 1850–1900* (Denver: Bibliographical Center for Research, Denver Public Library, 1954).

14. Certainly a well-recognized example is Donald N. McCloskey, *The Rhetoric of Economics* (Madison: University of Wisconsin Press, 1985).

15. Of course, one could present everything in this book without any reference to classical sources. However, doing so would be dishonest. It would also cause considerable difficulty for those who wish to extend their study of key concepts, which exist historically under their original names.

16. For example, the advice concerning jargon in Chapter 9.

RHETORIC AND   1

COMPETITIVE

ADVANTAGE

No existing management theory helps much in explaining the role of the customer in the prototypical excellent company. At most, recent theory talks about the importance of the external environment in influencing the institution. It misses by a mile, however, the intensity of customer orientation that exists within the top performers, and that intensity seems to be one of the best kept secrets in American business.

—Tom Peters, *In Search of Excellence*

A message must always be shaped in some measure, of course, to fit the audience; but in business and professional communications, the audience is more often than in many other kinds of specialized discourses the chief determinant of the means adopted to effect the end.

—Edward P. J. Corbett, *What Classical Rhetoric Has to Offer*

■ Classical Rhetoric in a Modern Business

This chapter offers a case study of a firm that found itself in a newly competitive environment and decided to assess its key communications with clients as part of its attempt to compete. MBT Associates, an award-winning architectural firm based in San Francisco, California, made this assessment of its interview presentation, its primary means of communicating its service and identity to its clients. During the course of this assessment, MBT discovered that its interview presentation was shaped primarily by the interests of the presenters and by an understandable emphasis on design, but all to the relative exclusion of the client as the receiver of the interview's communication. As a consequence of this assessment, MBT discovered the importance classical rhetoric placed on the receiver of messages, and it was able not only to re-design its interview for greater success with clients in the marketplace, but also to re-veal several defining and distinctive features of its own business.

Because this is a case study, it offers an example that may be generalized to busi-nesses in industries outside of architecture. The tendency of an architectural firm to concentrate on design and message to the exclusion of the audience is hardly limited to the field of architecture. For example, in medicine, the physician's focus on illness and on diagnosis as the primary service provided in health care can easily be main-tained, ironically enough, without much attention to the announced needs of the pa-tient.[1] For that reason among others, doctors and the medical profession in general have been criticized for being oriented toward the interests of the practitioner and not the patient, the audience of their medical care. This very criticism was the informing message of Touchstone Pictures' 1991 movie *The Doctor*. Based on the life of sur-geon Ed Rosenbaum, it tells the story of a doctor who practiced without concern or awareness of his client, the patient.[2] Eventually, he discovered his patient, and what it means to practice medicine, but only after he became ill himself, and became a pa-tient in his own hospital.

Personal computing and computer programming is another industry in which technicians and others are perceived as communicating with little attention to the au-dience, the "end user" of hardware systems and software applications. Complaints about the clarity of user manuals are legion as are laments about the unnecessary com-plexity of the software these manuals are supposed to explain. The failure of these manuals has resulted in most firms setting up elaborate and expensive technical as-sistance programs, only to provide assistance that most claim is "in the book." Al-though many significant changes have been made in the all-important "interface" in most computing platforms, personal computing continues to be a field in which ma-jor decisions about software and hardware technology appear to be made without much attention given to the audience that is expected to benefit from it.

In the examples above, in medicine and personal computing, the increase in industry competition is forcing a new appreciation for the receiver-client, whether that is the patient or the computer user. This is not simply to say, as Tom Peters and others repeatedly have, that American business is discovering the cus-tomer, but that businesses in competitive markets are beginning to discover the kind of communication—based in a full awareness of the audience—that customers in competitive markets require. This is certainly one of the discoveries made by MBT Associates, as it attempted to come to terms with competition in the architectural industry.

■ Communication and Competition

An increasing number of competitors and a growing awareness of the architectural firm as a business enterprise are both powerful forces, and they have pushed firms in the architectural business to seek new ways to increase their competitive advantage.[3] Although these firms will continue to market the quality of their traditional services by emphasizing design, many have found that this is simply not enough to differentiate them in a competitive marketplace. As a consequence, some firms have begun to look at a different kind of design—the design of their client interview—as a way of distinguishing their services from those of their competitors. Other things being equal—and firms report that clients do perceive that design services are comparable—the formal presentation of services, the architectural interview, can itself serve as an important source of competitive advantage.

Unfortunately, even architects would admit that they are unprepared to craft an oral presentation with the same degree of expertise and talent that they apply in designing buildings. Some have even recognized that their training in architecture may place them at a disadvantage because it orients them not to the interests of the client but to the requirements or aesthetic of the design.[4] For this reason, a way of understanding and assessing the design of the architectural interview should interest both those in the industry and those who study communication in the professions. This chapter attempts to provide both this understanding and assessment by describing the experience of one of the West Coast's more prestigious architectural firms. It explains *what* one might consider in assessing the design of an interview, *why* this is an important assessment to make, and *how* such an assessment can dramatically change the way a firm conceives of its business and conducts the kind of communication that is critical to its success.

■ Overview of a Firm

MBT Associates is an architectural firm with a forty-five-year history of specialized scientific laboratory design experience. Established in 1954, and based in San Francisco since 1964, MBT has carried out commissions throughout the United States and has been active internationally since the sixties. The firm enjoys a growing reputation for laboratory design, a reputation it has acquired through its projects such as the Life Sciences Building at the University of California, Berkeley, the IBM Almaden Research Center in San Jose, and Stanford University's Beckman Center for Molecular and Genetic Medicine. However, MBT has also completed a number of very large projects that represent a greater diversity of client interest. Its work on the Company Learning Center and Regional Headquarters for Pacific Gas and Electric, the seismic retrofitting and restoration of historic San Francisco City Hall, the Chevron Office Park, and IBM's Santa Teresa Programming Center, which is probably its best-known project, all suggest that MBT is not limited to scientific laboratory design. However, evidence of this greater diversity notwithstanding, MBT's primary reputation is still for laboratory design.

Not surprisingly, this image of MBT—as a firm specializing in scientific laboratory design—is the one it promotes in its responses to clients' requests for proposal (RFP) and from its more general promotional materials. MBT also emphasizes in its client proposals and its own promotional materials those features of service that it believes are of interest to its clients. The following passages are from a typical response to an RFP. This proposal offers information on the firm, a descriptive list of services, and then the following two paragraphs, which are marked as areas of service:

> **Excellence in Planning**: MBT's client services encompass the increasingly complex factors required to achieve success in long-range planning. The site selection, preparation of development and building programs, feasibility studies, existing building analysis, and master planning are all important considerations in establishing and defining the goals of the client.

> **Excellence in Management:** To aid clients throughout the development effort, MBT offers complete services in budgeting, selecting and administering the work of outside technical consultants, evaluating materials and construction methods, negotiating contracts, and often exercising full administrative responsibility during construction as required by the client. During the MBT process, the team remains together throughout the entire process, providing commitment to the client and cohesiveness to the project.[5]

Although these two paragraphs occupy most of the text space on this one-page introduction to the firm, they represent less important features of the firm's services than the following paragraph, which is announced as "the main objective of the firm":

> **Excellence in Design:** Quality architectural design is the main objective of the firm. MBT has been honored with highest national awards for the full range of its projects, from computer facilities to biological laboratories to corporate research and development facilities. Design at MBT reflects the user and the user's requirements rather than a given aesthetic. In any project, the first step is an understanding of the client. Quality design is appropriate design; it must take into account each project's particular factors: function, site, budget, and other considerations.

> MBT ASSOCIATES is proud of its reputation for design that is both responsive and innovative.

This view of the firm's most important offering, "quality architectural design," is also found in its other, more promotional materials. For example, MBT's most elaborate general-interest brochure opens with the following sentence: "The professional prestige of MBT Associates has been earned through nearly four decades of accomplished architectural design."[6] This is a view supported by other materials that characterize the firm, and it is the message presented through the many design awards that are displayed in the entry of MBT's San Francisco office. Perhaps most important, this view is consistent with the views voiced by the senior members of the firm, who, when asked what the interview is designed to sell, answered in majority by saying "architectural design."

▓ The Architectural Interview

Of course, one should not be surprised by MBT's strong concern with design. MBT is not in the business of selling cars or manufacturing fasteners. MBT is an architectural firm. Its business, its primary business, as it says, is providing "quality architectural design." And this perception of its business and service guided MBT's architects as they prepared for their interviews during the years 1975–1989. As long as this perception persisted, MBT's interviews remained essentially in the following format.

Typically, the interview team consisted of a panel of three to seven people drawn from MBT's senior architectural staff or a similarly sized combination of MBT architects and selected industry consultants in fields such as surveying, estimating, or construction engineering. This team represented to the client at least the partial if not the full membership of the team that would serve the client should the client select MBT. The team usually had one project principal, who had primary responsibility for the project and coordination of the team. The interview presentation was made either in MBT's conference room in San Francisco or at the client's place of business, and each interview involved the active participation of several to all of the panel members. On average, interviews were allotted one and one-half to two hours and varied in the time actually used. The format observed was less varied. Openings included a round of introductions, followed by the formal presentation and then the question-and-answer period.

The longest part of the interview, the formal presentation, usually relied heavily on visual aids. Because the team was attempting to establish the quality of architectural design as the desired end, the presentation usually opened with a discussion of the history of the company as a provider of quality architectural design. Then followed a lengthy slide show of past projects as graphic evidence of design quality. Finally, time was reserved toward the end to discuss particulars of the project at hand. This concluded the presentation, though prospective clients would often remain for similar presentations from competing firms.

▓ Rhetorical Design: Orientation

The strengths and weaknesses of MBT's interview become apparent when it is considered rhetorically, as an example of persuasive discourse open to the same forms of analysis as other discursive practices in the professions. Although the following rhetorical model has appeared in a variety of forms, its kernel has remained the same for decades. Used to study message communication, this model represents the three primary elements in communication: the source of the message, the message, and the receiver of the message. With pointers to indicate process and direction, the model typically appears in the following form:[7]

Message Source → Message → Message Receiver

This model is useful for examining general tendencies in acts of communication, and it has been used in interpersonal communication to identify speakers by their orientation toward an element of this model. For example, conversational narcissism may be seen as a speaker's preoccupation with or at least strong orientation toward the *source* of the message.[8]

Preoccupation with the *message* itself may result in textualism or the speaker's obsession with the medium of transmission, whether it is linguistic, visual, or kinesic. Critics at Toastmasters who count the number of times a speaker says "uh" or "ah" provide only a trivial example of the message-oriented communicator, now serving temporarily as listener.

Finally, the speaker who is obsessed with what the listener, the *receiver* of the message, may be thinking might be called deferential, ingratiating, or something even less kind. Of course, these examples represent extremes and thus are most useful in explaining the model, not the character of actual practice. In the actual practice of communication, we might expect less of the extreme and more overlap in the model's elements.

For MBT, no extreme in orientation was evident, though an orientation certainly was, and the model provided a useful means to identify it. MBT's concern with "quality architectural design" provides the first clue to orientation because in architecture, design is the intermediary between architect and client in the same sense that message is the intermediary between the source of a message and its receiver. But in MBT's case, the firm's message—that it provides quality architectural design—was itself derived from the source of the message: the MBT presenters. This became clear not only in interviews with the presenters but in disputes about technique in the presentations and in explanations about particular choices made. For example, when asked what the interview is designed to sell, most MBT senior architects responded "design," or more tellingly, "our design." When disputing whether slides should be included, most defenses were marked by personal preference. When asked why a topic was chosen for elaboration, the answer commonly referred to the speaker, another team member, the company, or the presentation itself. Because of this, we can repeat the model introduced earlier and emphasize with boldface the rhetorical orientation of the traditional MBT presentation:

$$\textbf{Message Source} \rightarrow \textbf{Message} \rightarrow \text{Message Receiver}$$

If we specify these elements for MBT, the model is more revealing and perhaps even a little startling:

$$\textbf{MBT} \rightarrow \textbf{Quality Architectural Design} \rightarrow \text{Client}$$

Remarkably, the rhetorical orientation is toward the source of the message (MBT) and the message (quality architectural design) rather than the client. Indeed, the message derives from what the presenters themselves thought was important (quality architectural design), or what they were trained in school to believe is important (quality architectural design), or what they spent most of their day working on (quality architectural design), or what they believed they were rewarded for (quality architectural design) by a variety of official groups or associations.

MBT's orientation is not surprising. It is not even uncommon among businesses more generally. However, such an orientation is unfortunate because the client figures in less than the source of the message or the message itself. When this happens, the interview, as an act of persuasion, can easily fall short of even the speakers' expectations if not fail to meet them entirely. Whether it will meet the receiver's or client's expectations may well be a matter of chance.

▓ The Importance of Rhetorical Design

Understanding the rhetorical design of an interview, or any other presentation for that matter, is important because it helps to determine not only the source from which messages have been derived but also the source from which messages *might* have been or might still be derived, in the case of those presentations which were not received well initially but which will be given again. In short, it allows us to see some activities (such as the architectural interview) that are essentially rhetorical *as* activities that are essentially rhetorical. Repairing a carburetor, for example, is not a rhetorical activity, nor would we probably benefit from seeing it as such. Shop mechanics routinely make such a repair without ever talking to or even making contact with the customer. Success or failure of the repair does not depend on any customer considerations but on following the "text" of the activity, and sometimes even the literal text of a repair manual. The service manager's job would be rhetorical because it would involve not only sharing responsibility for the repair but also insuring timeliness of job completion, perhaps as part of a larger program of customer satisfaction. The mechanic could afford to ignore the customer. The service manager could not.

Nor could MBT. And, in fact, MBT did not. As we have seen, MBT's concern about the customer is evident in both its promotional materials and its responses to RFPs. But this concern was so overshadowed by its concern for producing quality architectural design that MBT presenters had difficulty designing an interview that was client-oriented. To its considerable credit, MBT knew this, or at least it knew its presentations needed improvement, and this led to a company commitment in 1988 to do something about it. Late in that year, it hired a consultant and began an educational program that would take place over several years and eventually involve all of its executive management and senior architects.

▓ Reorientation: Discovering the Client

MBT's self-examination involved the guidance of a local consultant who was asked to review existing interviews and offer suggestions. Mock presentations were given to an MBT team that adopted the role of the client panel. The presentations were videotaped and played back for group commentary. This last step proved especially important. By asking MBT presenters to serve as clients, and by playing back the videotapes for critique, MBT presenters were actually able to become, if only in role play and for a short time, the people they were trying to persuade. For these people, the rhetorical orientation of the interview was quite different from that adopted by the presenters. The role players became more rhetorical in their view, and this represented quite a shift in attention, away from the source of the message, toward the receiver for whom the message had been designed. The model below represents this shift, which now places emphasis at the opposite end.

MBT → Quality Architectural Design → **Client**

This orientation, or stance, toward the message receiver, eventually produced a different understanding of the service MBT presenters had been trying to present through the interview. Until now the service-product was quality architectural design. Now it was becoming clear that, from the client's point of view, another concern was even more important: project management. Quality architectural design, while certainly important, no longer appeared as the firm's *distinctive* competence. As the presenters themselves admitted, though always with some reservation, quality design was available from many companies. What was most often in dispute or at issue was not the quality of the design but the quality of the project—the way it was managed, and the character, reliability, and professionalism of the people entrusted to manage it.

This reorientation was difficult to make, though the need for it had become apparent during preliminary discussions with each architect. When asked what service MBT provided the client, the most common response was "quality architectural design." However, when asked to account for those interviews that failed to sell that service, MBT presenters pointed to problems with "personality fit," "character clash," or the client's perception that "the team" was not convincing. In short, the first question was answered from the point of view of someone with graphical concerns; the second question, from the perspective of one whose concerns were behavioral. The models below illustrate the stages of this reorientation.

Message Source → **Message** → Message Receiver

MBT → **Quality Architectural Design** → Client

Message Source → Message → **Message Receiver**

MBT → Quality Architectural Design → **Client**

MBT → **Professional Project Management** → **Client**

By participating in the interview as receivers of the message, MBT presenters were able to see the interview as a more complete act of communication, one that involved not just presenters and messages (which characterize the one-sided clientless practice sessions they sometimes held) but the client as well. As a consequence, they were able to understand better not only the client but also the kind of message they would need to craft if they were to succeed in persuading that client. By becoming receiver-oriented, MBT became dramatically better acquainted with its own business. One could even say that this reorientation allowed MBT to discover its distinctive competence, the competitive service it really provides.

▓ Reorientation and Revision: Changing the Message

One might expect a change in MBT's perception of its service to result in a corresponding change in the way it presents that service in its interviews. However, such changes are seldom automatic. Old patterns of preparation and expected resistance to change are strong in any organization. Fortunately, MBT's executive management was committed to reasoned change in the firm's approach to the interview. With this support, MBT's approach to its interviews did change, and it changed dramatically, primarily because presenters now saw the interview rhetorically, from the point of view of clients, the very people the MBT presenters want to matter the most in their interviews.

MBT continued to present the client with evidence of quality architectural design, but it was no longer presented as part of an attempt to sell a competitive service, as one that would cause the client to determine whether MBT or a competitor would be the firm of choice. Instead, project management became the competitive service, and it became the service the interview would now be crafted to present. The potential change was enormous. Because selling project management might involve no visual presentation at all, MBT was faced with the possibility of giving a presentation without indulging in the chief orthodoxy of the industry—the slide presentation. This represented not just any change, but an unnerving and laborious one because it meant that material would have to be found to fill the gaping hole left by removing the slide show. It also meant that the comfort most speakers feel as narrators of slides in darkened rooms would probably have to be sacrificed for the sake of a change that might be seen as unconventional at best.

However, staying with the slides, at least as a mainstay in the presentation, simply does not make sense when one assumes the client wants evidence of quality project management. In the nonrhetorical presentation, the client, who is interested in the quality of architectural design, is interested primarily in the *quality of things*, the way structures are situated, the continuity of components, the way lines converge, the contrast of materials and shape, the interplay between light and space, color and texture. In the rhetorical presentation, the client, who is interested in the quality of project management, is interested primarily in the *quality of people*, their credibility and reliability, their ability to communicate and cooperate, to be patient and professional. Ironically, the very omission of the slide show, with its tendency to make members of the team anonymous and individual speakers invisible, provided MBT with exactly the opportunity it needed to feature its people, now through the vehicle of the oral presentation and the question-and-answer session. What was once an ineffective slide show soon became a presentation in which the MBT architects made every attempt to present themselves as a project management team—well organized, internally co-ordinated, and above all, rhetorically astute. This was a team that tried hard to show it paid attention to the client, and went beyond simply *stating* that, as many firms do in an age of customer service, to *demonstrating* it in the interview.

Because project management is essentially a rhetorical activity, with the client at the center, the MBT presenters found the interview, also essentially rhetorical, to be an especially effective vehicle to demonstrate evidence of project management simply because the *interview itself* could be presented as a well-managed project. In fact, the interview offered an extraordinary opportunity to showcase just about every important attribute of project management: control, credibility, team-work, time management, organization, responsiveness, and especially important, the ability to communicate. Particularly important in this was the client's presence and participation. By being a participant in the interview, a client panel could experience what it might be like to have members of the MBT team managing a project for them.

This is not to say that MBT ceased to appear to its clients as a firm known for and proud of the quality design it produces. Design was still discussed, of course, and at length. Visuals were also employed, though the darkroom slide show gave way to visual media (handouts, flip charts, and photo boards) that afforded the presenters greater control over the client's attention. And slides, when they were used, were used not because of their importance or value to the presenters but because they had predicted meaning for the client. In short, even those areas of MBT's previous approach to interviews had themselves been rhetorically reoriented.

The more formal differences between MBT's original orientation to its interview and the one it adopted after becoming more receiver-oriented were clear not only to members of the presentation team but also to the clients, as the two presentation formats at the end of this chapter will show. However, specifics of strategy, such as a technique employed to develop credibility used in the question-and-answer session, would not be conveyed very well by these formats. Nor would other changes, such as the experience reported by one presenter who felt for the first time that he was actually "talking to (his) clients" instead of "at the visual aids." These changes are no doubt very important, even though they may be difficult to show as an influence on the quality of the interview.

Even more difficult to establish is the influence of the reorientation on MBT's success with its interviews. Although most of the presenters are convinced that the more receiver-oriented approach has enhanced MBT's record of success, the number of competitive variables and lack of a control mechanism prevent making this connection in a way that might have considerably greater significance. Still, one thing is clear: as a consequence of redesigning the interview, the MBT architects are now more confident in their presentations, more responsive to the needs of the clients, and more careful about the way they craft their messages. They are also more knowledgeable about their own business. How could these changes not contribute significantly to the firm's competitive success?

▪ Discovering Audience: Some Conclusions

Communication theorists have for centuries recognized that audience is simply one of several important elements to consider in analyzing or composing messages. However, for businesses operating in competitive marketplaces or for individuals working in competitive environments, audience is probably the most critical element in communication. The audience is the closest rhetorical approximation of the client, and placing the audience at the center of communication enables the firm to balance its own interests with the interests held by arguably the most important members of its marketplace. By becoming the audience of its own product or service, a firm can understand its clients in a way that is probably not possible through any other means.

Unfortunately, audience-oriented communication is no easier for a firm to achieve than it is for a physician concentrating on diagnosis or a computer programmer on writing code. Any number of forces and conditions combine to discourage these communicators from becoming oriented toward those who receive their messages. For example, the physician may well adopt a skeptical stance toward the patient's concerns as a way of insuring objectivity or introduce distance to avoid personal involvement in what may become a painful situation. The computer programmer may find that the physical absence of the user in the process of writing code and the exclusive concentration required by this activity both make thinking about the user an unlikely event at best. As a consequence of these and other forces, not the least of which is the effort involved in determining one's own point of view, one may wonder if either has any cause to think of the receiver. Left to their own resources, each might very easily practice without any attention to the patient or the user.

Becoming audience-oriented requires a considerable effort, a familiarity with the practical applications of the discipline of rhetoric, and an appreciation for the emphasis classical rhetoric placed on the importance of audience in constructing messages. The rest of this book is devoted to developing such a familiarity and appreciation, and to offering reasons in support of working professionals making this effort.

PRESENTATION FORMAT I

Competitive Service: Quality Architectural Design

Emphasis is placed on the communication of design, and presenters serve the goal of design presentation. Most of this interview is devoted to one-way presentation. Presenters are responsible only for their own area of the presentation. Initiating and maintaining question-and-answer is the responsibility of the presenters.

Introductions—5 minutes

History of Company—10 minutes

Discussion of RFP and Client's Design (presenter 1)—15 minutes

Slide Show of Previous Designs (presenter 1 or 2)—40 minutes

Design Problems and Solutions (presenter 1, 2, or 3)—20 minutes

Question-and-Answer—20 minutes

PRESENTATION FORMAT II

Competitive Service: Quality Project Management

Emphasis is placed on the communication of skills and expertise in project management, and presenters attempt to embody those skills and expertise. Most of this interview is devoted to interaction in question-and-answer. Presenters are responsible for their own area of the presentation, for credentialing other team members, and for coordinating the transition of topics from one presenter to another. Initiating and maintaining question-and-answer is the responsibility of the presenters.

Introductions—5 minutes

Discussion of Project (project principal)—5 minutes

Discussion of Approach to Project (presenter 1)—10 minutes

Discussion of Approach to Project (presenter 2)—10 minutes

Discussion of Approach to Project (presenter 3)—10 minutes

Question-and-Answer—45 minutes

RELATED READINGS

These readings provide a very brief sampler of materials on the subject of competition as it appears in modern discussions of marketing and industry analysis. Among them are two works by Weld Coxe, one of only a few writers who have discussed the importance of the architectural interview. Also included are several studies of rhetorical orientation in communication.

Andrews, James R. *The Practice of Rhetorical Criticism*, 2nd ed. New York: Longman, 1990.

Benson, Thomas W. "The Senses of Rhetoric: A Topical System for Critics." *Central States Speech Journal* 29 (1978): 237–50.

Benson, Thomas, and Martin J. Medhurst. *Rhetorical Dimensions in Media*. Dubuque, Iowa: Kendall/Hunt Publishing Company, 1991.

Benson, Thomas W., ed. *American Rhetoric: Context and Criticism*. Carbondale: Southern Illinois University Press, 1989.

Black, Edwin. *Rhetorical Criticism: A Study in Method*. New York, 1965; Madison: University of Wisconsin Press, 1978.

Black, Edwin. "A Note on Theory and Practice in Rhetorical Criticism." *Western Journal of Speech Communication* 44 (1980): 331–36.

Bloom, Paul, and Philip Kotler. "Strategies for High Market Share Companies." *Harvard Business Review* (November–December 1975): 62–72.

Brock, Bernard L., Robert L. Scott, and James W. Chesebro, eds. *Methods of Rhetorical Criticism*, 3rd ed. rev. Detroit: Wayne State University Press, 1989.

Bryant, Donald C. *Rhetorical Dimensions in Criticism*. Baton Rouge: Louisiana State University Press, 1973.

Campbell, Karlyn Kohrs. *Critiques of Contemporary Rhetoric*. Belmont, CA: Wadsworth, 1974.

Campbell, Karlyn Kohrs. "The Nature of Criticism in Rhetorical and Communication Studies." *Central States Speech Journal* 30 (1979): 4–13.

Condit, Celeste. "Rhetorical Criticism and Audiences: The Extremes of McGee and Leff." *Western Journal of Speech Communication* 54 (1990): 330–45.

Coxe, Weld. *Strategies for Design Professionals: Superpositioning for Architectural and Engineering Firms*. New York: McGraw-Hill, 1987.

Coxe, Weld. *Marketing Architectural and Engineering Services*. Huntington, New York: Krieger Publishing Company, 1983.

Farrell, Thomas B. "Critical Models in the Analysis of Discourse." *Western Journal of Speech Communication* 44 (1980): 300–314.

Foss, Sonja K. *Rhetorical Criticism: Exploration and Practice*. Prospect Heights, IL: Waveland Press, 1989.

Hart, Roderick P. *Modern Rhetorical Criticism*. Glenview, IL: Scott, Foresman, 1990.

Leff, Michael C. "Interpretation and the Art of the Rhetorical Critic." *Western Journal of Speech Communication* 44 (1980): 337–49.

Leff, Michael. "Textual Criticism: The Legacy of G. P. Mohrmann." *Quarterly Journal of Speech* 72 (1986): 377–89.

Mohrmann, G. P., Charles J. Stewart, and Donovan J. Ochs, eds. *Explorations in Rhetorical Criticism*. University Park: Pennsylvania State University Press, 1973.

Porter, Michael E. *Competitive Advantage*. New York: Macmillan, 1985.

Porter, Michael E. *Competitive Strategy: Techniques for Analyzing Industries and Competitors*. New York: Free Press, 1980.

Thonssen, Lester A., A. Craig Baird, and Waldo W. Braden. *Speech Criticism: The Development of Standards for Rhetorical Appraisal*, 2d ed. New York: Ronald, 1970.

NOTES

1. For a recent but extreme example of this critique, see David Jacobsen and Eric D. Jacobsen, *Doctors Are Gods: Corruption and Unethical Practices in the Medical Profession* (New York: Thunder's Mouth, 1994). For a more balanced and qualified historical treatment, see Paul Star, *The Social Transformation of American Medicine* (New York: Basic Books, 1982). Both extreme and balanced accounts are reflected in varying degrees in journal and magazine articles such as the following: Michael Morris, "Gaps in Doctor-Patient Communication: A Patient's Response to Medical Advice," *New England Journal of Medicine*, 280 (1969): 535–40; B. M. Korsch, "Doctor-Patient Communication," *Scientific American*, 227 (2) (1972): 66–74; A. Segall, "Patient Evaluation of Physician Role Performance," *Social Science and Medicine*, 14 (1980): 269–78.

2. The reader may be interested in Dr. Rosenbaum's own account in *A Taste of My Own Medicine* (New York: Random House, 1988), the book on which the Touchstone Picture's movie *The Doctor* was based.

3. When I discuss MBT's attempt to gain competitive advantage, I have in mind its attempt at differentiation, one of three generic strategies for competitive advantage as they are

discussed in Michael Porter's work. See Michael Porter, *Competitive Strategy* (New York: Macmillan, 1980); Michael Porter, *Competitive Advantage* (New York: Macmillan, 1985). For a recent discussion of differentiation, one which reviews less recent discussion of this term, see Andrew C. Boynton, "Achieving Dynamic Stability through Information Technology," *California Management Review* 35, no. 2 (Winter 1993): 58–77.

4. David Lindemulder, Vice President, Marketing, interview with author, March 12, 1987, MBT Associates, San Francisco. Upon reviewing the present manuscript for this chapter, Mr. Lindemulder commented: "As I reflect back on the changes we made which you mentioned in the text, I am reminded how significant they were given the entrenched attitudes at the time. Although some backsliding is inevitable, we have been fortunately faithful over the years to the new approach. Even though our recent strategy sessions on firm direction, etc., determined the need to improve and emphasize quality design as most critical, our interview approach continues to be balanced as a result (of our earlier work on interviewing)."

5. MBT Associates, *Management and Technical Volume: Boeing Support Services. Materials Technology Complex*, 7 February 1992.

6. MBT (General Interest Brochure)—Laboratories.

7. Most models of this sort may be traced to their source in Claude Shannon and Warren Weaver, *The Mathematical Theory of Communication* (Urbana: University of Illinois Press, 1943). The one used here is a truncation of the model used in Ernest G. Borman and Nancy C. Borman, *Effective Small Group Communication*, 3rd ed. (Minneapolis, MN: Burgess, 1980), 11.

8. This emphasis on the sender of messages is at the heart of this study. For a discussion of a similar but more familiar emphasis in interpersonal communication, see H. Barrett, "Narcissism and Rhetorical Maturity," *Western Journal of Speech Communication* 50 (May, 1986), 254–68; Anita Vangelisti, Mark Knapp, and John Daly, "Conversational Narcissism," *Communication Monographs* 57 (December 1990): 251–73.

ORGANIZATION AND THE COMPETITIVE MESSAGE

2

Order in a World of Information

*From millions of sources all over the globe, through every possible channel and medium–light waves, airwaves, ticker tapes, computer banks, telephone wires, television cables, satellites, printing presses—information pours in. Behind it, in every imaginable form of storage on paper, on video and audio tape, on discs, film, and silicon chips–is an ever greater volume of information waiting to be retrieved. Like the Sorcerer's Apprentice, we are awash in information. And all the sorcerer has left us is a **broom**.*

—Neil Postman, *Technopoly*

Most working professionals, particularly those in middle and upper management, routinely produce a variety of messages, many of which are in the written form of memoranda, electronic mail, letters, reports, performance reviews, instructions, procedures, and proposals. Yet when these messages are judged according to the intentions of the writers, they traditionally fall into just two categories of writing: persuasive and informative.[1]

Of the two, persuasive writing is much more demanding because it attempts to bring about an important change in the reader's beliefs or actions. Thus writing persuasively requires giving considerable attention to a resistant reader, one who can be expected to challenge the writer's efforts. Writing persuasively also requires examining not only one's own beliefs but also the reasons one holds them and the reasons others do not. Because this form of writing is so demanding, and because it is usually recognized as the most advanced form of composition, it will be considered at length in the next chapter.[2] In the present chapter, we will look at a preparatory task: informative writing.

Writing informatively is the working professional's most frequent writing task, one that has an oral counterpart in voice mail and impromptu speaking.[3] Informative writing often takes the form of a memo, letter, or e-mail message, though sometimes a longer report or analysis will serve as the vehicle for presentation. Since informative messages can be about almost any topic, writers cannot use the content of a message to distinguish informative from persuasive messages. Compounding the problem of identifying the informative message is the fact that no message is purely informative. Each message is a mixture of intentions to inform and persuade.

Nevertheless, an important distinguishing feature of informative writing is a reader who is easier to satisfy than the resistant reader of persuasive messages. By definition, readers of informative messages do not resist the writer, primarily because they do not feel that the writer has a controversial point of view. Nor do they feel that the writer has a vested interest in overcoming their opposing point of view or the contrary interests of others. Because these readers do not appear as adversaries, writers can and usually do treat informative writing as if it existed without any serious competition.

■ The Competitive Character of Communication

Nevertheless, writers routinely run into trouble because they do not understand that informative writing is in fact competitive. And it is competitive because of the kind of resistance that characterizes readers in the professions. This resistance is the product of two conflicting forces in modern business: the rapidly increasing rate at which information is produced and disseminated and the dramatically decreasing amount of time the working reader has to spend on it. Writers need to understand this resistance and the conflicting forces that help to produce it.

The rate at which information is produced and disseminated has been the topic of many studies. Most of us know we are in the midst of an information explosion, one that continues to be fueled by rapid advances in technology.[4] While this is true of the world in which we all live, it is especially true for the world of business. Of all the professions, business is the primary consumer of technology and information, and a recognition of this underlies major studies of modern business culture, and even predictions about a new kind of product—information—and a new kind of worker, "the knowledge worker."[5]

Business will probably only increase its consumption of information. Those who have studied changes in the work force over the next decade argue that a cultural shift will continue to take place, one that will result in a greater sharing of information in the corporate setting: "The increased information sharing we are predicting for Workplace 2000 is the result of a consensus that emerged in the late 1980s that the danger of sharing information with employees was minimal compared to the advantage of having an informed work force."[6] Along with the increase in the sharing of information will be a new attitude of seriousness adopted toward messages that were previously viewed as peripheral. Newsletters, for example, will become more substantial carriers of important information. Thus, business will most probably increase not only its consumption of information but also the attention it is asked to pay to it.

Unfortunately, these developments come at a time when readers and other receivers of information have less time than ever before. Changes in the structure of the modern business organization, drastic and widespread downsizing, and increased competition have all reduced the time the manager was once able to devote to written messages. Readers in business can no longer afford to review material at relative leisure, and those who once had information processed for them in summaries, abstracts, or executive briefings find that they must now do it themselves.[7] As a consequence, many are developing techniques for "scanning" information, a phenomenon that has only recently received the attention of those who study communication. They are becoming more selective of the messages they read even as those messages compete more fully for their attention.

What writers need to appreciate about these recent and predicted developments is this: modern readers in business have to manage significantly more information than ever before, and they have significantly less time to spend on it. These are conflicting forces, but they are also *competing* forces, since they contend powerfully for the reader's attention. In practice, this means that writers will have to adopt special strategies for presentation, strategies that acknowledge the reader's resistance as well as the competing forces of increased information and decreased time.

Overcoming this resistance can take many forms. For example, writers could attempt to reduce the number of documents they produce, or not even write at all. This is probably a prudent course of action, at least in its tempered form, simply because the fewer the documents, the more attention they will receive as a matter of novelty. However, it is not a solution, even in its more tempered form, and writers who choose to produce fewer documents will find that the information may well need to be communicated in other, sometimes more time-consuming and less effective ways. They will also find that their reluctance to write can result in forfeiting their place of participation, record, and influence in the information community.

■ Competition and Organization

Although writers cannot meet resistance with reluctance, they can meet it with something else: organization. Organization, or *dispositio*, as it was called in classical rhetoric, is a powerful and time-honored solution to problems that result from increased information and decreased time. Without organization, readers will not be inclined to follow the writer from point to point and will not be able to retain the writer's message. In fact, the frustration and despair that can result from not being able to follow disorganized messages is only now becoming clear in the very publications that concern themselves with information. For example, in a recent issue of *PC Magazine*, chief editor Bill Machrone offers telling observations on his experience at a conference with a theme that "ignores the here and now in order to look farther down the road at the events and technologies that will shape the industry in the coming years":

> This year's theme was "Content Is Key," focusing on all the ways to infuse and extract meaning from the textual and data-oriented information bases that we all live

by. The amount of information available is exploding at an almost unimaginable rate. Without tools to organize and access it, meaning is irretrievably lost. Likewise, we need good authoring tools to impose order on the data and give the recipients choices of how to retrieve and use it.[8]

Here, information is presented as a force that will require "tools to organize" it if it is to have meaning. Unfortunately, Machrone continues by discussing one of these tools, one of his "favorite approaches to the information glut." This new software product possesses "a parsing engine that understands sentences and parts of speech." With the addition of considerable memory on disk, this program is supposed to be able to "extract the meaning and most important ideas from unstructured text."

Machrone certainly understands the importance of organization, though he may be a bit optimistic about the capability of software programs to produce it and thereby reveal meaning. However, good writers do just that. They provide their readers with "the meaning and most important ideas" when they organize their informative messages. By providing their readers with an organized message, writers can offer the promise of efficient reading and clear understanding. By consistently providing organized messages, writers can begin to earn a reputation for producing documents that are distinctive in quality and therefore appeal. Thus writers can gain an advantage over the forces that lead to resistance and thereby compete for their readers' attention.

Unfortunately, organization does not characterize business writing. This may be surprising to some simply because organization in many matters—personnel, finance, investment—is strongly associated with the business enterprise.[9] The popularity of software schedulers, project managers, and personal information managers suggests that organization is highly valued in most areas of practical business activity. Yet other evidence suggests that writing in business is no more and perhaps even less organized than writing done elsewhere. The task of this chapter, then, will be to discuss organization and its application to informative writing in business.

■ Organization and Arrangement

Understanding what organization is requires understanding what it is not, particularly in business writing. When asked how they organize their writing, working professionals in one long-term survey responded in ways that suggest they don't organize their writing at all.[10] Some never responded, and others who did respond candidly admitted that they simply do not organize their writing. Of those who did see themselves organizing their writing, most indicated that they organized while they were writing or that they worked from a list of points.

Since the writers who said they work from a list of points came the closest to providing any form of organization, this approach bears some comment. It also bears comment because of the prevalence of lists and listing devices in business writing. The listing device appears to provide organization but does not. Even though its alphabetical, numerical, or bulleted presentation may be familiar to the reader, a simple list only *appears* to organize. For example, in a list that is presented numerically, the number 2 certainly follows the number 1, just as the letter B follows A in the alphabetized version. However, nothing about the numerical or alphabetical version will show important relationships within the information the list contains. This is also true of the traditional college outline, which is essentially a listing device, and report headings that are used to increase readability. Simple lists, headings, and outlines *are* easy to read, and they should be used for that very reason, but this does not mean they provide organization to the material they contain.

If listing devices do not provide organization, we may well ask what does. Organization comes not from the *listing* of information but from the *arranging* of it. Because of that, we will come to expect two things from an organized document: first, that the arrangement of its parts be apparent; second, that the arrangement have an underlying principle that unites the parts of the arrangement. The difference between a list and an arrangement is illustrated by the following two simple examples. Each represents a kind of organization from which the writer intends to write. The topic concerns purchasing computers by direct mail:

1. Some people have used it.
2. Experience has been mixed.
3. Many people may become skeptical about it.

1. past opinions
2. present opinions
3. future opinions

Comparing the lists will usually result in a preference for the second, and most people will feel intuitively that the second is better organized simply because the items have words in common, and the pattern of repetition probably suggests greater design. The second is in fact better organized, though explaining why is another matter. Still, we can usually explain organization by testing for it. To do this, we remove the list's cosmetics, the numbers, letters, or bullets that stand before the information that will be developed. If we do that with the first example, nothing appears to unite the items, and no arrangement is *evident*. However, if we do it with the second example, we find that each has something *evidently* in common with the others, the *principle* of time. We could even present a reader with the first two ("past and present opinions") and reasonably expect the reader to predict the third ("future opinions") because the principle of organization would suggest it. Thus, organization exists as a principled and evident arrangement.

Such organization also exists as a critically important link between writer and reader because the principle behind the organization—time, balance, place, etc.—is one that *the reader brings to the reading experience*. Since the writer and reader both recognize this pattern of organization, it will serve them as a map they can travel along together.

In the example above, writer *and* reader need to acknowledge the principle of time if they are both to move without confusion from past to present to future.

Of course, knowing what organization is and does tells us nothing about where it comes from or how to select among different organizational options. Not many who study communication have written about this, and only a few have written about it in any detail.[11] Furthermore, the advice below, which represents much of the conventional thinking in this area, is probably not the best to follow.

> The first step in successful planning is a consideration of organizations with a view to eliminating those unsuited to the material. This selection is usually simple. For example, a writer rejects chronological order if there is no time sequence in his subject, geographical divisions if his topic has none, and climactic order if his main ideas have no suitable variations in importance.

> Second, a thoughtful writer considers his readers and does his best to select the organization that will be most helpful to them. This choice may involve more deliberation than does the selection of a plan suitable to the material, but it is not necessarily more difficult.[12]

While the content of this advice is good, it is backwards; at least it is for business applications. The first step is not oriented toward the interests of the reader, and the second step may well make the first one redundant or nonsensical. Since much that is written in business is solicited, this advice neglects the initial and important role the reader can play in helping the writer determine the appropriate organization, which ultimately is the organization that provides the reader with the kind of information the *reader* needs.

The guidelines that follow consider the reader in just this way, as the primary influence on choice of organization. These guidelines provide a systematic approach to informative writing, one that is particularly sensitive to the reader's resistance. They also present an organized approach, one that covers the writer's responsibilities *before, during,* and *after* writing.

▨ Before Composing

A significant amount of business writing is solicited by others, and the solicitation will often imply a way of organizing a written response. Because of this, writers will want to read or listen to their solicitations very carefully. For example, the following solicitation implies something about the reader's interests and the organization the writer's response might take:

> We are committed to purchasing a new folding machine for the Reprographics Department. Three machines work well for us: the Baumfolder 714, the MBM 352, and the Martin Yale Mark IV. Find out what you can about these machines, and give me a memo on their advantages and disadvantages.

Here the supervisor's request contains a clear structure, one the writer can use to organize the report. Any writer who chooses to respond to this request without considering advantages and disadvantages will probably not give the reader what the reader has requested. Although the request above presents an organization as part of the request, other solicitations are more subtle:

> Many of our personnel are urging us to move to flextime. Look into this, let me know what has caused them to feel this way, and what will happen if we go to flextime.

Although this is less straightforward, a careful reading will help the writer discern the structure. Two phrases in particular, "what has caused" and "what will happen" show the writer that the supervisor is interested in the *causes* and *effects* of going to flextime, and the writer can use this form of organization to frame a response.

When the request implies a form of organization, the writer should seriously consider using it because it helps to insure that the response is well organized and that the response will satisfy the reader's request. Much of the time, though, the request will be so vague and unhelpful that it implies nothing about how a written response might be organized. For example, an e-mail message might say the following:

> I just read the *Chronicle* piece on our contractors in Sunnyvale. What gives?

In this case, and in cases where writing is *not* requested, the writer may well wonder what to do about organization. Several options are available. First, the writer can use prior knowledge about the reader to select an appropriate form of organization. For example, if the reader has a known preference for balanced reviews, the writer may well select an organization of balance. If the reader usually expects information to have background as well as prediction, the writer may want to use some form of chronological organization.

If the writer simply has *no idea* what the reader may want, a quick telephone call or question on e-mail may help. Often a question that proposes a form of organization is best because it gives the reader something to accept or reject. At worst, the writer will know what the reader *does not* want, and that will help to determine what *is* needed. Should the writer be entirely unable to determine a form of organization appropriate to the reader, then turning to the subject matter for direction would make good sense. In either case, the writer will need to accept the responsibility for organizing the writing. Without a form of organization, the writer will lack direction, and the reader will be less able to follow and retain the information the letter, memo, or report contains.

Below are some common forms of organization. Writers can select from them a form that they believe would best match their reader's request or expectation. Notice that each has a unifying principle above it. Notice also that each form would most probably be recognized by both writers and readers.

TIME

Past—Present—Future
Before—During—After

PLACE

East—West—North—South
Top—Center—Bottom
Beginning—Middle—End

DEGREE

Least Important—Less Important—Most Important
Most Obvious—Less Obvious—Least Obvious
Least Urgent—Less Urgent—Most Urgent

BALANCE

Pro—Con—Conclusion
Advantages—Disadvantages—Conclusion
Benefits—Costs—Conclusion

INQUIRY

What—Who—When
Where—Why—How
(Other combinations)

Below are less common forms of organization that writers might use in three easily recognized professions: construction, education, and accounting. On the left are the principles; on the right are the organizational patterns.

Construction: Process	Plan—Frame—Finish
Education: Personnel	Faculty—Students—Staff
Accounting: Ledger Items	Credit—Debit—Balance

Least common are forms of organization that specialists might use within these three less easily recognized professions: auditing, house inspection, and automatic transmission repair. On the left are the principles; on the right are the organizational patterns.

Audit: Evaluation   Policy—Procedure—Compliance

Inspection: Areas   Substructure—Structure—Attic

Repair: Parts   Hard and Soft Components—Carriers

▣ During Composing

The writer who has selected a useful form of organization should be sure to *use* it and *communicate* it while writing the introduction, the body, and the conclusion of the paper.

The Introduction

The form of the introduction will depend partly on whether the writing has been requested. If it has been requested, then the writer should be content with a brief reminder: "Here is the opinion you requested on the recent changes in affirmative action." Writing that is unsolicited will require an explanation. A good if formulaic way to begin is this: "I am writing because I am concerned about the recent proposed changes in our affirmative action policy, and I believe you should know how they might affect us in Corporate Recruiting." Even better, and less formulaic, is this abbreviated opening: "I am concerned about the recent proposed. . . ."

Beyond providing the information above, the introduction should preview the *form of organization* and explain very briefly why the writer selected it. This is critical because the introduction serves as an orientation for the reader, who will have no idea what direction the writer will take unless it is explained. Although this suggestion may appear similar to already familiar advice—tell your reader what you will say, say it, then tell your reader what you have said—previewing the *organization* is entirely different. The following is a sample introduction written for a supervisor who requested a memo on employee attitudes toward decentralization of a company service (note: the entire memo is printed at the end of this chapter).

To:

From:

Subject:

Here is the memo you requested on our employees' attitudes toward decentralized word processing. Because their attitudes have changed since early May, and are expected to change even more in the next month, I have included in this memo a review of past, present, and future attitudes.

Notice the beginning of the second sentence and the word "because." This word begins not only the preview of the structure but also the reason the writer has selected it. This way, the reader will know not just *what* to expect from the writer's presentation but also *why* the writer has elected to present the information in this way. Because this provides a justification for the preview, it will help to overcome any resistance the reader might have had to the form of organization the writer selected.

The Body

Now that the writer has decided on a form of organization, both writer *and reader* must be able to follow it *in the body of the paper.* Many writers make the mistake of not working hard to communicate their organization in the presentation. They assume that because they know what the organization is and have announced it in the opening paragraph, the reader will be able to follow it through the document. Unfortunately, readers will not be able to follow the organization unless it is marked for them. Insuring they do is accomplished largely by using *organizational transitions* between major sections or paragraphs of the report. The introduction above is repeated below and followed with organizational transitions that indicate the major movements from one part of structure to another. Notice in particular the organizational transitions (in boldface here for emphasis only), which in a longer report might even be represented by formal headings:

To:

From:

Subject:

Here is the memo you requested on our employees' attitudes toward decentralized word processing. **Because** their attitudes have changed since early May, and are expected to change even more in the next month, I have included in this memo a review of **past, present,** and **future** attitudes.

We first became aware of a pattern in employee attitude toward decentralizing only at the end of **last April,** when several rumors about it started. **At that time,** people felt that decentralization had both **advantages and disadvantages.** Most saw the **advantages** in proximity and ease of distribution. **However,** others saw only **disadvantages,** particularly in problems with communication and storage.

Employee attitude has changed considerably since April, and things are much better **at present**. Some causes of the apparent disadvantages have now disappeared. **For example**, initial concerns about ease of distribution have been taken care of by our regular internal courier service. **As a consequence**, most people are looking for ways to benefit from the new arrangement. **Unfortunately**, a few of the key managers are resisting the change simply because they are so familiar with and accustomed to the traditional centralized service.

That is the current attitude toward decentralizing. What we can expect **in the near future** is unclear. **On the one hand**, our district managers believe most of our people will be supporting the change before summer vacations. **In addition**, they believe that even the more resistant key managers will support a decentralized service once they see how much more convenient and efficient it is. **On the other hand**, these managers have developed habits that are not broken easily, so they will still require some time to come around.

Note that each of the major sections above is introduced by a part of the writer's form of organization. Once the writer has provided this primary organization, the writer should consider extending it by providing a *substructure* to *organize ideas within* each section. For example, in the section on present attitudes, the writer may want to explain that some employees saw advantages while others saw disadvantages to decentralization. The principle of *balance* would thus lend further organization to the writer's report, and the appropriate transitions could then signal this organization within the paragraph, or between paragraphs if a major section requires several paragraphs to develop. Here is the body of the memo with the substructure of balance (in boldface) in the first and final paragraphs:

We first became aware of a pattern in employee attitude toward decentralizing only at the end of last April, when several rumors about it started. At that time, people felt that decentralization had both **advantages and disadvantages**. Most saw the **advantages** in proximity and ease of distribution. However, others saw only **disadvantages**, particularly in problems with communication and storage.

Employee attitude has changed considerably since April, and things are much better at present. Some causes of the apparent disadvantages have now disappeared. For example, initial concerns about ease of distribution have been taken care of by our regular internal courier service. As a consequence, most people are looking for ways to benefit from the new arrangement. Unfortunately, a few of the key managers are resisting the change simply because they are so familiar with and accustomed to the traditional centralized service.

That is the current attitude toward decentralizing. What we can expect in the near future is unclear. **On the one hand**, our district managers believe most of our people will be supporting the change before summer vacations. In addition, they believe that even the more resistant key managers will support a decentralized service once they see how much more convenient and efficient it is. **On the other hand**, these managers have developed habits that are not broken easily, so they will still require some time to come around.

These transitions are critically important for the reader who, even under the best circumstances, is trying very hard to follow the writer's message. For the resistant reader, who does not try this hard, these transitions can make the difference between continuing to read or doing something else. The idea behind these transitions, that they provide visible bridges within the writer's organization, may be extended to much more local concerns. Thus writers should attempt to provide transitions between sentences and even within them. The difference between providing them and not should be clear in the two paragraphs below. The messages are similar, except that the second paragraph has transitions (in boldface).

Employee attitude has changed considerably since April, and things are much better at present. Some causes of the apparent disadvantages have now disappeared. Initial concerns about ease of distribution have been taken care of by our regular internal courier service. Most people are looking for ways to benefit from the new arrangement. A few of the key managers are resisting the change simply because they are so familiar with and accustomed to the traditional centralized service.

Employee attitude has changed considerably since April, and things are much better at present. Some causes of the apparent disadvantages have now disappeared. **For example**, initial concerns about ease of distribution have been taken care of by our regular internal courier service. **As a consequence**, most people are looking for ways to benefit from the new arrangement. **Unfortunately**, a few of the key managers are resisting the change simply because they are so familiar with and accustomed to the traditional centralized service.

Below is a list of other transitions the writer can use to express specific relations between sentences within a paragraph and between words within a sentence.

Cause and Effect: as a result, because, consequently, hence, since, so, therefore, thus, for this reason.

Contrast: but, however, nevertheless, yet, on the contrary, on the other hand, although

Comparison: similarly, likewise, in the same manner, just as . . . so

Illustration: to illustrate, for example, for instance, as this shows, as this illustrates

Below is the memo with all of the organizational devices presented in boldface. These include the preview, justification for the preview, organizational transitions, substructure transitions, and sentence-level transitions.

To:

From:

Subject:

Here is the memo you requested on our employees' attitudes toward decentralized word processing. **Because** their attitudes have changed since early May, and are expected to change even more in the next month, I have included in this memo a review of **past**, **present**, and **future** attitudes.

We first became aware of a pattern in employee attitude toward decentralizing only at the end of **last April**, when several rumors about it started. **At that time**, people felt that decentralization had both **advantages and disadvantages**. Most saw the **advantages** in proximity and ease of distribution. **However**, others saw only **disadvantages**, particularly in problems with communication and storage.

Employee attitude has changed considerably since April, and things are much better **at present**. Some causes of the apparent disadvantages have now disappeared. **For example**, initial concerns about ease of distribution have been taken care of by our regular internal courier service. **As a consequence**, most people are looking for ways to benefit from the new arrangement. **Unfortunately**, a few of the key managers are resisting the change simply because they are so familiar with and accustomed to the traditional centralized service.

> That is the current attitude toward decentralizing. What we can expect **in the near future** is unclear. **On the one hand**, our district managers believe most of our people will be supporting the change before summer vacations. **In addition**, they believe that even the more resistant key managers will support a decentralized service once they see how much more convenient and efficient it is. **On the other hand**, these managers have developed habits that are not broken easily, so they will still require some time to come around.

The Conclusion

The writer is now ready for the conclusion. The writer should keep the conclusion uncluttered and resist the temptation to toss in ideas that have come to mind only as an afterthought. Summaries, which writers often provide because they have learned this in school, are not needed for documents only several pages long. For much longer documents, writers *may* want to review their form of organization, if only to reinforce the reader's recollection and retention of the material. In either case, writers will want to keep their conclusions or summaries free of any material that is irrelevant either to the topic or to the organization.

■ After Composing

Writers are routinely advised to put their writing away at this point and do something else before returning to it for editing. This advice is met with skepticism by those writers who feel they barely have enough time to write in the first place. For those whose time is extremely limited, a reasonable compromise would appear to be editing *while* writing. Although practiced writers will edit much of their work while writing, they will also reserve time after writing for a final revision and proofreading. This is important. A paper with a well-presented form of organization is almost useless to a reader who is constantly distracted and confused by problems in conciseness, word choice, word order, grammar, and punctuation. Fortunately, these matters are covered as individual chapters later in this book.

RELATED READINGS

Organization is easy enough to separate from format, which is often dictated by convention if not by the formal corporate design of letterhead and memoranda. However, as an area of study and description, organization is much less distinct from form, structure, arrangement, and invention as they are discussed by teachers and theorists of composition and rhetoric. For the

SAMPLE MEMO

To:

From:

Subject:

Here is the memo you requested on our employees' attitudes toward decentralized word processing. Because their attitudes have changed since early May, and are expected to change even more in the next month, I have included in this memo a review of past, present, and future attitudes.

We first became aware of a pattern in employee attitude toward decentralizing only at the end of last April, when several rumors about it started. At that time, people felt that decentralization had both advantages and disadvantages. Most saw the advantages in proximity and ease of distribution. However, others saw only disadvantages, particularly in problems with communication and storage.

Employee attitude has changed considerably since April, and things are much better at present. Some causes of the apparent disadvantages have now disappeared. For example, initial concerns about ease of distribution have been taken care of by our regular internal courier service. As a consequence, most people are looking for ways to benefit from the new arrangement. Unfortunately, a few of the key managers are resisting the change simply because they are so familiar with and accustomed to the traditional centralized service.

That is the current attitude toward decentralizing. What we can expect in the near future is unclear. On the one hand, our district managers believe most of our people will be supporting the change before summer vacations. In addition, they believe that even the more resistant key managers will support a decentralized service once they see how much more convenient and efficient it is. On the other hand, these managers have developed habits that are not broken easily, so they will still require some time to come around.

practitioner, the following should serve well as representative examples of books that cover organization as it is used in this chapter.

Adelstein, Michael E., and W. Keats Sparrow. *Business Communications.* New York: Harcourt Brace Jovanovich, 1983. Provides excellent coverage of different patterns of organization, though it does not show how they might figure into the presentation of the document.

Booth, Wayne C., and Marshall W. Gregory. *The Harper & Row Rhetoric: Writing as Thinking/Thinking as Writing.* New York: Harper & Row, 1987. Good collection of patterns of organization presented in paragraphs or short essays. Movement from pattern to presentation is not covered.

Friedrich, Gustav W., and Dan O'Hair. *Strategic Communication in Business and the Professions.* Boston: Houghton Mifflin, 1992. Different patterns of organization are converted into outlines. Outlines are not converted into documents.

NOTES

1. See, for example, the conventional division in Judith Bogert and Rebecca Worley, *Managing Business Communications: An Applied Process Approach* (Englewood Cliffs, NJ: Prentice-Hall, 1988), 2–5.

2. "Writing Is Thinking," *Selections: The Magazine of the Graduate Management Admissions Council* (Autumn 1987): 6–11.

3. See Marie E. Flatley, "A Comparative Analysis of the Written Communication of Managers at Various Organizational Levels in the Private Business Sector," *The Journal of Business Communication* 19, no. 3 (Summer 1982): 43–45.

4. See, for example, Neil Postman, *Technopoly* (New York: Knopf, 1992), 60–136.

5. See Peter Drucker, "The New Productivity Challenge," *Harvard Business Review* (November–December 1991): 70–79.

6. See Joseph Boyett and Henry Conn, *Workplace 2000* (New York: Penguin, 1992), 47–81.

7. For a discussion of organizational "flattening" and its influence on functions of this sort, see Janice Klein, "The Changing Role of First-Line Supervisors and Middle Managers," Bureau of Labor-Management Relations and Cooperative Programs, U.S. Department of Labor, *BLMR* 126 (1988): 7–17.

8. Bill Machrone, "Discontent with Content," *PC Magazine* (May 11, 1993): 88.

9. On the other hand, this may not be surprising because of the many unfavorable reviews of business writing. See, for example, J. W. Hildebrandt et al., "An Executive Appraisal of Courses Which Best Prepare One for General Management," *Journal of Business Communication* 19 (Winter 1982): 5–15. Also, Jean Evangelauf, "Business Schools Urged to Alter Curricula," *The Chronicle of Higher Education* (May 22, 1985): 16–18.

10. From a survey of approximately five hundred middle managers enrolled in the Executive MBA Program, Saint Mary's College of California. The survey was conducted as part of an in-class exercise from 1984 to 1992.

11. See Jack Selzer, "Arranging Business Prose," in *Writing in the Professions*, ed. Myra Kogen (Urbana, IL: NCTE, 1989), 37–64.

12. Harriet Tichy, *Effective Writing for Engineers, Managers, Scientists* (New York: Wiley, 1966), 65.

CLASSICAL ARGUMENT   3

AND MODERN BUSINESS

Now, previous compilers of "Arts" of rhetoric have provided us with only a small portion of this art, for proofs are the only things in it that come within the province of art; everything else is merely an accessory. And yet they say nothing about enthymemes which are the body of proof, but chiefly devote their attention to matters outside the subject; for the arousing of prejudice, compassion, anger, and similar emotions has no connection with the matter in hand. . . .

—Aristotle, *The Art of Rhetoric*

Modern business is typically an *argumentative* practice, in the best sense of the word, when people attempt to persuade by giving and assessing reasons.[1] It is an openly *competitive* activity, in which working professionals debate issues, defend positions, and evaluate the arguments of others. Because of this, we should not be surprised to find that written and oral communication in business, particularly when practiced at the middle and upper levels, is characterized less by a need to inform and more by an obligation to argue.[2]

This obligation to argue is one that many in business already acknowledge through much of their daily communication: it is present any time listeners or readers resist because they are intellectually competitive, because they have a competing point of view and are prepared to argue for it. For writers, these readers represent a distinct challenge. Not only will they expect writing that is well organized, they will demand of it reasons that are compelling enough to overcome their own competing point of view.

This does not mean that competition with readers will result in an unpleasant and uncooperative exchange, though argument is often thought of in just this negative way. Quite the opposite. As G. K. Chesterton once wisely said, "People generally quarrel because they cannot argue." As Chesterton suggests, argument offers an opportunity to avoid quarreling. As such, argument may be seen not as an impediment to cooperative interaction, but as a vehicle for promoting it. Understood in this way, argument will acquire a paradoxical character, one that is critically important to understanding its value to business and business organizations. And this paradox is implied, not surprisingly, in discussions of argument in interpersonal exchange:

> The need to supply supporting argumentation implies a difference between you and another person or group *and* a desire to eliminate or at least modify that difference: you want your audience to know what you know and to accept what you accept as true and desirable in that situation. However, you are unlikely to succeed in this attempt unless you can also demonstrate that you understand what your audience initially accepts as true and desirable about the situation. . . . Therefore, effective argumentation is a means of achieving cooperation and, insofar as it successfully addresses another's concerns, is itself a form of cooperation.[3]

Argument thus provides business with an extraordinary service because it is both a competitive *and* cooperative activity, one that is extremely well suited to an enterprise that today relies heavily on cooperative efforts to gain competitive advantage. However, changes in modern business will make argument an even more important part of business practice in the future, as markets become more competitive, as organizations become more culturally diverse, and as autocratic styles of management give way to efforts at empowerment.

As markets become more competitive, more emphasis will be placed on gaining advantage. However, the more successful companies will be those that can also persuade the customer that they possess advantage, particularly if this involves a differentiated product or service. Thus, business will depend more heavily on the tools of persuasion and therefore argument. Without the resistance produced by competition, a business could adopt a relatively relaxed stance and simply inform customers of products and services. In a competitive market, a business must persuade its customers that its products or services are the best or the best priced. With less competitive markets, some forms of persuasive communication might not even exist. For example, comparative advertising, which is openly persuasive if not argumentative, would be less likely in a market that is less competitive. This is not to say that advertising will become a more reasoned expression of business interest, but that competition will force businesses into a more persuasive stance. The greater the competition, the greater the need for argumentation.

As cultural diversity increases, so will the potential for misunderstanding and conflict. While this is often a reason for improving communication skills in general, it serves well as a particular cause for cultivating an ability to argue. Argument is most useful when differences exist, and it is well employed when differences exist for reasons that may not be readily apparent. Since many of these reasons are related to individual cultures, argument may be expected to help reveal them and thereby increase awareness if not acceptance of diversity. Thus, argument may be expected to gain greater prominence as an important form of exchange employed at the workplace.[4]

The use of argument will also increase as autocratic styles of management give way to empowerment, and as attempts at direction are replaced with efforts toward facilitation. Managers who once issued directives that were followed without question or discussion are already finding themselves inviting discussion as a vehicle for selling their directives to others. If unsupported statements characterize the discourse of the autocratic manager, argument may well become the most characteristic form of discourse for empowerment. However, argument will probably have the strongest initial appeal to those managers in transition from one style to another: even if they remain autocratic in disposition, they will not be able to depend on unsupported directives to carry the day. And as soon as they begin to give reasons or support for their directives, they will be arguing. So too will their staff members, since empowerment requires participation, and argument more than one point of view.[5]

The trends above indicate that the world of business will provide greater opportunities for argument in the future, both in the larger environment, as a consequence of competition, and in the organization, as a consequence of diversity and empowerment. Unfortunately, few managers have received any training in argumentation or even brief exposure to it. Courses in argument are uncommon at most universities and colleges, where even formal debate, a thoroughly competitive event, has become an extracurricular activity. MBA programs, including executive versions designed for working professionals, generally offer no instruction in it. And in the traditional corporate training curricula, courses in argument simply do not exist.[6]

One should expect that argumentation would be of considerable interest to managers not only for the reasons already mentioned but also for one that may be much more apparent: the ability to argue well is an important professional asset, and it is generally recognized as such. As one writer on management communication has said, "Generally speaking, argumentativeness in the workplace is a positive and constructive strategy. Arguing for causes, positions, and ideas within organizations is often viewed favorably because people who are effective arguers achieve their goals more often."[7] Thus, if managers have an interest in understanding argument, they have it for good reasons. This chapter responds to that interest. The following sections begin by providing a general understanding of argument and a description of its parts. Subsequent chapters then consider how to assemble these parts into a plan for presentation.

■ Understanding Argument

Understanding what argument is involves understanding what it isn't, especially since the word admits of many possible meanings. One of these meanings is "quarrel," and it is responsible for the negative connotation "argument" can have. This sense, which usually appears as a secondary dictionary entry, is the one that is most consistent with other negative senses when the word is used in common conversation. For example, when people say "Don't argue with me," they normally mean "Don't disagree with me" or "Be quiet." When someone says "I got into an argument," it usually means "We fought."

Of course, the word "argument" has several less negative meanings, including "a reason given in proof or rebuttal," "discourse intended to persuade," and "a coherent series of statements leading from a premise to a conclusion." Although these meanings are used less in conversation, they serve well to describe argument as something that is positive and constructive.[8] They also bring us closer to the sense of argument used at the beginning of this chapter, that of "persuading by giving reasons." Thus *argument is a form of persuasion, one that proceeds by giving reasons.* However, this does not tell us how argument works. For that, we will need to understand the principle of exchange.

■ The Principle of Exchange

At the heart of all argument is the principle of exchange: to receive something, something must be given. This means that if Jones wants to persuade Smith to accept her point about a financial investment, she will need to "give" something to Smith in exchange for her assent. Of course, Jones can "give" any number of things—a slap on the back, lunch or dinner, flattery about Smith's racquetball game, and so on. Or, Jones may give nothing at all. Jones may not even buy lunch but sit in Smith's office and simply repeat the same point in several different ways. If Jones does *any* of these, she will still be attempting to persuade Smith, and she may even be successful, but she will not be arguing.

Argument is the form of persuasion that proceeds by giving reasons, and reasons are statements that serve to support other statements. In argument, *reasons* are exchanged for assent. For example, Jones may be interested in gaining support for a new program that she believes will increase productivity in her department. She knows she will get this support if she can convince others that the program stands a good chance of doing what she claims it will. Thus, Jones would like to gain their assent or their agreement with her projection of increased productivity. In *exchange* for their assent, Jones will give one or more reasons. She may say that the program will foster cooperation and teamwork. She may say that it will enhance job satisfaction. She may say that it has increased productivity for another company. Notice, though, that in each case, Jones has provided a reason, a statement in support of her belief that the program will increase productivity.

By offering one or more reasons in support of her belief, Jones has met the minimum requirement for producing an argument. However, whether she has produced a good argument and whether the exchange will be successful are matters that depend on much more than simply issuing some statements in support of others. They will depend on knowing what to look for in these statements and their support, and on an ability to assemble these statements into a plan that can be used for writing. The following section will help writers to understand the parts of an argument as they appear in an argumentative plan. The next section will describe a logical procedure for constructing the plan. In a later chapter, the plan will be converted into a document.

▨ Planning an Argument: The Claim[9]

Since the quality of an argument is determined in large part by the quality of its parts and their connections, probably the best place to begin is with the most fundamental part: the claim. The claim is the statement the writer intends to support. If the argument goes well, it is also the statement the reader will eventually accept. Although the claim will be put forward in writing, it can be understood by thinking about its familiar use in conversation. The following expressions in conversation all signal that the speaker is about to offer a claim:

The main point I am trying to make is . . .

What I am arguing here is . . .

All I am saying is . . .

Thus, the writer's claim will represent the point the writer is trying to make as opposed to the points the writer will offer in support of it. Of course, writers will often want to make many points. For example, they may want to show that a product is safe, effective, and inexpensive. Or they may want to show that a plan will both comply with regulations and generate additional revenue. However, these multiple points almost always support a single one: in the first case above, that the product should be purchased; in the second, that the plan should be implemented. Most claims are of this singular sort. For this reason, writers may think of the claim as *the singular* statement that other statements will be offered to support.

▨ The Form of Claims

Even as a singular statement, the claim can take many different forms simply because writers will argue many different things.[10] For example, the writer who argues for increasing job fulfillment is obviously arguing *about* a different subject than one who argues for increasing profits. Job fulfillment and profits are different subjects. However, in addition to differences in the *subject* of the argument, claims display differences in *form,* in the way they are constructed. These are particularly important because they can contribute to the strength of the claim as well as to the way the claim is connected with other parts of the argument.

One important element of form is word order and whether the claim is in the active or passive construction. Although the topic of active and passive is covered at greater length as an editing concern in Chapter 9, the two examples below will be enough to distinguish between the two forms as they may be used in argument. In each case, the claim is about whether a company should sponsor an on-site daycare center:

An on-site daycare center will increase productivity.

Productivity will be increased by an on-site daycare center.

The first statement is in the active construction, which means that the sentence's subject, "An on-site daycare center," appears first and acts, through the verb "will increase," on the sentence's object, "productivity." The second statement is in the passive construction, which means that the object appears first and is acted on by the subject. Although the difference between the two might seem minor, it is not.

Passive constructions in argument are problematic for two reasons. First, the causal relationship that the writer will argue is less clear in the passive, and thus the direction of the claim may not match the direction of action the writer will argue. This will cause big problems when the writer supports the claim later. Second, the passive construction allows for, and sometimes even invites, omission of the subject. Once the writer has started the passive above, nothing would prevent a more severe expression:

Productivity will be increased.

Although this may not cause problems in this statement, omitting the subject *will* cause problems when the writer is unclear about what the subject is. Then, the passive construction will only make this lack of clarity more probable. The omission of the subject is most problematic in arguments in which the subject is an important part of the controversy. For example:

The company should be reorganized.

Not providing the subject in this statement only delays thinking through this part of the controversy. Thus, as one element of form, the active construction provides the writer with a preferable structure for the claim.

Another important element of form is verb tense: claims can take the form of past-, present-, or future-tense statements. Some are easily associated with some professions. In the practice of law, for example, many arguments involve claims in the past tense because controversy usually concerns the past: whether injury *was* done, whether a law *was* violated, whether a contract *was* breached, or whether a particular state of mind *did* exist. In audit, arguments often involve present-tense statements because concern is usually about whether an organization *is* complying, whether it *does* follow procedure, or whether it *adheres* to a particular policy.

Although a particular profession may be inclined to produce an argument in one tense or another, *all* of the tenses are *available*. However, one has a formal advantage over the others, one that becomes amusingly clear in the following collection notices in an advertisement from Microsoft Corporation.[11] The company issuing the notices is the fictional Bob's Tropical Fish & Grubs, a company that is trying to collect payment from a customer that ordered twelve Tahitian Swayback Guppies. Notice the progression of tenses as the reminders become more urgent:

A Friendly Reminder

Unfortunately, we have not received payment for the 12 Tahitian Swayback Guppies you ordered. It may have just slipped your mind. Or more likely, you've already sent in your payment, so just ignore this notice. We don't know what got into us. Sorry to bother you. You're special to us.

2nd Notice

Your account is now 60 days PAST DUE. We hope you are paying more attention to your guppies than you are to us. Remit your payment to avoid further action. Please pay your bill so we can pay our bills.

3rd and FINAL NOTICE

Your account is now Seriously Delinquent. If you do not pay the total amount due by Friday midnight, your guppies will be repossessed, your credit damaged and your fishing license revoked. Remember, we know where your guppies live.

Thank You

Here is an outlined progression of tenses from the first notice to the last:

(PAST)
We have not received payment.

(PRESENT)
Your account is now 60 days past due.

(FUTURE)
Your guppies will be repossessed, your credit damaged and your fishing license revoked.

The final statement here is important. It is a *statement of consequences,* and it serves as a basis for action. For this reason, the consequential statement preceded this thank-you-for-payment note:

We appreciate your prompt payment. As always, we value your patronage and we look forward to seeing you soon. P.S. By now, you've discovered the phenomenal rate at which a Tahitian Swayback Guppy grows. Coincidentally, for a limited time, our 100-gallon aquariums are now on sale. Have a nice day.

Writers in business will do well to strive for a similarly consequential claim in their writing. A claim that is consequential insures that the writer will have a strong basis for recommendation and helps to avoid structural problems that may arise when the writer takes the next step and combines the claim with a reason.

▇ **Planning an Argument: The Main Reason**

Of course, a claim does not make an argument, and even the strongest claim will be worthless unless the writer can support it. Support provides the reader with a basis for exchange, and if the argument goes well, the support will be exchanged for the reader's acceptance of the claim. This support has been called by various names, including "evidence," "data," and "minor premise." However, since it provides the reader with a reason to accept the claim, and since argument proceeds by giving reasons, the term "main reason" appears to be an appropriate one. The term "main" here simply signifies that other reasons may be added or subordinated to it.

Like the claim, the reason should take the form of an active construction. This will help to avoid the same problems that active constructions prevent when writing claims. It also greatly facilitates making a logical connection between claim and main reason. The main reason below is offered in support of the earlier claim about day-care centers. Notice that the word "because" precedes the main reason and defines the relationship between it and the claim it supports:

(Claim) An on-site daycare center will increase the working parent's productivity

because

(Main Reason) an on-site daycare center will reduce the working parent's anxiety about whether the child is receiving quality care.

Notice also that the subject of the claim, "an on-site daycare center," is repeated as the subject of the main reason. This is necessary and important because it provides a basis for making a logical connection between the two. Without this connection, nothing guarantees that the reason will support the claim, even though the *writer* might suppose it does:

(Claim) An on-site daycare center will increase the working parent's productivity

because

(Main Reason) people distrust caretakers who cannot be readily monitored.

Here, the connection between the two may well exist (e.g., by monitoring, you reduce stress and thereby increase productivity), but only in the writer's mind. Thus, repeating the subject helps to insure that the *reader* will see the connection between claim and main reason as readily as the writer does.

With a repeated subject, the writer can now assess the quality of the main reason by determining whether it is sufficient to support the claim. Of course, the *writer will think* that it is simply because it is the *writer's* main reason. However, since the main reason is offered to the reader in exchange for acceptance of the claim, its sufficiency to support the claim will have to be clear to the reader. The writer *can* assess the reader's sense of whether the main reason is sufficient, but only by recasting the argument (claim and main reason) into a form that will permit this assessment. This form is called a *syllogism*, and it consists of three statements: the claim, the main reason, and the assumption that is produced by connecting the two.[12] To produce the syllogism, the writer begins with the standard form we have already seen:

> (Claim) An on-site daycare center will increase the working parent's productivity
>
> because
>
> (Main Reason) an on-site daycare center will reduce the working parent's anxiety about whether the child is receiving quality care.

Next, the writer reverses the order of the statements so that the claim is last. Notice that the "because" is replaced with "therefore" to show that the direction of reasoning has changed:

> (Main Reason) An on-site daycare center will reduce the working parent's anxiety about whether the child is receiving quality care.
>
> Therefore,
>
> (Claim) an on-site daycare center will increase the working parent's productivity.

The last statement that is needed to produce the syllogism is the assumption behind the argument thus far. The writer will need to ask: how can I expect my reader to accept my claim if what I am giving *in exchange* is this main reason? The answer will always be the assumption behind the exchange; in this case, the short version is "reduction in anxiety will increase productivity." Below is the full version of this syllogism, with the assumption placed at the top:

> (Assumption) A company benefit that reduces the working parent's anxiety about the quality of child care will increase productivity.
>
> (Main Reason) An on-site daycare center will reduce the working parent's anxiety about whether the child is receiving quality care.
>
> (Claim) An on-site daycare center will increase the working parent's productivity.

Should the writer want to express the syllogism in its traditional format, little would change except for the labels that are used to mark each statement. In the traditional form, two of the statements are called *premises*, and one is called a *conclusion*, but the syllogism as a conceptual model of reasoning remains in the form it took earlier:

(Major Premise) A company benefit that reduces the working parent's anxiety about the quality of child care will increase productivity.

(Minor Premise) An on-site daycare center will reduce the working parent's anxiety about whether the child is receiving quality care.

(Conclusion) An on-site daycare center will increase the working parent's productivity.

▨ Judging Assumptions

Whether one calls the uppermost statement in the syllogism an "assumption" or a "major premise," judging it is a critically important part of constructing the argument, since it indicates the foundation on which the entire line of reasoning rests. It is also important because it represents a common ground between writer and reader, one that the writer will rely on to move the reader toward accepting an initially controversial statement. For example, in the argument above, the writer would have to assume that the reader would accept the assumption that "a company benefit that reduces working parents' anxiety about the quality of child care will increase their productivity." Otherwise, the writer would have no way of being certain that the main reason could be exchanged for the reader's acceptance of the claim.

Because assumptions are so important, writers will want to be sure to identify and evaluate them fully. Part of this can be done mechanically by considering the argument in its standard form:

> An on-site daycare center will increase the working parent's productivity because an on-site daycare center will reduce the working parent's anxiety about whether the child is receiving quality care.

The writer will begin by working with the subject after the "because" in the main reason. This is "an on-site daycare center." The writer can generalize this by calling it "a company benefit," which provides the beginning of the assumption, since it is always a more general category than any of the syllogism's other statements. All the writer needs to do now is follow this through to the end of the main reason. This produces "a company benefit that reduces the working parent's anxiety about whether the child is receiving quality care." To complete this, the writer needs only to go to the claim and consider the consequence there: "will increase productivity." Thus, the full assumption is "A company benefit that reduces the working parent's anxiety about the quality of child care will increase productivity."

Another, even more mechanical but perhaps more reliable way of identifying the assumption begins by numbering the parts of the argument. Here is a fresh example for the writer to consider:

(Claim) Purchasing laptop computers will increase our revenues because

(Main Reason) purchasing laptop computers will boost the morale of our salespeople and the satisfaction of our customers.

The parts of the argument are numbered in the following way. First, in the claim, all
words to the left of the verb, which taken together constitute the subject of the sentence, are given the number 1. Second, still in the claim, all words to the right of the
verb, which taken together constitute the object of the sentence, are given the number 2. Third, now in the main reason, all words to the left of the verb, which taken
together constitute the *repeated* subject of the sentence, are given the number 1R.
Fourth, and finally, still in the main reason, all words to the right of the verb, which
taken together constitute the object of the sentence, are given the number 3. In this
way, the argument would appear as it does below, with a single underline to help represent the subjects and a double underline to help represent the objects. The verbs in
the argument are not underlined.

                    1   2
Purchasing laptop computers will increase our revenues because

                    1R   3
purchasing laptop computers will boost the morale of our salespeople and the
satisfaction of our customers.

This numbering shows a defining feature of the argument: it consists of three parts
distributed over four possible positions. The task now is to reveal the assumption by
presenting the relationship between 3 and 2. This is a *causal* relationship. Because
of that, the writer can use this formula: "That which *causes* the verb and 3 of the
main reason will *cause* the verb and 2 of the claim." Thus in the example above,
the assumption is "That which boosts the morale of our salespeople and the satisfaction of our customers will cause the increase of our revenues." Although this appears clumsy as a statement, it does represent the assumption on which the argument rests. Here it is in its full syllogistic form, with the assumption (the major
premise) "cleaned up":

(Major Premise) Any purchase that will boost the morale of our salespeople and
the satisfaction of our customers will increase our revenues.

(Minor Premise) Purchasing laptop computers will boost the morale of our salespeople and the satisfaction of our customers

(Conclusion) Purchasing laptop computers will increase our revenues.

Although the writer does not need to clean up the assumption to have a reliable understanding of the basis of the argument, it will help to show how the subjects are

consistent since they are all expressions of a purchase, except that they range from general ("any purchase") to particular ("purchasing laptop computers"). Still, in either of these cases, the writer will have correctly identified the assumption.

Determining whether the assumption is acceptable is not quite as easy as identifying it. This will require the writer to think solely about the reader and about any objections the reader might be able to voice against the assumption. This may require time, but the time will be well invested. Only by determining if the assumption is acceptable to the reader will the writer be able to tell if the main reason is sufficient to support the claim. If it isn't, the writer will need to strengthen the main reason. If it is, the writer can use this structure as a plan to develop the argument at much greater length, whether it is in the form of a memo, letter, report, or a document form that is less familiar.

■ Testing the Argument: Common Fallacies

Of course, eventually the writer will want to develop the plan into a full document, and the next two chapters will consider just this development, both in the stages of further planning and final presentation. However, before writers move beyond the argument in its present three-part form, they should be certain that it is in a form *worth developing further*. Developing the plan further would be pointless if it contains flaws in its present form. Happily, several tests exist for avoiding flaws in reasoning and thus for insuring the quality of the plan in its present and critically important initial stage.

The writer should acknowledge that one major test is available simply through the mechanism of the syllogism, which has traditionally provided a way of evaluating the quality of an argument. The writer who has been able to construct a plan and derive the assumption behind it can be reasonably certain that its ideas are related in a particularly coherent way. However, that alone will not insure that the ideas are worth developing. Even if the writer can express the argument syllogistically, it may still contain problems or *fallacies* that will only become more severe and troublesome when the ideas are eventually developed. Just as enlarging an image will make graphical flaws more apparent, so will developing an argument reveal flaws of reasoning that may be more difficult to see at the planning stage.

Although catalogues of fallacies of reasoning may be found in a variety of works on logic, rhetoric, and composition, the following are representative of the more common problems that arise at the stage of constructing the argument and its underlying syllogism. What follows is thus intended as being specific to this stage of constructing the argument. Other fallacies, those which occur more commonly in the presentation of the argument, will be taken up specifically in a later chapter devoted to ethical argument and fallacious reasoning.

The word "fallacy" is used in a very general sense to include not only conventionally recognized formal flaws in reasoning but also those problems that can "deceive" the writer into thinking an argument is better than it really is. Irving Copi describes the concept of fallacy very well:

Many arguments, of course, are so obviously incorrect as to deceive no one. It is customary in the study of logic to reserve the term "fallacy" for arguments which, although incorrect, are psychologically persuasive. We therefore define a fallacy as a form of argument that *seems* to be correct but which proves, upon examination, not to be. It is profitable to study such arguments, for familiarity and understanding will help keep us from being misled by them.[13]

These fallacies may be divided into two types: structural and semantic. Structural fallacies concern the structure of the argument, the relationship between the claim *and* the main reason, as opposed to matters that concern only the claim *or* the main reason, such as the form of a verb or the abstractness of a word. Writers will want to become familiar with one major structural fallacy: the fallacy of circular reasoning, and one major semantic fallacy, the fallacy of assumed specifics.

Circular Reasoning

Formally known as the *petitio principii*, and less formally as "begging the question," the fallacy of circular reasoning can be understood by recognizing that an argument must have at least a claim and a reason supporting that claim. What this means in practice is that the two must be different. Otherwise, the writer will be offering support for the claim that is itself the claim. For example, the writer who intends to support the claim "This product will fail in the marketplace" by offering the reason "This product will not be purchased" only rewords the idea of the claim in the main reason.

Although spotting circular reasoning can be tricky, writers can catch most instances of circularity by becoming familiar with the six conditions that follow.

1. Plans with present-tense claims will be circular. When the claim is in the present tense, the main reason will almost always offer detail to the claim. For example, one might argue that

The controller is a crook because the controller embezzled company funds.

In this argument, the writer is intending to prove the crookedness of the controller simply by stating the form the crookedness took. Another, more revealing, way to cast this argument is:

The controller is a crook because the controller is a crook.

or

The controller embezzled company funds because the controller embezzled company funds.

Of course, calling the argument "circular" is one way of describing it, and describing it in this way is important if the writer is to see the circularity. However, if the writer is entirely aware of this and chooses to provide the claim's detail in the main reason, then a more generous description is possible. Thus, we might say the writer is arguing a *definition*. While this is an acceptable argument to make, it will be predictably limited when consequences are available. In the case above, the writer wishing to lead toward a recommendation about the controller would do better to predict what will happen as a consequence of the embezzlement.

2. Plans that explain, describe, restate, or define the claim in the main reason will be circular. For example, the writer of the following argument explains the meaning of "hurt the quality of patient care" by saying that it will "cause physicians to perform unnecessary operations."

> Cost containment in medical care will hurt the quality of patient care because cost containment in medical care will cause physicians to perform unnecessary operations.

Of course, the writer *might* have something else in mind with the expression "hurt the quality of patient care." If that is the case, then the writer will want to state specifically the meaning of "hurt the quality of patient care" in a way that has little to do with performing unnecessary operations. By doing this, the writer would be better able to avoid the circularity.

3. Arguments with *objects* that are *both* descriptive of actions can easily be circular. Notice that the verb in the previous sentence is "can," which indicates that circularity is less probable here than it was in the two cases already discussed. In the following argument, the objects of the claim and main reason are italicized:

> The company's reputation for unsafe practices will cause *a reduction in product purchases* because the company's reputation for unsafe practices will cause *customers to boycott its products.*

Since the objects are conceptually similar, the argument has a greater chance of being circular. Note that in both cases, the writer appears to be saying the same thing, that sales will be reduced.

4. Plans with objects that are both descriptive of belief, attitude, feeling, or perception can also easily be circular. Again, the verb is "can," which indicates that circularity is less probable here than it was in the first two cases discussed. In the following argument, the objects of the claim and main reason are italicized:

> The division's refusal to accept a proposal on flextime will cause *low morale* because this refusal will produce *employees who are unhappy with their working conditions.*

Since the objects are also conceptually similar (though they concern themselves with expressions of nonaction), the argument also has a good chance of being circular. Note that in both cases, the writer appears to be saying the same thing: low morale is simply a less specific way of saying "unhappy with working conditions." "Low morale" here *means* "unhappy."

5. Plans with a belief, attitude, feeling, or perception expressed in the main reason and an action expressed in the claim will probably not be circular (note that probability is all that is available here). This amounts to saying the reverse of what has been said in the four preceding examples. To avoid circularity, the writer needs to differentiate the objects of the claim and main reason. One way to do this is by selecting objects that are conceptually different, as *internal* beliefs, attitudes, feelings, and perceptions differ from *external* actions, such as improved performance. For example:

> Establishing quality circles within this division will improve employee performance because establishing these circles will cause employees to perceive that management values their ideas about and participation in the running of the company.

6. Plans with a clear cause-to-effect relation will probably not be circular. This is an extrapolation of the previous point. By insuring that the argument has a cause (main reason) and effect (claim) relationship, the writer will also insure a noncircular argument simply because causes and effects are conceptually so different. For example:

> A policy that restricts smoking because of pressure from a small group will result in smokers disregarding the policy because a policy that restricts smoking for this reason will cause the majority of smokers to believe they are being victimized by a minority.

Assumed Specifics

The other major fallacy we want to consider here, the fallacy of assumed specifics, is related to circular reasoning because it can prevent writers from being able to detect circularity. This fallacy recognizes that argumentative plans are useful because they help writers to determine most of what they want to say before they actually have to say it. What this means in practice is that writers will benefit from the direction their plans can give them to the extent that their plans *specify* this direction through the concreteness of the language used in the claim and main reason. The fallacy occurs either when the writer *assumes* specifics or when the writer chooses to wait to provide specifics in the presentation.

Simply telling writers to be more specific doesn't help when they are puzzled about what "specific" means in writing. However, writers can become more specific in their expression by becoming familiar with the *ladder of abstraction*, which is discussed at length in a later chapter, where it is used to discuss editing, ethos, and word choice. Here it is introduced in abbreviated form because it is important enough to be considered as a separate matter in reasoning.

The ladder of abstraction shows how words and phrases gain specificity by reducing their references. Note in the following ladder how expressions on the lower levels ("rungs") refer to *fewer* things. These words are more specific than the words that are higher on the ladder.

enhanced performance

improved communication

better ability to speak effectively

acquired a skill at oral argument

A feature of the ladder of abstraction is that each term includes the term below it. "Enhanced performance" is simply a more general or abstract way of saying that someone has "improved communication," which is more abstract than saying the person has a "better ability to speak effectively." That, of course, is the abstract way of saying specifically that the person has "acquired a skill at oral argument."

Although writers will always want to use specific verbs, the ladder of abstraction is used primarily for other parts of speech. Writers can use it to insure that they have specified the subjects and objects of their arguments. This will help them to produce arguments that will give them much more direction in the written presentation of the case. The examples that follow will show how the subjects and objects of the original plan become refined until the writer arrives at an argument that is specific in the direction it will offer in presentation. The writer's first and most abstract version is this:

(Claim) Hiring new employees will help our business

because

(Main Reason) hiring new employees will make us more efficient.

In the form above, the argument is more representative of the writer's first general opinion about hiring than it is of the steps that will guide the writer in the presentation. In fact, it is so general (abstract) that it could easily be hiding circularity in the terms "help" and "make us more efficient." For that reason alone, the writer should strive to move the terms down the ladder of abstraction. This writer has wisely chosen to do that and begins by asking whether the first term, "Hiring new employees," can be made more specific by reducing the number of people to which the expression refers. After some thought, the writer realizes that not all "new employees" are being sought but only those for a particular position and with a particular kind of knowledge:

(Claim) *Hiring new programmers with a knowledge of C5 graphical interfaces* will help our business

because

(Main Reason) *hiring new programmers with a knowledge of C5 graphical interface* will make us more efficient.

The writer has effectively moved the subject of the claim down two rungs on the ladder of abstraction: one rung represents reduced reference by specifying a particular knowledge; the other rung reduces the reference even more by specifying that programmers are being sought. Since the subject of the argument is repeated, the writer will want to be sure to make the change, as it is made above, in both the claim and the main reason. With the writer starting on the top rung, this is how the change would look on the ladder of abstraction:

Hiring new employees

Hiring new programmers

Hiring new . . . with . . . interfaces

Once the subject has been specified (the writer may want to specify this one further), the next step is to consider doing the same with the objects of the argument. The first object is "will help our business." The writer begins by acknowledging that business can be helped in many ways. This acknowledgment is important because it means that the expression can be specified further. Of course, the writer can always decide to provide the specifics while writing, but that would be a mistake. If the writer is involved in the writing and cannot provide the specifics, much will have to be changed. By making the meaning more specific in the planning stage, the writer can be sure that specifics exist. If they do exist, they will be ready when the time comes to present the argument at length. Realizing this, the writer wisely decides to make "will help our business" more specific now. After some thought, the writer produces this less abstract version:

(Claim) Hiring new programmers with a knowledge of C5 graphical interfaces will enable us to *increase our sales of both DOS and Windows versions of our software*

because

(Main Reason) Hiring new programmers with a knowledge of C5 graphical interfaces will make us more efficient.

This will help considerably when the writer begins to present the argument because the specific ideas now contained in the claim will translate into specific direction in the paper. Also, since the claim is ultimately the conclusion of writing, the writer will now have a much clearer idea of what to work toward. What now remains is the abstract expression "make us more efficient," which is the object of the main reason. After considerable thought, the writer is able to explain in this part of the argument the more specific idea behind efficiency in this case: these programmers will help with deadlines for product releases. In its slightly more refined form the writer produces this:

(Claim) Hiring new programmers with a knowledge of C5 graphical interfaces will enable us to increase our sales of both DOS and Windows versions of our software

because

(Main Reason) hiring new programmers with a knowledge of C5 graphical interfaces *will enable us to meet our projected deadlines for software releases that we have promised to our customers.*

The writer now has a much more specific (less abstract) argument and consequently a much better idea of what to say when the time comes to begin writing at length. The writer also has a very clear idea of *one* side of the argument. What the writer does with the *other* side is the subject of the next chapter.

RELATED READINGS

The materials below consist of theoretical works and books about practical application. Readers will find that most works that emphasize argument do not consider its use in business communication. Readers will also find that most works about business communication do not emphasize the use of argument.

Aristotle. *Rhetoric.* Trans. J. H. Freese. Loeb Classical Library. Cambridge, MA: Harvard University Press, 1982. Any serious study of argument should probably start here.

Bogert, Judith, and Rebecca Worley. *Managing Business Communications: An Applied Process Approach.* Englewood Cliffs, NJ: Prentice-Hall, 1988. Useful introduction to the proofline but without an application to composition.

Booth, Wayne C., and Marshall W. Gregory. *The Harper & Row Rhetoric: Writing as Thinking/Thinking as Writing.* New York: Harper & Row, 1987. Contains a section on enthymemes and syllogisms as well as one on fallacies of argument.

Brandt, William. *The Craft of Writing.* Englewood Cliffs, NJ: Prentice-Hall, 1969. An extended application of the syllogism to writing in college.

Brandt, William. *The Rhetoric of Argumentation.* Indianapolis: Bobbs-Merrill, 1970. Excellent work on argumentative analysis with an emphasis on enthymemes and syllogisms.

Cicero. *De Oratore, Books I and II.* Trans. E. W. Sutton and H. Rackham. Loeb Classical Library. Cambridge, MA: Harvard University Press, 1976. Representative of Roman rhetoric and argumentation. Any serious study of argument should probably continue here after Aristotle's *Rhetoric.*

Gage, John. *The Shape of Reason: Argumentative Writing in College.* New York: Macmillan, 1987. Excellent recent work on the use of enthymeme-based argument in college writing.

———. "An Adequate Epistemology for Composition: Classical and Modern Perspectives." *Essays on Classical Rhetoric and Modern Discourse.* Ed. Robert J. Connors, Lisa S. Eds, and Andrea A. Lunsford. Carbondale: Southern Illinois University Press, 1984.

———. "Teaching the Enthymeme: Invention and Arrangement." *Rhetoric Review* 1 (1983), 83–96.

Green, Lawrence D. "Enthymemic Invention and Structural Prediction." *College English* 41 (1983), 20–27.

Micheli, Linda, Frank V. Cespedes, Donald Byker, and Thomas J. Raymond. *Managerial Communication.* Glenview, IL: Scott, Foresman, 1984. Good introduction to the proofline, though it is not converted into a written presentation.

Toulmin, Stephen. *The Uses of Argument.* Cambridge, MA: Cambridge University Press, 1958. Practitioners may regard this with some suspicion because it engages several audiences with more theoretical interests. Still, this is a good book to begin studies of prooflines.

Toulmin, Stephen, Richard Reike, and Allan Janik. *Introduction to Reasoning.* New York: Macmillan, 1979. An extension of earlier work, this text considers the analysis of argument in a variety of disciplines. Includes a section on arguments in management.

NOTES

1. Any number of working definitions of argument may be adopted here. The one I have selected is a modified version of the one used in Stephen Toulmin et al. *An Introduction to Reasoning* (New York: Macmillan, 1979).

2. See, for example, the survey of business writing tasks in Judith Bogert and Rebecca Worley, *Managing Business Communications: An Applied Process Approach* (Englewood Cliffs, NJ: Prentice-Hall, 1988), 2–5.

3. Linda Micheli, Frank V. Cespedes, Donald Byker, and Thomas J. Raymond, *Managerial Communication* (Glenview, IL: Scott, Foresman, 1984), 34. Not surprisingly, argument is considered as part of cooperative negotiation in Dan O'Hair and Gustav W. Friedrich, *Strategic Communication in Business and the Professions* (Boston: Houghton Mifflin, 1992), 349–76.

4. In more specialized terms, argument may be expected to assist greatly in making "subjective cultures visible." On this, see George A. Borden, *Cultural Orientation: An Approach to Understanding Intercultural Communication* (Englewood Cliffs: Prentice-Hall, 1991), 209.

5. On argument, empowerment, and participative management, see Joseph Boyett and Henry Conn, *Workplace 2000* (New York: Penguin, 1992), 156–60.

6. Corporate training directories are generally regarded as highly proprietary. However, readers who are able to review them may expect to find nothing on argumentation as it is described in this chapter.

7. Dan O'Hair and Gustav W. Friedrich, *Strategic Communication in Business and the Professions* (Boston: Houghton Mifflin, 1992), 350.

8. For a dedicated discussion of "cooperative argument," see Josina Makau, *Reasoning and Communication: Thinking Critically about Arguments* (Belmont, CA: Wadsworth, 1990), 43–58.

9. This begins a discussion of a device that rhetoricians will recognize as an enthymeme. For much more on this, see Book II of Aristotle's *Rhetoric.* For less but with a direct application to writing, see the following: William Brandt, *The Rhetoric of Argumentation* (Indianapolis: Bobbs-Merrill, 1970); William Brandt, *The Craft of Writing* (Englewood Cliffs, NJ:

Prentice-Hall, 1969); John Gage, *The Shape of Reason: Argumentative Writing in College* (New York: Macmillan, 1987); Lawrence Green, "Enthymemic Invention and Structural Prediction," *College English* 41 (1980): 623–24.

10. What follows is not the conventional classification of claims according to statements of fact, value, and policy. Although I believe I appreciate this classification, I do not believe that it is particularly useful for explaining argument as it is presented in this chapter for this audience. For a discussion of the more conventional terms, see Makau, *Reasoning and Communication: Thinking Critically about Arguments* (Belmont, CA.: Wadsworth, 1990), 62–63.

11. Microsoft Advertisement, *Byte* (December 1992): 37.

12. Standard terms here are major premise, minor premise, and conclusion. I have substituted more familiar terms because the final terms for these statements will accord those in the proofline.

13. Irving Copi, "Informal Fallacies," in Richard Young, Alton Becker, and Kenneth Pike, *Rhetoric: Discovery and Change* (Harcourt, Brace & World: 1970), 251.

ethos — character credibility

word, language

logos — logic appeals to

reasoning

organization

p ethos — emotions

REFUTATION 4

Argument as Inquiry

In the case of any person whose judgment is really deserving of confidence, how has it become so? Because he has kept his mind open to criticism of his opinions and conduct. Because it has been his practice to listen to all that could be said against him; to profit by as much of it as was just, and expound to himself, and upon occasion to others, the fallacy of what was fallacious.

—John Stuart Mill, *On Liberty*

Some theorists of argumentation seem to believe that we should consider the purpose of argumentation to be persuasion. Although persuasion is a purpose of argumentation on some occasions, we must recognize that argumentation can and does fulfill another equally important purpose, namely inquiry.

—Jack Meiland, *Argument as Inquiry*

▓ Planning an Argument: Opposition

As we have seen, writers may expect to increase their chances of success in reasoned persuasion if they construct an argumentative plan, test the plan by examining the syllogism it is based on, and check for weaknesses by examining it for several fallacies. By doing this, writers will have determined the strongest case they can make, and they will have considered many of the options available to engage and influence the thinking of their skeptical readers. They will also become aware of the more critical assumptions on which they must rely in the course of presenting their case.

Nevertheless, writers who do not move beyond the plan that represents their point of view will probably fail to win the assent of their readers. Although the plan as it stands does a very good job of representing the writer's point of view, it represents *only* the writer's and not the reader's opposition to it. Of course, the argument itself is born from opposition, so we must assume the writer has a reason for arguing. We

61

must also assume that someone, either the reader or an important third party, disagrees with the writer's point of view.

However, the existence of disagreement does not automatically result in its incorporation into the argument. The writer will need to *build it in.* This will require a strong effort because three circumstances will influence the writer to ignore opposition entirely. First, writing is itself a private activity. Unlike an oral presentation, in which the listeners are physically present, writing is done in the almost total absence of the reader. Since the reader is literally out of sight, chances are greater that the reader will also be out of mind, the writer's mind. Second, argument always involves conflict or disagreement, states most people find unpleasant and literally *disagreeable.* Just as most people will avoid conflict in general, so too will the writer of a particular argument. Third, the writer of argument is primarily engaged in presenting his or her own line of reasoning. Thus, the harder the writer works to present one point of view, the greater will be the temptation to exclude any view that might threaten it or interrupt the effort. For these reasons, writers should view the inclusion of opposition as a task that requires extraordinary effort.

Fortunately, the writer who builds opposition into the argument will be rewarded by a greatly increased likelihood of success. Numerous studies in an area of communication known as *message-sidedness* indicate that the inclusion of opposing points of view increases the credibility of the arguer (though certain conditions, which we will discuss later, will need to be met). These studies also indicate a link between including opposition and the arguer's success in changing the attitudes of those who hold the opposing point of view.[1]

A very good example of the persuasiveness of entertaining opposing points may be found in one mail-order distributor's open-letter attempt to overcome the skepticism of consumers who are concerned about shopping by mail. Here is a section in which the distributor's point of view is presented:

> Nationally, mail order sales are growing at a greater rate than store sales. This is because mail order provides you with the best way to get quality merchandise at consistently low prices. Therefore, don't deny yourself the convenience and savings of this type of shopping because of the mail order myth. Please realize that the vast majority of the businesses in our industry maintain the highest ethical standards and are sophisticated enough to recognize that the secret to their success is satisfied customers.[2]

Of course, the distributor could continue to present its point of view and argue for the benefits of ordering through the mail, but that may or may not convince readers who have their *own* concerns about mail-order purchases. For example, the passage above has nothing directly to say to those customers who are concerned about getting a product that does not meet their expectations. Nor does it speak to customers who have chosen not to purchase through mail order because of their concerns about slow or poor service. Of course, these are the very concerns we have in mind when we discuss opposition. Fortunately for the distributor, these are also the very concerns this distributor apparently had in mind when the original message was crafted. Here they are as they were expressed in the original letter:

> The first fear which consumers apparently have is that they will be defrauded. Actually, this is extremely unlikely in today's society. Principally because of tough mail fraud laws, we feel that you have more legal protection buying from a mail order firm than from any other type of retailer. Since mail order companies depend on the mails for soliciting and receiving their orders, fraudulent sales practices can be easily reported to a local Postal Inspector who can initiate a formal mail fraud investigation. Also, a consumer complaint can be made to the Federal Trade Commission in Washington or the Attorney General's office of the state in which the mail order company operated. Consequently, almost all of the fraudulent mail order schemes are very short lived.

> The second and more justified concern with mail order is the fear of slow and poor service. Fortunately, this is becoming less of a problem as mail order retailers adapt to changes in the public's attitude. In the past, people shopped mail order either for price or because it was the only way in which they could get what they wanted. Therefore, service was not the overriding concern of the seller or buyer. However, people are now shopping mail order for convenience and service as well as price. With the widespread use of credit cards, toll-free WATS lines and UPS shipments, it is now possible for a customer to receive his purchase within a few days after ordering it. Smart mail order merchants recognize this and are finding that fast, efficient service is vital to their business success.

An important relationship exists here between the distributor's announced interest in the customer and the way that customer is treated in the letter. The distributor has in fact treated the customer well here because the customer's concerns have been raised as the concerns of the reader of the letter. Although we might simply assume at this point that the letter will be much more persuasive with the opposition entertained than with it omitted, we will find later that good reasons exist to support this supposition. As long as other conditions are met, messages that include the opposing point of view will be more persuasive than those that don't.

However, the persuasiveness that the writer gains by including opposition may well not be the most valuable contribution that opposition can make to the process of writing. Recent writers on argument have even been moving away from discussing its persuasive character and have instead begun to emphasize the function of argument and especially opposition in inquiry. Jack Meiland is one of these. Meiland is interested in "developing the notion of argumentation as a method of inquiry and contrasting this notion with the prevailing idea that the main purpose of argument is persuasion."[3] Meiland defines inquiry as "the process of discovering what (if anything) is rational to believe about a topic," and offers the following set of steps in the argumentative process of inquiry:

1. Determining a question or problem to be inquired into
2. Formulating a hypothesis or position on the question or problem

3. Constructing an argument for the hypothesis or position
4. Developing objections to the argument for the hypothesis or position
5. Devising replies to these objections

Steps four and five are the ones most relevant to our interests here because they reveal in the process of argument the role of the opposing point of view. If argument is to provide the greatest utility to writers, it will of necessity involve more than one point of view. The writer who is satisfied with arguments in which only one point of view is represented will also need to be satisfied with an undeveloped and probably inaccurate point of view on an issue or problem. The invaluable function of opposition, then, is to provide a test for ideas, a way of checking the writer's point of view against others so that the strengths and weaknesses of each may be considered. Writers who abandon or revise an initial claim in the face of opposition may experience pain, but they will do better in the long run because they will have a better understanding of the issues and a clearer idea of what they think about them. They will also have a better understanding of their readers. Opposition thus provides for inquiry into both the subject and the audience.

Although including opposition represents a significant addition to the writer's work, it can easily make the difference between success and failure in inquiry as well as persuasion. For that reason, the writer will want to include it in the structure of the plan. This will help the writer to overcome the temptation to avoid opposition for the reasons mentioned at the beginning of this chapter. It will also insure that opposition is viewed as part of the argument proper and not just something that the writer will want to remember "not to forget about."

Because incorporating opposition into the argument represents a significant addition, it will require a more elaborate schematic for the plan. One that has been widely used for the *analysis* of arguments should also prove useful for their composition. This is the formulation of English logician Stephen Toulmin.[4] As we will see, Toulmin's diagram can accommodate both the argument plan in its present state as well as any predictable opposition that may be brought against it. With some refinement, it will also help the writer to anticipate not simply opposition in general but also some of the forms it will probably take.

Toulmin understands argument in much the same way we have already described, as a form of reasoning in which some statements are offered in support of others. He also uses some of the same terms to describe the argument's parts. The claim of the argument is still the statement the writer is attempting to support with others. However, the main reason, the statement offered as support, is called the *data,* a term that signifies the possible addition of other reasons for support. Finally, the assumption that allows the writer to move from data to claim is called the *warrant,* in the sense that it "warrants" the movement from data to claim. In addition, Toulmin provides for support to the warrant in the form of *backing*. This allows the writer to argue with a provisionally acceptable assumption. Together, these elements constitute the *proofline*, the writer's main line of reasoning.

Although the labels used in Toulmin's proofline are time honored, we will want to keep our terms consistent. For that reason, we will continue to use the terms we have used earlier in this book. However, we will adopt Toulmin's use of the term "backing" because it does not exist in formal syllogistic logic, and eventually, we will use "rebuttal," a term Toulmin uses to represent a view that opposes a line of argument. To this, we will add a term, *recommendation*, which does not exist in Toulmin's original proofline but which will help us to distinguish statements about policy from statements about consequences.

One of the many strengths of Toulmin's diagram is the way its dynamic design helps to communicate the *movement* of the argument and the relationship between its parts. Few other schematics do this. Figure 4.1 shows the three parts of the argument constructed earlier. The movement of the argument is clear here. Still, the proofline in Figure 4.1 represents only the writer's point of view. To include the reader's opposing view, we will want to notice two features of the argument thus far. First, the claim is always controversial. Second, the main reason is often controversial. What this means is that the claim will always have opposition, and the main reason will often have opposition. Thus, an efficient way to determine opposition is to challenge the statements in the main reason and claim by representing them in the proofline. Toulmin's term for this opposition is *rebuttal*. The proofline in Figure 4.2 shows two rebuttals: one for the claim and the other for the main reason. Notice in each case that the language originally used in the claim and the main reason is used again to frame the rebuttal. The word "unless" in each of the rebuttals signifies something very important about this argument and about opposition in general: *unless* the writer con-

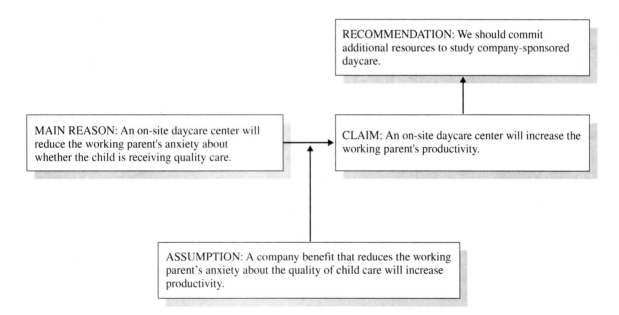

FIGURE 4.1

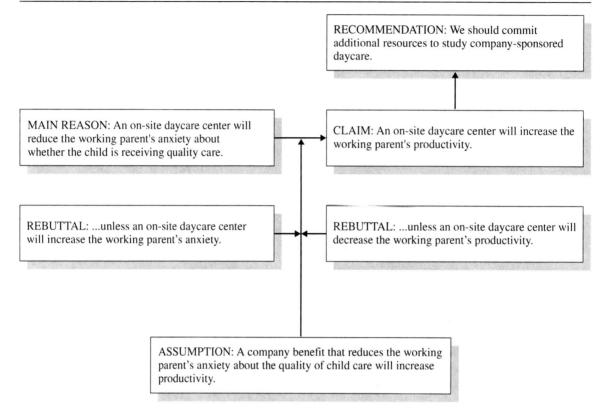

FIGURE 4.2

siders these opposing points of view, they may well *prevent* a successful movement to the claim. Representing this threat graphically are the two arrows that intersect the otherwise continuous line from the assumption to the main reason and claim. Rebuttals can interrupt this movement and halt it entirely.

Successful management of rebuttal is essential. One study indicates that rebuttals that the writer does not respond to get roughly the same reader reaction as a one-sided argument. Of course, managing the rebuttal, including the response, will occur primarily in the writing, and we are still at the planning stage. However, the writer can prepare for the rebuttal by including in the proofline a reason for the opposing point of view. This will help to develop the opposition when the time comes to write the document. Figure 4.3 shows the proofline with the reasons added to the rebuttals. Notice the word "because," which is used here to provide support for the opposing point of view.

At this stage of the planning, the writer possesses a very useful "map" that can be used later to generate the presentation of the argument. It includes the writer's claim and main reason for it, the assumption behind the writer's argument, the reader's or third party's point of view, and the reason or reasons behind it. However, before the writer begins to present the argument in writing, two more items must be added to the proofline, or at least considered as options to add. The first is a recommendation. Of course this assumes that the writer will recommend or indicate a course of action the reader should take. Since a significant part of writing in business is designed for action as opposed to timeless contemplation, this item will probably be included most of the time. The second item, which is more optional, is support for the assumption. Much of the time the assumption will function as it is supposed to, as an authorization for the movement from main reason to claim. Since this has to be assumed, the assumption will seldom be discussed in the document. However, anything can be challenged, and sometimes writers may not know their readers well enough to assume the assumption confidently. In these instances, *backing* can be used to provide support to the assumption. The writer may never need the backing in writing, but as the musical team ZZ Top has said about money, "It's better to have it than to need it and not." Figure 4.4 shows the proofline with the addition of these two items. Notice that the backing supports the assumption in the same way that the main reason supports the claim. Notice also that the claim, because it is *consequential*, gives the reader a reason to accept the writer's recommendation statement.

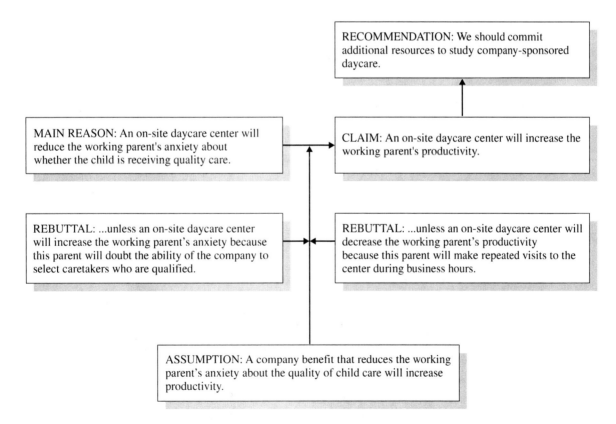

FIGURE 4.3

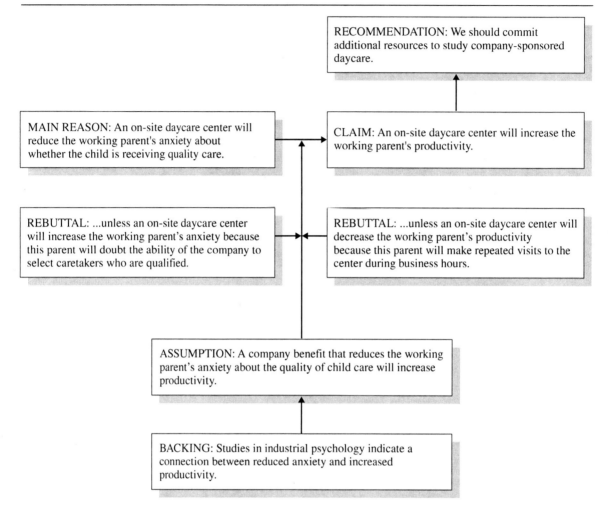

FIGURE 4.4

▧ Prooflines and Procedure

Discussion thus far has concentrated on explaining the *parts* of an argument that will be found in a comprehensive plan. We have yet to consider the best *procedure* for assembling those parts. The following is offered as a logical procedure for constructing a proofline because steps that others will depend on are considered first. At each stage, the parts of the proofline are described by providing a question that the writer can ask to produce them. The example used for illustration, the purchase of microcomputers, is gradually constructed in proofline boxes until the end, where the proofline appears in its entirety.

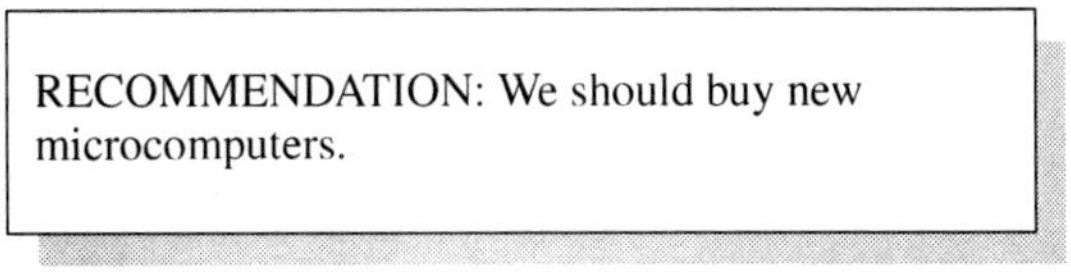

RECOMMENDATION: We should buy new microcomputers.

FIGURE 4.5

Constructing the Recommendation

Recommendation (Figure 4.5) answers the question: what do I want my reader to do as a consequence of reading my argument, and in particular, as a consequence of coming to accept my claim? This is usually a recommendation and will contain policy verbs such as "should," "ought," or "must." For example: "We should buy new microcomputers."

Constructing the Claim

Claim (Figure 4.6) answers the question: What do I want my reader to believe, to be persuaded of, after reading my argument? This statement will almost always be consequential: it will tell the reader what *will happen* if the reader does or does not follow the course of action indicated above. The claim will always be controversial to the reader. The claim will also take the form of an active or subject-verb-object sentence. For example: "Buying new microcomputers will increase employee performance."

Constructing the Main Reason

Main reason (Figure 4.7) answers the question: What reason(s) can I give my reader to accept my claim? The reason(s) may be in the form of facts: more often, the rea-

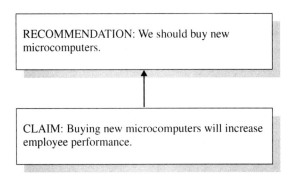

FIGURE 4.6

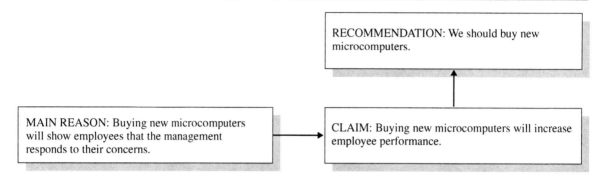

FIGURE 4.7

son(s) will take the form of point(s) to be developed in writing. Writers should provide reasons that are in the active construction (subject-verb-object) and begin with the same grammatical subject of the statement(s) in their claim. For example: "*Buying new microcomputers* will show employees that the management responds to their concerns." The diagram above represents the reasoning to this point.

Constructing the Assumption

Assumption (Figure 4.8) answers the question: What must I assume, or what must my reader assume, if I am to argue from my main reason to my claim? The assumption

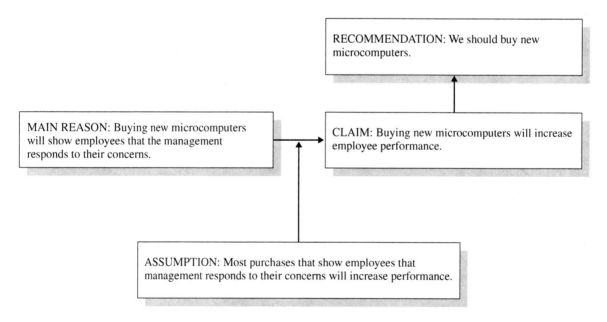

FIGURE 4.8

will always be a general assumption and is similar in concept to the major premise of the syllogism, discussed earlier. For example: "Most purchases that show employees that management responds to their concerns will increase performance." Since the assumption is supported by backing, the writer may want to produce backing as part of the construction of the assumption.

Constructing the Backing

Backing (Figure 4.9) answers the question: How can I expect my reader to accept my assumption? Writers may never need to argue their backing (or even their assumption, for that matter), but they should have it ready in case they are not sure about the acceptability of their assumption or in case their reader questions its basis. For example, the assumption is generally acceptable because "This relation between management concern and increased performance is established in studies of organizational behavior and personnel management." The proofline below adds both assumption and backing.

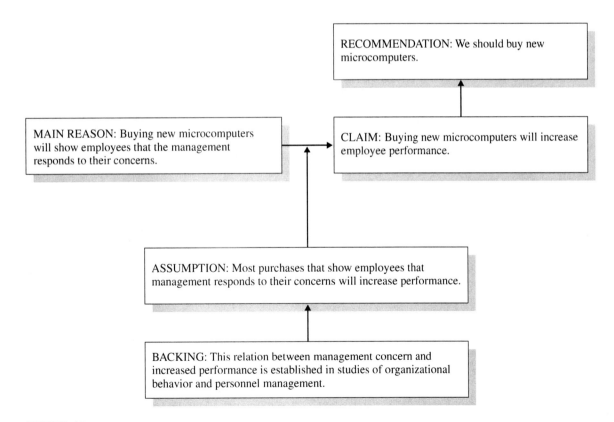

FIGURE 4.9

Constructing the Rebuttals

Rebuttal answers the question: What will my reader say in opposition to my line of argument? Any argument worth making will have an opposing point of view, and this will represent it. The rebuttal will be to the claim, to the main reason, or to both. If the rebuttal is to the assumption, the writer will supply backing. Only rarely will the rebuttal be to the recommendation.

Writers should provide a reason (with the word "because") for each point of opposition: this will help them to avoid "straw arguments," those which appear worthwhile to the writer but not to the reader. If the writer has a straw argument, a reason will be difficult if not impossible to produce. This is important because straw arguments, while tempting and easy to manage, can do irreparable damage to the writer's case. Some theorists feel so strongly about the damage of straw arguments, they treat them as fallacies of reasoning:

> This common fallacy is characterized by an underestimation of opposition. *Straw arguments* present weak versions of opposing views. This form of misrepresentation is often used to avoid refuting more difficult opposition arguments. However, straw arguments addressed to the composite audience are likely to weaken the arguer's effectiveness. The audience members reading or hearing the misrepresentation of their views are likely to become hostile and thereby less receptive to the arguer's reasoning. Additionally, critical listeners and readers of straw arguments may assume that the advocate's own position results from inadequate understanding of alternative points of view.[5]

Here is an example of a rebuttal (with its reason) to the claim:

> . . . unless buying new microcomputers will decrease performance *because* of the time needed to become familiar with the new operating systems.

Providing a reason will also give writers a better sense of what they will need to do with opposition when they have to raise it in their writing. The writer has decided that the most important rebuttal is to the claim, and has provided that rebuttal in the completed proofline in Figure 4.10. Of course, another rebuttal is available, to the main reason of the proofline. In this example, the writer might raise opposition to the statement "Buying new microcomputers will show employees that management responds to their concerns." The writer might consider this: ". . . unless employees will not believe that management is responding to their concerns because the purchase of new computers will be seen as a normal development in scheduled office automation." However, the writer will not always need to raise opposition to the main reason because the main reason will be developed at length in the document.

To some writers, the time required to produce a complete proofline may seem extraordinary, particularly when it turns out to be little more than a one-page diagram.

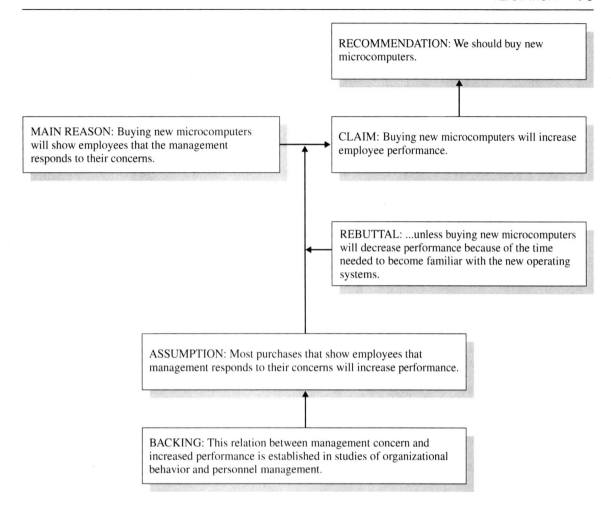

FIGURE 4.10

Part of the reason for this is that writers in business are not in the habit of planning their writing. As a consequence, they can easily become impatient with the plan and eager to get to the presentation of it. However, planning the argument is the *better* use of requisite time, time that will be consumed either in the plan or later in the presentation. Writers who have not planned their argument will not know where they are going in their presentation. Nor will they know what their readers will voice as opposition. Thus, the time that goes into planning saves time in making these determinations in the presentation. It can also save additional time if the writer has to rewrite a poorly written argument, one that the reader has rejected.

With a completed and sound proofline, the writer can now turn to the task of presenting the proofline in the document, the subject of the next chapter.

RELATED READINGS

In addition to the writings listed in the notes to this chapter, the materials below consist of works that emphasize argument as discovery or inquiry and the application of Toulmin's proofline. Readers will find that most of these works are not in the mainstream of business publications or even in the mainstream of publication in management communication.

Aristotle. *Rhetoric.* Trans. J. H. Freese. Loeb Classical Library. Cambridge, MA.: Harvard University Press, 1982. Any serious study of argument should probably start here.

Booth, Wayne C., and Marshall W. Gregory. *The Harper & Row Rhetoric: Writing as Thinking/Thinking as Writing.* New York: Harper & Row, 1987. Contains a section on enthymemes and syllogisms as well as one on fallacies of argument.

Brandt, William. *The Craft of Writing.* Englewood Cliffs, NJ: Prentice-Hall, 1969. An extended application of the syllogism to writing in college.

Brandt, William. *The Rhetoric of Argumentation.* Indianapolis: Bobbs-Merrill, 1970. Excellent work on argumentative analysis with an emphasis on enthymemes and syllogisms.

Cicero. *De Oratore, Books I and II.* Trans. E.W. Sutton and H. Rackham. Loeb Classical Library. Cambridge, MA: Harvard University Press, 1976. Representative of Roman rhetoric and argumentation. Any serious study of argument should probably continue here after Aristotle's *Rhetoric.*

Gage, John. *The Shape of Reason: Argumentative Writing in College.* New York: Macmillan, 1987. Excellent recent work on the use of enthymeme-based argument in college writing.

Toulmin, Stephen. *The Uses of Argument.* Cambridge, MA: Cambridge University Press, 1958. Practitioners may regard this with some suspicion because it engages several audiences with more theoretical interests. Still, this is a good book to begin studies of prooflines.

Toulmin, Stephen, Richard Reike, and Allan Janik. *Introduction to Reasoning.* New York: Macmillan, 1979. An extension of earlier work, this text considers the analysis of argument in a variety of disciplines. Includes a section on arguments in management.

NOTES

1. See, for example, M. Allen et al., "Testing a Model of Message Sidedness: Three Replications," *Communication Monographs*, 57 (1990): 275–90; S. Jackson and M. Allen, "Meta-analysis of the Effectiveness of One-Sided and Two-Sided Argumentation," Paper presented at the International Communication Association Convention, Montreal, Canada, 1987.

2. *Crutchfield's*, July 1984.

3. Jack Meiland, "Argument as Inquiry and Argument as Persuasion, *Argumentation* 3: 186. See also J. Meiland, *College Thinking* (New York: Mentor–New American Library, 1981) and John Gage, "A General Theory of the Enthymeme for Advanced Composition" in *Teaching Advanced Composition*, ed. Katherine Adams and John Adams (Portsmouth, NH: Boynton/Cook-Heinemann, 1991). These are worth contrasting with the more traditional view of argument as persuasion in Jerry M. Anderson and Paul J. Dovres, *Readings in Argumentation* (Boston: Allyn and Bacon, 1968).

4. For more on Toulmin's proofline, see Stephen Toulmin, *The Uses of Argument* (Cambridge, MA: Cambridge University Press, 1958); Toulmin et al., *An Introduction to Reasoning* (New York: Macmillan, 1979); Wayne Brockriede, "The Contemporary Renaissance

in the Study of Argument," in *Argument In Transition: Proceedings of the Third Summer Conference on Argumentation*, ed. David Zarefsky, Malcolm O. Sillars, and Jack Rhodes (Annandale, VA: Speech Communication Association, 1983), 17–26; Wayne Brockriede and Douglas Ehninger, "Toulmin on Argument: An Interpretation and Application," *Quarterly Journal of Speech*, 26 (February 1960): 44–53.

    5. Josina Makau, *Reasoning and Communication*. (Belmont, CA: Wadsworth, 1990), 196.

STRATEGIC DISPOSITION

Presenting the Case

Despite the countless number of composition and rhetoric texts dealing with arrangement, we know very little about order in composition. In many texts, arrangement is either neglected or its treatment is woefully inadequate.

—Frank D'Angelo, *A Conceptual Theory of Rhetoric*

Audience probably matters more than anything when a good writer orders business prose. In fact, writers through the centuries have devised (usually on psychological grounds) a number of arrangement strategies (several of them related) calculated to win the assent of neutral or skeptical readers.

—Jack Selzer, *Arranging Business Prose*

Just as planning the proofline follows a procedure, so does presenting the plan in a document. Whether the document is a memo, report, or letter, the procedure will be the same, and the writer will use the parts of the proofline to generate the parts of the document. This means that words and sentences within the proofline will become sentences and paragraphs within the document. When the document is completed, it will still represent the ideas of the proofline, but it will represent them in a fully developed form, in a form that is strategically intended for the *reader*.

Illustrating a procedure for presenting the proofline in the document will require a proofline. For this example, the writer will be using the proofline in Figure 5.1. The argument is about a familiar topic in modern business, telecommuting, an activity that involves employees working at home with a computer and modem to send and receive work. The writer's reader is skeptical about this proposal because telecommuting is an activity that is difficult to supervise.

■ Beginning with the Claim

The writer will use the claim *first* but will place it almost *last* in the document. After the recommendation statement, the claim is the first element the writer produces

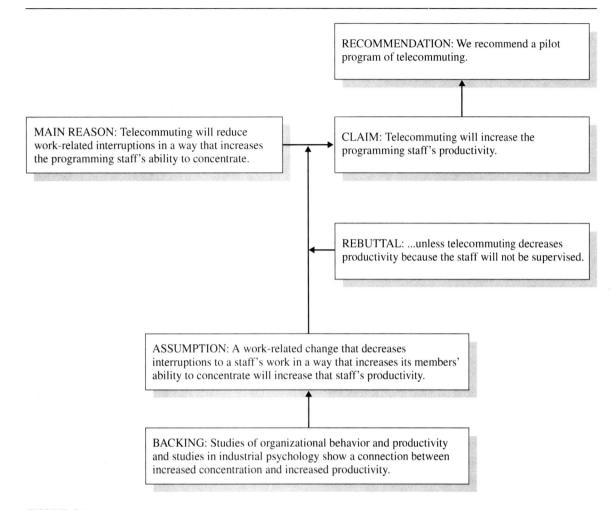

FIGURE 5.1

when *planning* the argument; however, the *presentation* of the claim should come nearly last, immediately before the statement of recommendation. This suggestion will surprise those writers who follow the popular formula "Tell your reader what you will say, say it, and then tell your reader what you have said." It may even shock those who use this formula to get the main point "up front" for their busy executive readers. Such a formula may work well for other writing tasks, if the writer doesn't mind the inevitable redundancy and lack of organization, but to follow it in writing an argument is to commit at least two mistakes.

The first mistake is organizational: by placing the claim at the beginning, the writer will always be writing away from the statement that needs support. After all, the claim is the *conclusion* of the argument: it is that final point that all others support. As a consequence of placing the claim at the beginning, the argument will be forced to proceed backward by producing reasoning for a statement that has already been offered for acceptance. The writer who places the claim at the end has something to work toward and can then evaluate each step of the presentation according to how well it contributes to supporting the claim.

The second mistake is strategic, and it is more serious. By placing the claim at the beginning, the writer will be presenting to the reader the argument's most controversial statement at a time when the reader will be the least prepared to accept it. The reader has yet to be exposed to the writer's supporting arguments, and the writer has yet to demonstrate an awareness of the reader's opposing point of view. Presenting the claim first is to invite from the reader a reaction that is entirely the opposite to the writer's intention in the argument. The writer wants the reader to accept the claim, not to reject it.

The problems above thus suggest that the writer should withhold the claim from the opening of the document and present it at the end, after the reader has had an opportunity to assess the quality of the writer's arguments and the fairness with which the writer treats the reader's concerns in opposition. However, if the writer does not begin with the claim, what is left? The writer will need to let the reader know what the document is about. This is a requirement of both convention and courtesy, and the kind of preview that is required for informative writing also has a place in argumentative papers.

The solution here is to provide the reader with a statement of the problem or issue the document will solve or resolve. This is easy if the writer is using a proofline because the same statement that is used in the claim can be recast to state the issue. Starting with an issue statement has the advantage of opening the document by engaging the reader's attention, since the reader is presumably *interested* in the issue, even while being initially opposed to the reader's eventual claim about it. It has the further advantage of defining the scope of the document; matters not directly related to addressing the problem or issue may thus be avoided.

By presenting the claim at the end of the document and by placing the issue or problem form of it at the beginning of the document, the writer will have accomplished several things. First, the statement of least controversy, the issue statement, will appear at the beginning, to engage the reader's interest and attention. Second, the most controversial statement, the claim, will appear at the end, to solicit acceptance at a time when the reader will be best informed and most prepared to accept it. Third, since the issue statement and the claim are formed from the same sentence ("Telecommuting will increase the programming staff's productivity"), the writer will be able to work within a very clear framework, one that requires moving the reader from the problem (issue statement) to the resolution (claim). The following example shows how the issue statement and the claim can provide this framework. Notice that the issue statement is simply the question form of the claim, and that the downward direction, represented by the dotted lines, indicates the movement from issue statement to the claim.

Will telecommuting increase the programming staff's productivity?

. . . .

. . . .

. . . .

. . . .

. . . .

. . . .

Telecommuting will increase the programming staff's productivity.

Of course, the writer will want to prepare the reader for the issue statement, or *question at issue*. This is necessary because any number of questions *might* be asked at the beginning of a document, and the reader will want to know why *this one* in particular is being asked. To prepare the reader, the writer will want to provide a basis or reason for asking the question. In this case, the writer knows that the topic of telecommuting is one that has been discussed in the department and that some disagreement exists about whether it will increase productivity. The introduction could then be drafted this way:

> Telecommuting is a continuing subject of discussion among members of our programming staff, and many of them want to know if we plan to engage in telecommuting activities. Some of the managers are concerned that work performed under this activity would be difficult to supervise and would therefore be less productive. Others claim that telecommuting will actually increase productivity. Therefore, to see if telecommuting is appropriate for our department, **we must determine its effect on productivity.**

. . . .

. . . .

. . . .

. . . .

. . . .

Telecommuting will increase the programming staff's productivity.

Notice that the opening has one function here, and that is to explain why the question at issue is a good one to ask. In this case, the question arises from different points of view about telecommuting and productivity. Notice also that the question at issue, now in boldface, has changed from the original. It no longer uses the exact wording of the claim in question form. In fact, it is not even asked as a direct question. However, it still functions well as a question at issue because it does two things: first, it provides the issue to which the claim is a direct resolution; second, it is asked in a neutral form, which means that it does not telegraph any bias toward the eventual claim.

The writer now has a more complete framework within which the remaining parts of the proofline will appear and develop. For example, the recommendation statement may now be added since the claim that motivates the reader to take action has been presented. The recommendation statement will usually have one of two transitions depending on whether the consequence in the claim is positive or negative. If the consequence is positive, the transition from claim to recommendation will be "To insure (claim), I recommend. . . ." If the consequence is negative, the transition from claim to recommendation will be "To avoid (claim), I recommend. . . ." While variations on these transitions are certainly possible, the writer will probably want to preserve the logical connection. The consequence provides the reader with a *reason* to accept the recommendation. The recommendation is added in boldface in the example below.

■ Developing the Main Reason

With the document framed as it is, the writer has a very clear *rhetorical* task: to move the reader from the question at issue to the claim. Once there, the reader will be in the best possible position to take the action the writer recommends. Moving the reader from main reason to claim is a procedure that consists of two events: one, the development of the main reason, the writer's "side" of the argument; two, the management of the rebuttal, the reader's competing argument. Although the two may be mixed, presenting them separately will keep them distinct and lend clarity to the argument.

> Telecommuting is a continuing subject of discussion among members of our programming staff, and many of them want to know if we plan to engage in telecommuting activities. Some of the managers are concerned that work performed under this activity would be difficult to supervise and would therefore be less productive. Other managers claim that telecommuting will increase productivity. Therefore, to see if telecommuting is appropriate for our department, we must determine its effect on productivity.
>
> . . . .
> . . . .
> . . . .
> . . . .
> . . . .
> . . . .
>
> Telecommuting will increase the programming staff's productivity. **To insure this increase in productivity, we recommend adopting the following pilot program in telecommuting.**

Either way, the writer will want to think of them as separate because they represent two quite different points of view.

Developing the main reason is almost always necessary, and it represents one of the major writing tasks in argument. If the writer assumes acceptance of the assumption, then the main reason will become the chief means by which the reader will be brought to the claim. After all, the main reason continues to be the currency of exchange in the document even more than it was in the proofline: it is now offered *at length* to the reader in exchange for the reader's eventual acceptance of the claim. Because so much depends on developing the main reason, the writer will want to give this part of the document careful attention.

Fortunately, many resources are available for developing the main reason. Numerous works on rhetoric, both classical and contemporary, provide a wealth of techniques, methods, even entire systems for inventing, developing, and supporting controversial statements.[1] The more sophisticated and complete systems are even designed with the proofline or a similar logical structure at the center.[2] Serious writers of argument will want to become familiar with these resources. However, the writer of the telecommuting proofline will be content with a simple but useful system for developing the main reason.

This is a system of invention by inquiry, and it involves the use of the well known journalistic questions: *what, who, why, how, where,* and *when.*[3] The advantage of asking these questions lies in their comprehensiveness, and that is why they are used to insure initial coverage in the news. Thus, the writer will have a good opportunity to develop the main reason by asking these questions. However, the goal here is not to provide an answer for each question but rather to determine whether a given question is *relevant and helpful* to developing the main reason. For example, the "what" question concerns definition or description, concepts that are useful in explaining to someone *what* something *is.* In this case, the writer will ask specifically of the main reason whether definition or description is necessary. To be certain that the question is asked of the main reason, the writer may frame it in this way (the main reason is in italics):

WHAT?

(Definition and Description)

Will developing the main reason require the reader to know anything about *what* telecommuting is? Will information about *what* telecommuting is help the reader to see that *telecommuting will reduce work-related interruptions in a way that increases the programming staff's ability to concentrate?*

If nothing needs to be said about telecommuting that will help the writer develop the main reason, the writer can move on to the next question. However, this writer decides that the reader will need to know something about *what* telecommuting is to understand how it will reduce interruptions. The writer will probably want to make a note of this before asking the remaining questions, which are listed in similar form below.

WHO?

(Agency and Party)

This is a question about people, about the agents or parties involved in this issue. The writer will want to ask: Will developing the main reason require the reader to know anything about *who* is involved in telecommuting? Will any information about *who* is involved in telecommuting help the reader to see that *telecommuting will reduce work-related interruptions in a way that increases the programming staff's ability to concentrate*?

WHEN?

(Time and Timing)

This is a question about time and timing. The writer will want to ask: Will developing the main reason require the reader to know anything about *when* telecommuting will be instituted or *when* interruptions occur? Will information about *the timing* of telecommuting help the reader to see that *telecommuting will reduce work-related interruptions in a way that increases the programming staff's ability to concentrate*?

WHERE?

(Place and Location)

This is a question about place or location. The writer will want to ask: Will developing the main reason require the reader to know anything about *where* telecommuting will be instituted or *where* people are interrupted? Will information about *the location or place* of telecommuting help the reader to see that *telecommuting will reduce work-related interruptions in a way that increases the programming staff's ability to concentrate*?

WHY?

(Reason and Cause)

This is a question about cause, reason, or motivation. The writer will want to ask: Will developing the main reason require the reader to know anything about *why* telecommuting will be instituted? Will information about *reasons* for telecommuting help the reader to see that *telecommuting will reduce work-related interruptions in a way that increases the programming staff's ability to concentrate*?

HOW?

(Means and Manner)

This is a question about means and manner. The writer will want to ask: Will developing the main reason require the reader to know anything about *how* telecommuting will be instituted or *how* it will work? Will information about *the way* telecommuting will work help the reader to see that *telecommuting will reduce work-related interruptions in a way that increases the programming staff's ability to concentrate*?

The writer *may* find that all of these questions yield information that will be useful in developing the main reason, or the writer may find that only some of them do. The writer's task is to *ask* all of these questions to stimulate thought and produce supporting arguments for the main reason. The task is not to wring every possible bit of information from them simply for the sake of producing information. A writer who finds only a few questions productive can develop a main reason just as well as one who has found all of them productive.

The writer of this proofline finds that in addition to the question of definition, asking three others has been productive. The question about place (where?) has revealed that location provides a special invitation to interruptions. The question about agency (who?) has revealed that programmers are the kind of people who require a special level of concentration. Finally, the question about manner (how?) helps the writer to see a special need to discuss the way in which telecommuting will reduce the distractions and increase concentration.

Because each of the questions that has been asked concerns a separate concept (e.g., *why* is quite different from *who*), the information from each should provide material for at least one paragraph. If the information is important enough to use to develop the main reason, it should be sufficient enough to develop into a paragraph. This way each paragraph will be unified internally by a specific concept (manner, for example) but unified externally by its contribution to developing the main reason.

Of course, developing the paragraphs in this way says nothing about the order of their presentation. The writer will want to think about this, about which paragraphs should be presented earlier, and which ones later. However, research has produced very little that can serve as a guide here. Nevertheless, the writer can depend on one guideline for arrangement: matters of definition or description (what) should be presented before other points that depend on them. This means that discussing *how* telecommuting works will not make much sense if the writer hasn't already discussed *what* telecommuting is. The following example is the document with the descriptive (what) paragraph added immediately after the question at issue.

Telecommuting is a continuing subject of discussion among members of our programming staff, and many of them want to know if we plan to engage in telecommuting activities. Some of the managers are concerned that work performed under this activity would be difficult to supervise and would therefore be less productive. Other managers claim that telecommuting will increase productivity. Therefore, to see if telecommuting is appropriate for our department, we must determine its effect on productivity.

Simply defined, telecommuting is performing work on company time at a noncompany location, typically the user's home, through a computer which is connected over a telephone line to a company computer system. The activities performed at the user's home are done in place of coming into the company location to perform the work. For telecommuting to work over our datacom network and on our system, our staff will use an IBM-compatible personal computer, a copy of the Handshake software package, and a cable modem. Once connected, users at home can perform all the functions normally done on their terminals at their work location.

. . . .

. . . .

. . . .

. . . .

. . . .

. . . .

Telecommuting will increase the programming staff's productivity. To insure this increase, we recommend adopting the following pilot program in telecommuting.

Notice that the topic of this paragraph is previewed for the reader in the opening sentence: "Simply defined, telecommuting is. . . ." This tells the reader that the information will be about *what* telecommuting is. Notice also that the writer has worked hard to insure that this paragraph contains *only* information that describes or defines telecommuting. Other matters are important certainly, but they will have their time and paragraphs later. Notice finally the transition between the end of the first paragraph and the beginning of the second. This is the result of the claim and main reason having the subject in common. It helps to keep the writer on track after leaving the first paragraph:

Therefore, to see if **telecommuting** is appropriate for our department, we must determine its effect on productivity.

Simply defined, **telecommuting** is performing work on company time at a noncompany location, typically the user's home, through a computer which is connected over a telephone line to a company computer system.

The writer is now ready to supply the remaining paragraphs of development. They are added on the following pages, with their first sentences in boldface to indicate which question has produced them. Notice that the paragraphs attempt to do two things: first, they try to remain unified by a single point (means, location, etc.); second, this attempt is in service of another, the development of the main reason. Consequently, key terms from the main reason ("interruption," "concentration," etc.) will constantly appear. The dotted lines have almost disappeared because more of the argument has been written.

Telecommuting is a continuing subject of discussion among members of our programming staff, and many of them want to know if we plan to engage in telecommuting activities. Some of the managers are concerned that work performed under this activity would be difficult to supervise and would therefore be less productive.

Other managers claim that telecommuting will increase productivity. Therefore, to see if telecommuting is appropriate for our department, we must determine its effect on productivity.

Simply defined, telecommuting is performing work on company time at a non-company location, typically the user's home, through a computer which is connected over a telephone line to a company computer system. The activities performed at the user's home are done in place of coming into the company location to perform the work. For telecommuting to work over our datacom network and on our system, our staff will use an IBM-compatible personal computer, a copy of the Handshake software package, and a cable modem. Once connected, users at home can perform all the functions normally done on their terminals at their work location.

Telecommuting becomes important once we consider where our programming staff spend most of their time. They spend most of their time on their terminals **where** they perform such tasks as program coding and error detecting, file interrogation, job scheduling, and word processing. They also spend most of their time in open offices, **where** they are fully exposed to the routine noise and interruptions of our department's activities. All of these tasks can easily be done while telecommuting because the only difference would be the **location** where they are performed—the employees' homes. The big difference is that they would perform these tasks without office interruptions and distractions.

These interruptions are especially troublesome for **our programmers**, **people who** must maintain an extraordinary level of concentration to perform their tasks. Merely using the COBOL and ALGOL programming languages that support our systems requires high concentration, but when our programmers are designing or retracing the embedded logic of a program (nested IF-statement, GOTOs, etc.) as well, they require even more intensive and uninterrupted concentration. Any interruption will delay the completion time of the task because of the start-up time required to get back into the task each time the programmer is interrupted.

How can telecommuting help to avoid these work-related interruptions and provide our programmers with the concentration they need? **By** removing the programmer from the distracting environment, telecommuting will help them to perform their tasks with fewer interruptions and with much more concentration. **By** telecommuting, programmers have much more control over their working environment. The distracting background noises of the work location and other interruptions can be almost completely eliminated **in this way**.

. . . .

. . . .

. . . .

Telecommuting will increase the programming staff's productivity. To insure this increase in productivity, we recommend adopting the following pilot program in telecommuting.

▓ **Presenting the Reader's Rebuttal**

The writer's "side" of the argument, the main reason, has now been developed. Yet a considerable space still exists between it and the claim. This is the space reserved for the reader, or more accurately, for the reader's point of view. Entertaining the reader's point of view *in writing* is critical for the argument to succeed. It is a good example of the principle of exchange in action: by managing opposition, the writer considers the reader's point of view in implicit exchange for the reader considering the writer's point of view.

Not only does the writer stand to gain by including opposition, but much will be lost if the writer neglects it. Without opposition, the reader will be less inclined to see things from the writer's point of view. Without it, the writer will appear only partially aware of the full issue. Without it, the writer will produce reasoning that is one-sided at best. And without it, the writer will never really know just how strong the case on the other side really is. Without presenting opposition in writing, the writer may be sure of convincing only one person: the writer.

Although the rebuttal has already been identified in the proofline, it will need to be managed at greater length in the document because that is where it will meet the reader's resistance. This is accomplished in three parts. First, the writer will want to *signal* that the opposition is in fact someone else's point of view, different from the one held by the writer. Second, the writer will want to *develop* that point of view to demonstrate greater understanding of the reader's perspective. Third, the writer will want to *refute* the opposing point of view to prepare for the claim and statement of recommendation.

Signaling Opposition

Signaling opposition means marking it as someone else's competing opinion. Otherwise, the reader will assume that it is a continuation of the writer's reasoning. For example, the following would *not* be a good way to signal opposition in the document on telecommuting:

> Telecommuters could be difficult to supervise, and this lack of supervision might reduce productivity. The inability to monitor closely the telecommuting programmers' work efforts could easily cause this.

Nothing here informs the reader that this is a competing opinion, one held by someone other than the writer. Consequently, this passage will appear to run contrary to everything the writer has said, and the reader most probably will not know what to do with it. What is seriously missing here is a signal *to the reader* that this is not the writer's opinion. This signal is supplied in the passage below. Note that the phrases "nevertheless," "some managers," and "they" show that the competing view belongs very clearly to someone other than the writer:

Nevertheless, some managers will object to telecommuting. They feel that telecommuters might not be as productive as those who work on site and that this lack of productivity. . . .

Writers routinely make the mistake of not signaling opposition because *they* know very well that the opposing point of view belongs to someone else. Because they know this so well, they can easily neglect to pass this knowledge along by signaling the reader.

Developing Opposition

After signaling the opposition, the writer will want to develop it. This is important for several reasons. First, it will help the writer to avoid "straw" opposition, which is opposition that is particularly attractive to some writers because it is weak and easily dismissed. The writer will be better able to identify straw opposition because any attempt at developing it will usually be futile. While straw opposition can easily be stated, it cannot be easily supported or developed without seeing how groundless it is. Second, developing opposition will help to convince the reader that the writer is capable of adopting the reader's perspective. This is important because the act of arguing is an attempt to reconcile divergent points of view. Anything that represents a common ground (such as the assumption of the proofline), can only contribute to this attempt. And finally, developing the opposition will give the writer the first real glimpse of the case the reader might make against the writer's argument.

Developing the opposition begins with the proofline and the rebuttal. The "because" clause that the writer provided to represent the reader's reason for the rebuttal is now used to develop the opposition. Here is the rebuttal as it appears in the proofline: ". . . unless telecommuting decreases productivity *because* the staff will not be supervised." This reason ("because") for objecting to telecommuting is one the writer will now need to develop in the document. The development follows the signaling of the opposition, and it is in italics below. Note that the writer has chosen to develop this opposition by using one of the topics that was employed in developing the main reason: the topic of location (indicated by boldface):

Nevertheless, some managers will object to telecommuting. They feel that telecommuters might not be as productive as those who work on site and that this lack of productivity will go unnoticed until it is too late. *They feel this way because of the programmers'* **location, which is away from the work site**. They feel they will not be able to monitor closely the telecommuting programmers' work efforts **off site**. They believe that the programmers will not work as hard as they do when they are under supervision.

Refuting the Opposition

Once signaled and developed, opposition will need to be refuted. Doing this successfully will require a combination of several techniques already discussed. The writer will need to *signal* that the refutation is beginning and *develop* it to counter fully the reader's concern in voicing it. To do this, the writer will once again want to consider the topics for development. In this case, the writer selects the topic of *agency* to counter the topic of *location* used above. The refutation is presented in italics, with the topic of agency represented in boldface.

> Nevertheless, some managers will object to telecommuting. They feel that telecommuters might not be as productive as those who work on site and that this lack of productivity will go unnoticed until it is too late. They feel this way because of the programmers' location, away from the work site. They feel they will not be able to monitor closely the telecommuting programmers' work efforts off site. They believe that the programmers will not work as hard as they do when they are under supervision. This is a reasonable and cautious concern. *However, we must bear in mind that our programmers are **people who** take considerable pride in their work. They are company leaders in program production. They also have an established record of accomplishment and a documented ability to produce without considerable supervision. During last year's reorganization, when departmental supervision was at its lowest, our programmers were among **those** few **who** showed no decrease in productivity. Some of them even increased their productivity, and this suggests that they may be the **kind of people who** work even better without direct supervision.

After the brief compliment to the reader for the "reasonable and cautious concern," the writer signals the beginning of the refutation with "however." The rest of the refutation develops agency as a counterargument to the initial opposition that programmers would be less productive if they did their work off site.

The management of this opposition is now added to the document to complete the argument, not only from the writer's point of view but also from the reader's. After completing the argument, the writer will want to take the same steps as those taken by the writer of informative writing. The writer will want to put the argument away and do something else before returning to it. This is especially important with argumentative writing because writers have considerable difficulty gaining an objective distance from the ideas they are arguing. Nevertheless, this distance is necessary for effective editing.[4] Sentence-level problems in conciseness, word choice, word order, grammar, and punctuation may only distract in informative writing; in an argument, they can easily damage the writer's credibility and call into question the writer's competence. For that reason, the remaining chapters of this book are devoted to helping the writer avoid those problems.

On the following pages, the entire argument is presented without interruption, this time in the format of a corporate memo, with some attention given to the business environment that produced the issue and with some detail given to the recommendation statement. Note that the format here is only a cosmetic addition, and it could as easily be formatted as a letter or report. Thus, the argument and its presentation exist as a persuasive enterprise that is independent of company or industry formats.

INTER-OFFICE MEMORANDUM

To: Matthew Nathan

From: Nicholas James

Subject: Telecommuting

Date: 1/11/99

As you know, our last managers' meeting indicated a continuing interest in telecommuting. It is a continuing subject of discussion among members of our programming staff, and many of them want to know if we plan to engage in telecommuting activities. Some of the managers are concerned that work performed under this activity would be difficult to supervise and would therefore be less productive. Other managers claim that telecommuting will increase productivity. Therefore, before we make any decisions about it, we will want to determine its probable effect on productivity.

Simply defined, telecommuting is performing work on company time at a noncompany location, typically the user's home, through a computer which is connected over a telephone line to a company computer system. The activities performed at the user's home are done in place of coming into the company location to perform the work. For telecommuting to work over our datacom network and on our system, our staff will use an IBM-compatible personal computer, a copy of the Handshake software package, and a cable modem. Once connected, users at home can perform all the functions normally done on their ET1100 terminals at their work location.

Telecommuting becomes important once we consider where our programming staff spend most of their time. They spend most of their time on their terminals where they perform such tasks as program coding and error detecting, file interrogation, job scheduling, and word processing. They also spend most of their time in open offices, where they are fully exposed to the routine noise and interruptions of our department's activities. All of their tasks can easily be done while telecommuting because the only difference would be the location where they are performed—the employees' homes. The big difference is that they would perform these tasks without office interruptions and distractions.

These interruptions are especially troublesome for our programmers, people who must maintain an extraordinary level of concentration to perform their tasks. Merely using the COBOL and ALGOL programming languages that support our systems requires high concentration, but when our programmers are designing or re-tracing the embedded logic of a program (nested IF-statement, GOTO's, etc.) as well, they require even more intensive and uninterrupted concentration. Any interruption will delay the completion time of the task because of the start-up time required to get back into the task each time the programmer is interrupted.

How can telecommuting help to avoid these work related interruptions and provide our programmers with the concentration they need? By removing the programmers from the distracting environment, telecommuting will help them to perform their tasks with fewer interruptions and with much more concentration. By telecommuting, programmers have much more control over their working environment. The distracting background noises of the work location and other interruptions can be almost completely eliminated in this way.

Nevertheless, some managers will object to telecommuting. They feel that telecommuters might not be as productive as those who work on site and that this lack of productivity will go unnoticed until it is too late. They feel this way because of the programmers' location, away from the work site. They feel they will not be able to monitor closely the telecommuting programmers' work efforts off site. They believe that the programmers will not work as hard as they do when they are under supervision. This is a reasonable and cautious concern. However, we must bear in mind that our programmers are people who take considerable pride in their work. They are company leaders in program production. They also have an established record of accomplishment and a documented ability to produce without considerable supervision. During last year's reorganization, when departmental supervision was at its lowest, our programmers were among those few who showed no decrease in productivity. Some even increased their productivity, and this suggests that they may be the kind of people who work even better without direct supervision.

All things considered then, we can expect telecommuting to increase the programming staff's productivity. To insure this increase in productivity, we recommend adopting the following pilot program in telecommuting.

The program should begin with two or three carefully selected employees from each district. These programmers should telecommute only one day

a week to begin with, and they should plan to perform the tasks that require the most concentration from them. After approximately six weeks,
both the telecommuting employees and their supervisors will evaluate their
experiences. If the program successfully demonstrates increased productivity, the program should be implemented more widely throughout the department.

RELATED READINGS

In addition to the writings listed in the notes to this chapter, the materials below consist of
works that emphasize the relationship between argumentative plans and presentations of those
plans.

Aristotle. *Rhetoric.* Trans. J. H. Freese. Loeb Classical Library. Cambridge, MA.: Harvard
   University Press, 1982. Any serious study of argument should probably start here.
Booth, Wayne C., and Marshall W. Gregory. *The Harper & Row Rhetoric: Writing as Think-
   ing/Thinking as Writing.* New York: Harper & Row, 1987. Contains a section on enthymemes and syllogisms as well as one on fallacies of argument.
Brandt, William. *The Craft of Writing.* Englewood Cliffs, NJ: Prentice-Hall, 1969. An extended application of the syllogism to writing in college.
Brandt, William. *The Rhetoric of Argumentation.* Indianapolis: Bobbs-Merrill, 1970. Excellent work on argumentative analysis with an emphasis on enthymemes and syllogisms.
Gage, John. *The Shape of Reason: Argumentative Writing in College.* New York: Macmillan,
   1987. Excellent work on the use of enthymeme-based argument in college writing.

NOTES

1. See, for example, Aristotle, *Rhetoric,* trans. J. H. Freese, Loeb Classical Library (Cambridge, MA.: Harvard University Press, 1982); Cicero, *De Oratore, Books I and II,* trans. E.W.
Sutton and H. Rackham, Loeb Classical Library (Cambridge, MA: Harvard University Press,
1976); Chaim Perelman and L. Olbrechts-Tyteca, *The New Rhetoric: A Treatise on Argumentation,* trans. John Wilkinson and Purcell Weaver (Notre Dame, IN: University of Notre
Dame Press, 1969).

2. This is the system described by Aristotle in his *Rhetoric.* See Aristotle, *The "Art" of
Rhetoric,* trans. J.H. Freese, Loeb Classical Library (Cambridge, MA.: Harvard University
Press, 1982).

3. Interestingly enough, these questions are used to prepare prospective journalists for *interviews,* where comprehensiveness is critical. Although not all of the information the questions reveal will be used in a story, they help to insure that important items will not be overlooked.

4. Distant and dispassionate review may also reveal a need for more important revisions.
For example, in the argument about telecommuting, a disabling rebuttal (to the main reason)
has been overlooked: "Telecommuting will only introduce interruptions to the work environment because familiar surroundings of home contain a personal choice of distractions."

6 ETHICS IN ARGUMENT

Classical Fallacies

We are all of us preachers in private or public capacities. We have no sooner uttered words than we have given impulse to other people to look at the world, or some small part of it, in our way. Thus caught up in a great web of intercommunication and interinfluence, we speak as rhetoricians affecting one another for good or ill.

—Richard Weaver, *Visions of Order*

It is customary in the study of logic to reserve the term "fallacy" for arguments which, although incorrect, are psychologically persuasive. We therefore define a fallacy as a form of argument that seems *to be correct but which proves, upon examination, not to be. It is profitable to study such arguments, for familiarity and understanding will help keep us from being misled by them.*

—Irving Copi, *Informal Fallacies*

Once a discipline struggling for recognition and acceptance, business ethics is now well established as an important subject of study among management scholars and as a topic of considerable concern to practicing managers.[1] However, it is still relatively new as an area of interest in the field of management communication, where discussions of business ethics are only now beginning to appear routinely in books and journal articles, and at professional conferences.[2] While an examination of ethics within this field appears to have been welcomed by everyone, the extent to which ethics has been considered so far has been very limited. Discussion has focused primarily on popular notions of good and bad business behavior, and often those reported dramatically by the press. Thus, concerns are organized around Beech-Nut selling infant apple juice that contains no apple, E. F. Hutton committing two thousand counts of mail and wire fraud, and Johnson & Johnson profiting by using the trade secret of one of its rivals.[3] While all of these instances certainly invite discussion of appropriate behavior, what is missing here is a way of defining ethics so that it has a particularly relevant meaning for those who study management communication as well as those who practice it. One way of providing such relevance is by defining ethics in relation to argument.

A consideration of ethics and argument is relevant for several reasons. First, if we understand ethics in a popular sense, as the study of good and bad behavior, we will need to acknowledge that much of what constitutes behavior at the workplace is essentially linguistic in both process and product. Working professionals spend *most* of their time communicating, as many surveys, studies, and interviews have established.[4] Because of this, we should not be surprised to find that much of their behavior, both good and bad, becomes apparent through their uses of language and their daily acts of communication. Since argument characterizes those communicative acts that are designed to influence others, it should be a favored candidate for ethical examination. Considering the ethical dimension of argument is thus relevant to communication theorists and practitioners because it recognizes the central role of linguistic behavior at the workplace and because it draws our attention to possible abuses of the medium.

Second, if we consider ethics in a less popular though perhaps more significant sense, not simply as the study of moral behavior but as a process that helps us determine what moral behavior is in the first place, we will find that ethics and argument are related in almost inseparable ways.[5] Discussions of right and wrong behavior cannot take place without conflicting points of view and advocates prepared to debate them. Since these discussions are characterized by controversy, the use of argument, even poor argument, is unavoidable. Arriving at the "right" decision about behavior, which is one way ethicists have characterized the goal of ethics, is simply not possible without engaging in a process that is fundamentally argumentative.[6] As a matter of *practice*, then, ethics cannot exist without argument.

Nor can argument, depending on how it is conceived, exist without ethics, unless one regards it as a mechanical device that is unrelated to the people it is designed to persuade. However, argument is much more than syllogistic modeling, and reducing it to such would greatly diminish its value as a form of inquiry as well as persuasion. At best, such a reduction would hinder one from noticing and appreciating the different points of view that characterize the discussion of problems and issues. At worst, it would result in qualitatively inferior arguments because they would be self-serving and one-sided. Of course, this is argument in its most limited sense. Understood more fully, as a form of rhetorical action in which one person seeks ways to persuade another, argument acquires at least as much of an ethical dimension as any other behavior that affects people involved in reasoned exchange. Because of that, argument should be particularly relevant to those who study ethics as part of their interest in management communication.

■ Ethical Argument

For the practitioner, the relevance of argument and ethics is perhaps even greater than it is for the scholar because of the consequences one might directly suffer in the world of work. Here, several more practical points might be made about the relevance of argument and ethics, and about the need for considering them in a combined form, in a form that might be called *ethical argument.*

Ethical argument refers to the practitioner's attempt to discover and provide support that is relevant to the claims that are stated or implied. For example, a writer states a problem exists with the newly hired supervisor. The writer adds that after the supervisor was hired, more accidents occurred on both day and night shifts. If the writer gives the second statement as support for the first, we may be able to say that the writer is arguing *unethically*, if we can show that the reason as it stands is not relevant to the claim. At the very least, we can say that the argument is ethically suspect and save our comments about the writer until we know something more about his or her intention. Notice that the argument here is not *about* moral behavior (though it could be); the argument *is* the behavior itself, and as such can be discussed as having an ethical dimension of its own, quite apart from the subject it may be about.

Defined in this way, as an expression of behavior, ethical argument is important to the practitioner for at least three reasons. First, and perhaps most importantly, it helps to avoid self-deception. By becoming aware of the various ways in which one can argue points with only apparent support, the practitioner will acquire a familiarity with and understanding of spurious arguments which Irving Copi, at the beginning of this chapter, suggests will "help keep us from being misled by them." Being misled includes misleading ourselves, which is all too easy if we do not recognize the spuriousness of our own lines of reasoning.

Second, an understanding of ethical argument is important because it provides the practitioner with another form of defense, one that extends well beyond self-deception. An awareness of ethical argument will make more apparent the unethical attempts of others, from poorly reasoned performance reviews written by some supervisors to the manipulative messages produced by some advertisers. This provides a form of protection against those who might mislead us through something Copi calls "a form of argument that *seems* to be correct but which proves, upon examination, not to be."

Third, by becoming familiar with one's own as well as others' unethical arguments, the practitioner will become a better judge of ethical argument. By separating ethical from unethical arguments, practitioners can reserve the former for presentation to an audience that could reasonably be expected to appreciate the effort. Thus, the practitioner should expect the same kind of benefits in the form of audience appreciation and respect that some have argued accrue to those who demonstrate more conventional ethical behavior through nonargumentative means. The ethical arguer stands to gain in the same way that the ethical manager in general does. This analogy, used here for illustrative purposes, is based on an argument recently made by LaRue Tone Hosmer. This is the abstract of his proposition:

> It is proposed that managers have to be moral, have to be concerned about the distribution of benefits and the allocation of harms brought about by their decisions and

actions, in order to build trust, commitment, and effort among the stakeholders of the firm. Trust, commitment, and effort on the part of all of the stakeholders are essential for long-term corporate success, given the economic conditions of intense global competition that now exist for the foreseeable future.[7]

Just as the ethical manager might "build trust, commitment, and effort among the stakeholders," so might the ethical arguer build similar beneficial relations with an audience of readers or listeners. Of the three reasons offered for becoming familiar with ethical argument, this one may well have the most consequential appeal to the practicing manager.

However, these reasons may not be the most compelling. In addition to them are others usually regarded as more important in the more general course of life, and for that reason, they are considered as applying to ethical behavior more generally. For example, one can argue that ethical behavior, revealed through argument or not, is important to observe because it is consistent with one's sense of self-respect and respect for others. One can argue similar importance because ethical behavior follows from adherence to a set of religious or personal beliefs or principles. And certainly one can point to the need for order and continuity in the community, which would be disrupted and diminished by unethical action. Such reasons apply also to ethical argument, since it too is a form of moral behavior, but they are not confined to it. Nevertheless, combined with the reasons given earlier, they provide strong cause to become familiar with ethical argument as a form of ethical behavior.

All previous reasons aside, one thing is relatively certain: a greater understanding of ethics and argument will result in greater accountability. If one is not familiar with the ethical dimension of argument, then one cannot hold anyone responsible for fair treatment in argumentative exchanges. Once one gains a familiarity, one also gains accountability because of the responsibility for what one knows and the recognition that it may be confusing, misleading, or even harmful to others. Therefore, yet an additional reason for becoming familiar with ethical argument is to develop a greater accountability among those who depend on argument as an important form of exchange and influence.

■ Analyzing Ethical Argument

As we have seen, several sound reasons argue for a familiarity with ethical argument. Unfortunately, those who wish to produce an ethical argument, much like those who wish to demonstrate ethical action, will find that they face a challenge. Unlike more easily recognized forms of unethical behavior—cheating on tax forms, lying to a supervisor, or stealing from the company—unethical argument is more difficult to discern and therefore more difficult to avoid. This is true if only because examining unethical argument *assumes* an understanding of argument and the uses of language in reasoning. For example, we can apply to our analysis of ethical problems an orthodox set of three principles: ideals, obligations, and consequences.[8] But using them to evaluate moral behavior assumes we are able to discern and understand the problematic behavior in the first place.

In the end, we will probably find that the vocabulary we use to discuss behavior that is normally regarded as unethical is simply not specialized enough for use in the analysis of language and argument. For example, we know what to call an act that involves the removal of an item without right or permission—we call it stealing—but what do we call a persuasive ploy that misrepresents blame by confusing causal and temporal connections (see *post hoc ergo propter hoc* below)? How are we to identify this ploy in language and argument, and how are we to understand its rhetorical operation? As working professionals, most of us are unfamiliar with the terms and concepts that might be employed in determining ethical quality in an argument.

Even those who are very familiar with both ethics and argument have struggled in their attempts to determine what constitutes ethical discourse in general and ethical argument in particular. A rich intellectual debate of over two thousand years includes contributions from the disciplines of rhetoric, philosophy, logic, and others. The discussion continues today, and it shows no sign of diminishing in the near future. On the contrary, recent writings on ethics and discourse provide evidence of a rich diversity of opinion and approach to judging the ethics of argument.

For example, some recent writers have argued that the ethics of argument should be judged from two points of view, from the means employed and the ends sought.[9] What matters in this approach is both the medium employed and the intent of the writer or speaker. Others have argued that ethical action should be judged from "the consequences, intended or otherwise, of a given persuasive message."[10] From this point of view, means and ends are almost irrelevant, and intention is a matter of choice.

Still others have moved entirely away from conceptual frameworks in which means and ends, for example, have much meaning and have chosen instead other vehicles for expressing their opinions on ethical discourse and argument. Richard Weaver, whose writings on ethics and rhetoric have been enormously influential in this century, presents ethical archetypes as a way of assessing ethics in argument and discourse.[11] Distinct from this is the view adopted by Henry Nelson Wieman and Otis Walter, in which ethical discourse and argument become a form of discovery, much as rhetoric was for Aristotle: "the discovery of the means of symbolism which lead to the greatest mutual understanding and mutual control."[12] The topic of ethical discourse and argument is thus today characterized by a diversity of viewpoints and little agreement on a singular approach.

Fortunately for the writer, considerable agreement does exist on some areas of argument that have ethical dimensions. One area in particular constitutes an entire category of rhetorically unappealing behavior that is available for examination, though we will have to reach outside the field and profession of business proper, if we are to benefit from it. However, it will be worth the interdisciplinary effort. By examining this category, *the fallacies of reasoning,* we will come to understand better at least one characteristic of ethical argument, as it has been agreed upon by many writers.[13] Although the fallacies may be treated in many ways, we will consider them, as we have other matters of thought and expression, in the context of practical argument and the written presentation of a reasoned case.

■ The Ethically Suspect: Fallacies of Reasoning

We have already seen that writers will increase their chances of success in reasoned persuasion if they construct an argumentative plan, test the plan by examining the syllogism it is based on, and present the plan according to a strategy that recognizes and seeks to overcome the predictable resistance of their skeptical readers. By doing this, writers will have determined the strongest case they can make, and they will have considered many of the options available to engage and influence the thinking of their skeptical readers. They will also become aware of the more critical assumptions on which they must rely in the course of presenting their case.

These steps having been taken, the course of presentation still affords the writer many opportunities for error as well as unethical practice. Not all matters of reasoning and discussion are determined by argumentative plans, syllogisms, and prooflines. Even with the line of reasoning and opposing point of view well determined, the writer will still need to construct the individual paragraphs and sentences that serve to present the argument in its extended form. During this presentation, the writer will want to guard against common mistakes in reasoning and indulgence in sophistry, not at the level of global organization that is determined by the proofline, but at the more local level of expression that occurs in paragraphs and sentences.

Errors of this sort, in the presentation of the argument, are generally classified as *fallacies*, much like those mentioned at the end of Chapter 3. In fact, those fallacies apply equally to the planning of an argument and the presentation of it. However, in this chapter, we will want to consider problems in reasoning that are less likely to occur at the planning stage but which can prevent the writer from presenting a compelling argument.

As we consider these fallacies, we will want to be careful about two matters of judgment. First, the presentation of fallacies in the context of ethics may suggest that the presence of a fallacy also indicates the presence of an unethical act. However, simply because a writer's argument may be fallacious does not mean that the writer is unethical. The writer may simply have made an honest error in reasoning. Thus, to assume that "fallacious" equals "unethical" might well be to commit a further fallacy because it would confuse coincidence and design. Nevertheless, fallacies are called fallacies for a reason, and they have long been recognized as such precisely because they can mislead and because they are open to if not inviting of abuse in argument. Perhaps the best way to characterize them, then, is by referring to them as Richard Weaver has referred to other forms of argument, as *ethically suspect*.

The second matter of judgment concerns how seriously and absolutely we consider the fallacies. Simply because they have traditionally been labeled fallacies, we will have a tendency to see the weaknesses in them and perhaps even reject them entirely as being useless in the process of writing. This would probably be a mistake, though unfortunately only a few composition theorists have pointed this out. Two of them, Wayne Booth and Marshall Gregory, put the matter well:

> Certain kinds of bad reasons, called "fallacies," have destroyed so many arguments that they have been labeled and banned by logicians and rhetoricians. All educated people know the names of at least some of these, but too often their names are used as unexamined weapons in argument, without sufficient thought about what is bad about them. Booth can remember as a college student being silenced in an argument when an opponent shouted at him, "False dichotomy"; it was the first time he had heard the word "dichotomy," and it was years before he realized that some dichotomies are not false at all but useful.[14]

The authors go on to point out that the very use of the word "false" suggests that some dichotomies may not be false. On the contrary, they may be very useful to the writer. So too with the following list of fallacies. Analogy, for example, may well cause problems when used as a form of proof, and certainly when it's used as the exclusive form of proof. However, analogies can be very useful during moments of exposition and at times when the writer needs additional though not critical support for a point. This is true of most of the "fallacies" which follow.

Assumed Authority (argumentum ad verecundiam)

Known classically as *argumentum ad verecundiam*, this is particularly tempting to those managers whose management style may be described as "autocratic" or "traditional." Because they are accustomed to giving direction without explanations or reasons, they may not readily see the need for supporting reasons in their attempts at persuasion. Without a reason, the reader is left with only the "authority" of the writer as a basis for accepting controversial statements. Whether this is politically sufficient is one matter. Its argumentative sufficiency is another. The appeal to *the writer's* authority is one form of this fallacy, and it occurs when the writer offers no support other than that writer's say-so. Here is an example:

> All of us know that going to flextime is not without its share of problems, but I think it is the best thing for us to do. I am concerned that the other options presented will simply not work. I have given the matter plenty of thought, and considering the alternatives, this strikes me as the most efficient way to structure our schedules. I have decided to recommend flextime at the Monday manager's meeting, and I would like your support at that time.

Two things are worth noticing here. First, the writer has simply repeated statements that may appear to give support but in fact do not (flextime is the best thing because it's the most efficient thing; in this case, "best" equals "most efficient"). Because of this, the fallacy is closely related to begging the question, a fallacy covered in detail in Chapter 3. Second, the frequent use of the first-person pronoun ("I") indicates that support here relies heavily on self-reference. Although the reader may not openly oppose the writer because of the political implications, little exists here to provide the reader with an understanding of the writer's claim and recommendation. Such an understanding would certainly help the reader appreciate the writer's point of view and help to secure the reader's informed support.

We have just seen one form of assumed authority, in which the writer relies on his or her own authority. This is *primary* authoritative support. Just as popular is another form, in which the writer relies on the authority of another. This is *secondary* authoritative support. To support a point, the writer now relies on the opinion of another:

> Our people are very concerned that this program will add time to their job assignment. Their concern is valid because many of these programs don't require the client to enter a number or device reading while at the station. However, the program we're considering has been broadly accepted among marketers, among them Roberts and Associates, and they are confident that the transaction information will not add time and money. Therefore, we do not really see a problem in this area.

Although Roberts and Associates may well be a recognized authority on this matter, the writer's reference to it will probably not satisfy the reader. Nor should it. Even though the reference may carry considerable strength from the *writer's* point of view, it need not carry any weight from the *reader's*. After all, nothing in the name Roberts and Associates proves anything about the additional burden that may be caused by the transaction information. That Roberts and Associates has an established reputation for being knowledgeable in these matters means only that it has a history of useful opinion. It says nothing directly about the case at present.

Writers can often avoid problems with assumed authority simply by asking whether a reason exists for the authority's opinion. This reason, if it does exist, is one the writer may be able to present to the reader. For example, instead of urging a particular investment because Jones thinks it's a good idea, one might urge it because the investment carries little risk in an industry that is extremely stable (Jones's reason for endorsing it). The difference here is significant: risk and stability are directly relevant to judging the value of the investment; Jones's credibility is relevant only indirectly if at all.

Assumed authority is commonly found in journalistic coverage in which testimony in some form is invoked. In the following passage, the writer is attempting to show that the "communications giant" Pacific Telecom would be in a position to dictate rates if it purchased the Anchorage Telephone Utility:

> Yet the prospect of inviting in Pacific Telecom, a communications giant that already owns several Alaska telephone exchanges as well as Alascom, the state's sole instate long distance carrier, raises fears that it would gain a virtual monopoly here. The company would be in a position to dictate rates, Assembly Chairman Bill Faulkner said Thursday.[15]

Nothing in the article is offered to support the remarkable assertion that "inviting in Pacific Telecom . . . raises fears," unless one accepts the hidden assumption that any company that one assembly chairman says would be in a position to dictate rates will raise fears. That this assumption is not universally accepted is made clear in the very next sentence, in which the mayor is quoted as saying that "Rates would be regulated by the Alaska Public Utilities Commission." In fact, rates *would be* regulated by the Public Utilities Commission, just as they are in every other state in the country. Although the reporter has not used the passive voice here, the passage has a similar effect because it suppresses the logical subject of "fear." As a consequence, the reader does not know for whom the invitation would raise fears, only that one assembly chairman believes the company would be in a position to dictate rates. The reader is thus asked to associate Pacific Telecom with "fears," but is given no evidence for the association, except the "authoritative" endorsement of an assembly chairman.

The example above notwithstanding, writers will need to appeal to authority at times, particularly when the authority's reasons are unavailable, and if the writer still wishes to provide human testimony. In those cases, some guidelines are useful. The following are from the authors mentioned earlier and will guide the writer in determining whether the authority cited is likely to be relevant to the reader.

1. Is the authority *known* to the relevant audience?
2. Is the authority genuinely expert on the subject in hand, or merely well known in some other domain?
3. Is the authority known to be trustworthy? As Senator Sam Irwin said about ex-President Nixon, winning a point in the Watergate hearings, "It is not entirely unlikely that a man who has been found lying when under oath would lie when *not* under oath!"
4. Is the authority *representative* of the more authoritative opinions in the subject being discussed? Would other authorities concede that this person is an authority?[16]

Assumed Causal Connection (post hoc ergo propter hoc)

In its classical form, this fallacy is called the *post hoc ergo propter hoc*, which is Latin for "after this, therefore as a result of this." Known also as "false cause," this fallacy involves a confusion of the time of an event or action and the results of that event or action. Simply because something happens at a particular time, and something else happens after it, the two need not be related in any way but temporally. The following is an example of this fallacy in practice:

The Warehouse Project was initially very successful. To begin with, a multidisciplinary project team was formed to develop a project timeline and project management structure. In just two weeks after the first project team meeting, final packaging options were selected, and a project completion deadline and budget were established.

The problems didn't start until the team from marketing became involved. Only two weeks after they joined the effort, people started having second thoughts about not just the packaging options but also about whether the budget we originally agreed on is still adequate. It may well have been a mistake to have marketing involved at this early stage.

The causal connection suggested here is between the involvement of the marketing team and the problems that ensued. Thus, from the writer's point of view, marketing *caused* the problems. Of course, marketing *may* have caused the problems, but nothing in the writer's reasoning supports this. Any number of other causes are just as likely until the writer makes the causal connection for the reader. For example, the original team may have come to have reservations independently of marketing's efforts. Someone in a position of external review could have brought packaging and budgetary matters to the attention of the team. The writer above has only given the reader a temporal sequence, and that is quite different from a causal link.

To avoid this fallacy, writers will want to be careful not to assume the causal connection, but to argue for it. For example, the writer of the previous passage might have said:

The Warehouse Project was initially very successful. To begin with, a multidisciplinary project team was formed to develop a project timeline and project management structure. In just two weeks after the first project team meeting, final packaging options were selected, and a project completion deadline and budget were established.

The problems didn't start until the team from marketing became involved. Only two weeks after they joined the effort, several of their members openly challenged our plans on packaging, and their team leader pressed repeatedly for a larger budget to accommodate their special interests in the project. It may well have been a mistake to have marketing involved at this early stage.

Of course, a causal link may not exist at all; only the writer will know after examining the line of reasoning. At the very least, the writer who is sensitive to this fallacy may discover it and wisely choose not to present it to the reader in the first place.

Unfortunately, discovery of this fallacy is not always easy, and it will often go unnoticed when it appears in the writing of more experienced practitioners. The following example is from a major newspaper. Note that the reporter relies on this fallacy as the major part of his attempt to show that the mayor's executive assistant was involved, as an act of political favoritism, in influencing the sale of the Anchorage Telephone Utility to the telecommunications company, Pacific Telecom:

The company has other ties to the Fink administration. Henry Pratt, a long-time friend of the mayor and a long-time political consultant to Alascom, was hired as the mayor's executive assistant in March.

> In March and again Thursday, Fink said Pratt has nothing to do with the ATU sale issue, but Pratt was on hand in the city purchasing department Thursday morning as the deadline for bids came down.[17]

In the paragraphs above, the fact, as presented, is that the mayor's assistant was "on hand," an abstract phrase signifying little more than being "physically present." However, the corrective conjunction "but" indicates that the clause will be in opposition to the claim that "Pratt has nothing to do with the ATU sale issue." The fallacy is thus the reporter's sole resource as he attempts to show that Pacific Telecom is unethically relying on political favors to insure a protected acceptance of its ATU bid.

Value of Community (argumentum ad populum)

In its classical form, this fallacy is called the *argumentum ad populum*, or the "argument to the people." In its more familiar expression, it is referred to as the "bandwagon." Here the writer relies on the assumption that a community of opinion indicates proof of or support for a controversial point. Commonplace in advertising and in teenage efforts at peer-pressure persuasion, this fallacy occurs when the popular is allowed to replace the arguable. Thus, what others think is a good idea must in fact be a good idea. This should not be surprising to find in business environments that rely heavily on teamwork and cooperative community effort. For example:

> Almost everyone in this organization favors this project, and quite frankly some of them are beginning to wonder why we have not joined in. As you know, many of our managers strongly supported the project during the planning and execution phases and praised the project team for its work to date and for the way it has invited departments to buy in. We can join this effort if we make our case for it now, along with the others. If we do not, we may well find that we will have considerably more difficulty making the case alone later. I recommend that we move forward on this, at our earliest opportunity.

The writer may well be right. Sometimes delay can be costly. However, the popularity of a project does not itself provide support for the writer's recommendation. While many may favor a particular project or course of action, they may simply be wrong in their endorsement, or their favor may result from needs not shared by the reader.

Yet if this fallacy is commonly found in cooperative environments, it is also at home in competitive industries. Fear of being left out, of losing competitive advantage to another company can make this fallacy almost unavoidable. The idea here is that "others are doing it, so we should do it too." Here is an example:

> Soon after deregulation, Northwest Telephone decided to automate all of its services in this area, and that included customer telephone support. Soon after it switched, the

directory department alone reported a 15 percent increase in efficiency. NT was the last to switch to this method of providing support. All of our competitors now offer this form of support. We are the only ones who do not. If we are going to remain competitive, I think we should seriously consider going to automated telephone support soon.

Although reasons may well exist for adopting automated telephone support, the only explanation given above is that others have done it. Of course, one might point out that a 15 percent increase in efficiency is reason enough, but that may simply be an example of the fallacy of assumed causal connection (see above).

A good way to avoid this fallacy begins by asking whether good reasons might exist for the popularity of an idea. Presumably, the widespread use of automated support is not simply a matter of coincidence (though that too *is* possible). The writer who takes the time to discover these reasons will then be in a position to present them to the reader.

False Division

The fallacies of "false division" and "false composition" (discussed next) both proceed from assumptions about the relationship between individuals and larger collectives, from small groups to entire communities. Of the two, false division is perhaps the more poisonous because it borders on outright bigotry. This fallacy attributes to an individual a characteristic popularly attributed to a group or larger collective. If the popular notion is that technicians from TechService really don't know how to work on anything but mainframe computers, then one would be committing this fallacy by saying "We shouldn't be surprised that he didn't have a clue what was wrong with the workstation—after all, he's from TechService." Here is another example:

> Regarding the information transfer aspect of the project, this evaluation has been underway for at least three months and will be concluded in two weeks. The cost effectiveness of the work and validity of all contracts and costs were substantiated in the preliminary audit, and are not expected to be an issue in the regulatory audit. The only opposition has come from Reynolds. However, I think we can safely put his concern to one side. His objection is what we might expect from a recently minted MBA, and it will take a while before he gains some real world experience.

The working assumption here, of course, is that what is often said of some MBAs, that they lack real-world experience, is attributable to Reynolds simply because he *is* a brand-new MBA.

To avoid this fallacy, writers need to be careful about making their reasons as specific as their claims. The writer may well claim that Reynolds's objection is trivial or impractical, but this will not carry much force until something else is said about Reynolds and not about his membership in a graduate community.

False Composition

This is the other side of false division, and it works, as one might expect, by attributing to a group something that is characteristic of an individual. The fallacy here becomes clearer when we acknowledge that group behavior or the characteristics of a collective can be quite different from the behavior or characteristics of one person. Of course, unions offer the very promise that a community can afford to act in a way that individuals cannot. In the following passage, the writer assumes something about the behavior of a fifteen-member advisory committee:

> I had an opportunity to discuss this individually with several of the committee's members, and I am pleased to say that they support it. To be candid, it's hard to believe that they would oppose it since they will benefit from it in both the short and long run. Once others see the benefit, we can expect a vote in favor of our proposal.

The writer has assumed here that what is true of individual members of a group will be true collectively. No doubt, the members of the committee have things in common—interests, concerns, and so on. However, nothing above shows why the reader might expect the group to mirror the attitude of the several individuals. One might just as reasonably expect the opposite, that the group would reject what the individuals value because doing so would allow them to deny the predictable charge of individual self-interest.

False Dilemma

Not much different from the false division mentioned earlier, the "false dilemma" is probably a better label since it brings out the sense of a situation that requires a choice between two equal and often unpleasant alternatives. Of course, the point of this fallacy is that other alternatives are available, even if the writer has not thought of them or has chosen to conceal them. For example, in the following remarks from a company's spokesperson, other alternatives would probably be apparent to everyone except those in upper management:

> As everyone knows, we have enjoyed an unprecedented six years of growth. Our product lines have several times been the envy of our competitors, and our corporate programs in human resources have won industry acclaim. Because of our success, the recent drop in revenues caused by bad press from our recent legal entanglements has been all the more difficult to accept. Unfortunately, we now find ourselves in a position that other companies have found themselves in. To remain responsible to our shareholders, we must maintain profits, and we can do that in only two ways: either by downsizing middle and lower management or by taking salary reductions at all levels. Since the second is not acceptable, we have, regrettably, opted for the first.

"Opting for the first" will appear especially regrettable to those who know that other alternatives, perhaps even many, exist but have not been mentioned because concealment protects special interests such as job security in top management.

The false division or false dichotomy is simply one expression of this fallacy and differs only in its lack of a necessary dilemma. Sometimes called the fallacy of "black and white" or "either . . . or," it assumes a world in which problems, methods of analysis, and solutions are all binary. Once that assumption is made, argument is reduced to making a case for one choice. "If you are going to motivate your sales team," a supervisor might say, "you have only two choices: the carrot or the stick." Here the dichotomy has to do with perspective, and the only choice permitted by the false construction is between two ways of viewing motivation. In fact, many exist.

False Analogy

Analogies work by comparison whether they assume it or argue toward it, and this very function of the analogy is its greatest strength and weakness. Used to illustrate or explain, the analogy is a wonderful tool of informative discourse. Especially when writers suspect that their readers will be unable to grasp a concept, a well-constructed analogy, one that is designed to make the unfamiliar familiar, can be enormously helpful to comprehension. However, in argumentation, the conditions are very different, and analogies can easily be abused when writers compare matters that are critically different. The following record of exchange from *Newsweek* provides an interesting example:

> Tobacco companies continue to deny that nicotine is addictive as they defend lawsuits over smokers' deaths. The most famous was brought in 1983 by the family of Rose Cippollone. Soon after Philip Morris quashed its nicotine studies, James Johnston of RJR Tobacco told a House panel that calling nicotine addictive meant "characterizing virtually any enjoyable activity as addictive, whether it is eating sweets, drinking coffee, playing video games or watching TV." "You and I know that Twinkies don't kill a single American a year," Rep. Henry Waxman responded. "The difference between cigarettes and Twinkies . . . is death."[18]

When Johnston compared cigarettes to the enjoyable activity of eating Twinkies, Waxman's memorable response immediately pointed out the weakness of the analogy.

Not all analogies are as straightforward as the one above. In the passage that follows, a reporter is suggesting that unfortunate consequences could well face Anchorage voters should they support the sale of the Anchorage Telephone Utility to Pacific Telecom. The first analogy is in the lead paragraph, where it will demand the reader's greatest attention:

> Other towns have sold publicly owned utilities and banked the cash, the choice being offered the Anchorage voters on the Oct. 3 ballot. But some of those cities found the funds set up with the proceeds from the sales did not pay off quite as hoped.

> A Florida town found that when interest rates plunged, the earnings it had counted on to help run the city were cut in half. A Texas town spent its fund on a swimming pool. And in Fort Wayne, Ind., a former mayor filed a lawsuit to stop the city administration from ladling money out of its utility trust fund to bail out a failing hotel project.
>
> If more than 60 percent of local voters approve, the municipality will sell Anchorage Telephone Utility to Pacific Telecom Inc. for $412 million.[19]

The analogies compare the previous sale of publicly owned utilities in other states and the proposed sale of ATU. The analogies are faulty in at least several respects. First, items compared could well be more different than similar, and no attempt is made to establish a basis for similarity. Second, the assumption that Anchorage may suffer consequences similar to those of voters in Florida and elsewhere is actually denied later in the article. The reader who continues to read that far will discover that the Florida fund is secure and paying in excess of the previous utility, that the Texas fund was never really a trust fund in the first place, that the fund in Indiana is just fine, and that Kansas has a fund that is working very well. Given the extreme weakness of the analogy, one should not be surprised to find the reporter arriving at the conditional statement below instead of a solidly supported conclusion:

> If the experience of some other cities makes the future of Anchorage's proposed utility trust iffy, the way the proposal was put on the ballot doesn't help. Unless the voters approve two propositions, Anchorage's fund could be self-liquidating.

The conditional preposition "If" is worth noting here because it allows the writer to introduce a danger to Anchorage's utility trust without actually substantiating it or presenting it as a probability. This is also true of the final sentence above, where the verb "could" introduces only a possibility.

Invective (argumentum ad invidiam)

Known popularly as "name calling," this usually involves an attack either on the arguer or someone or something else. Because it can be directed at something other than the arguer, it is different from the *ad hominem* (discussed later). However, it shares with it this: invective is seldom directed toward the argument at hand, unless it is used to disparage it. Invective can occur in both literal and figurative forms. In its literal expression, invective dispenses with all pretense to civility, and the "names" are simply "called":

> The State of California has completed the audit of the firm's overhead expenses for the fiscal years 1989 through 1991. The results of this audit were that significant amounts of employees' reimbursable expenses have been disallowed. I don't know what else we could have expected from such an obviously incompetent and ignorant review of our records.

This is both direct and irrelevant. The reader still does not know why the writer has a problem with the review or why the expenses have been disallowed.

In its figurative form, invective is less direct and sometimes more sophisticated, but it is just as irrelevant. The following example is ostensibly a story about possible city liability. Note that the assumed culprit, Pacific Telecom, is positioned in a way that suggests it is involved in behavior that is both impure and forbidden. This occurs at and following the lead, where the reader's attention is greatest:

> Anchorage could get stuck paying up to $30 million for disputed long-distance billings to Alascom Inc. unless its parent company agrees to take over all debts if it buys the city phone utility.
>
> And if it doesn't, the city could be liable even after it sells Anchorage Telephone Utility to Pacific Telecom, Inc. PTI, a $1.1 billion communications conglomerate, which owns Alascom.
>
> These strange and incestuous outcomes are the result of a big-bucks legal fight that has frazzled lawyers, embarrassed the Fink administration and left everybody wondering where ATU would scratch up tens of millions of dollars to pay off its legal debts.[20]

The problem here is one of reference, arrangement, and the misuse of figurative language. By placing Pacific Telecom in the second paragraph (the writer could have placed it in the third or even first), the reporter is able to attribute to Pacific Telecom "These strange and incestuous outcomes." The reporter probably didn't mean "incestuous *outcome*" simply because that would be nonsense, but instead meant something like "unlawful or uncustomary behavior that had resulted in the city's present liability." Unfortunately, the reporter did not say that, perhaps because he would then be obligated to show an actual breaking of law or custom. This is also true of the abstract adjective "strange," which stands only as an indication of the reporter's point of view. The confusion of cause and effect and the referent pronoun "These" emphasize the metaphor of incest, in which Pacific Telecom has become a direct participant.

What is especially troublesome about the metaphor and its place in the article is that it is neither explained nor supported later on. All the reporter is able to show, or even attempts to show, is that many people with overlapping interests and business have been involved in the many discussions and disputes that have led to the city's present liability. Yes, this is a complex issue of liability, and the reporter has done a good job of communicating that. Yet the reader will be left with the sense that Pacific Telecom has been involved not in something complex, but in something unsavory and prohibited.

At the most basic level, avoiding invective involves developing an ability to play fair and treat others with respect. In the practice of argument, it involves a commitment to limit the grounds of debate to the issues at hand. This means that calling others names, either directly or indirectly, is a departure from the issue at hand.

Red Herring (ignoratio elenchi)

Classically labeled *ignoratio elenchi*, the "red herring" is so called because it applies to the practice in hunting in which a herring is dragged across the track to distract hounds from their pursuit. It serves a similar function in argument when the writer attempts to distract the reader from the issue at hand by introducing something that is not relevant to the line of reasoning.

> There has been a lot of discussion about our current policy and new proposal governing smoking in enclosed facilities. Most of the people who are upset about this are smokers who agree that the quality of air should be improved but already feel that they are being punished because of their habit. They are concerned that if the new and more restrictive proposal is adopted they will have to leave the building entirely if they are to smoke. I agree with them and wonder if we wouldn't all do better to concentrate our efforts on the pollution produced by automobiles, since they contribute more damage to the quality of our air than smoking does.

The air pollution caused by automobiles is the "red herring" here since it is being used to redirect the reader's attention from the issue at hand, the new nonsmoking proposal, to an unrelated matter, automobile pollution. Even if the reader were to grant that automobile pollution presents a greater danger to air quality, the issue of smoking in enclosed facilities would remain as an issue.

Appeal to Ignorance (argumentum ad ignorantiam)

Known classically as the *argumentum ad ignorantiam*, this fallacy exists whenever someone argues that a statement is true simply because it has not been shown false. For example, someone might state that an out-of-body experience follows directly after death. When challenged, this person shrugs and says that no one has ever proved that it doesn't. This fallacy has another side, which involves arguing the falseness of a statement based on the absence of a proved truth. Thus those who might snicker at the person who argued for out-of-body experiences above would be committing this fallacy if they held that these experiences *don't* occur because no one has proved that they do.

A very interesting and extended example of this fallacy is apparent in one episode of the *Anchorage Daily News* and its coverage of Pacific Telecom's table negotiations with Anchorage Telephone Utility. Notice how the writer's "argument" is built on this fallacy, which is introduced in the passage below, and how it becomes the assumption behind the logic of the entire article:

> "We were unable to come up with a scenario that would justify them spending that money, " said Jeff Sinz, ATU's finance manager. "They obviously have some plans that aren't on the table."[21]

This is, of course, one person's opinion, but even if it were true, nothing can be deduced from what the speaker *does not know*. This is the appeal to ignorance, and it is soon adopted by the reporter in subsequent paragraphs, where the metaphor of table negotiations is extended:

> What PTI has on the table is a sketchy bid to transform ATU into a private company. It has promised that for five years, it won't fire anybody or jack up phone rates higher than already contemplated by the Anchorage Assembly which has approved a 56 percent rise in rates by the end of 1993.

> A million-dollar marketing campaign has accentuated the positive aspects of the sale. Advertising, promises, and political testimonials have created an appearance of forthrightness, an appearance belied by PTI's refusals to explain its business plans.

> Citing corporate confidentiality, PTI has repeatedly refused to discuss ATU's future. As voters stroll behind the curtain Oct. 3, they won't possess any real knowledge about how PTI plans to reach into their wallets to get back its investment.

The line of reasoning here is faulty and relies on unacceptable assumptions, and unsupported premises, all of which are easily diagrammed according to the syllogistic logic covered elsewhere in this book:

> (Assumption) If a company does not discuss its plans, and others cannot explain those plans, then that company's intentions must be suspect.

> (Premise) Pacific Telecom does not discuss its plans for ATU, and others have not been able to explain those plans.

> (Conclusion) Pacific Telecom's intentions for ATU are suspect.

Without acceptance of the assumption, this line of reasoning is worthless (it will not enable the conclusion to be drawn). However, even if someone were to accept this assumption, the reporter would still have to support the premise. Since the rest of the article offers many different explanations of Pacific Telecom's plans, it actually removes any force this line of reasoning might have. As a result, the only "support" remaining takes the form of several sentence-level misrepresentations. The first is the use of the phrase "sketchy bid" to describe the seventy-six-page *Assets Purchase Agreement*, a legally binding contract. If anything is "sketchy" about this agreement, the reporter leaves it unstated. The second is the metaphor "reach into their wallets to get back its investment." This is certainly the more serious allegation, and it is nowhere supported or explained in this article. By inserting this charge within the statement ". . . they won't possess any real knowledge about how PTI plans to reach into their wallets," the reporter implies that Pacific Telecom will exact payment from the public, as perhaps the only predictable action one could expect from a company whose intentions have been portrayed as so suspect.

Although writers and readers alike need to watch for this fallacy, particularly when it appears in the form above, at least one exception exists to the general rule, as the logician Irving Copi indicates:

> This mode of argument is not fallacious in a court of law, because there the guiding principle is that a person is presumed innocent until proven guilty. The defense can legitimately claim that if the prosecution has not proved guilt, this warrants a verdict of *not guilty*. But since this claim is based upon the special legal principle mentioned, it is consistent with the fact that the *argumentum ad ignorantiam* constitutes a fallacy in other contexts.[22]

Appeal to Pity (argumentum ad misericordiam)

This fallacy involves replacing support of a claim with an appeal to the pity of the reader or listener. Although this would not be spurious if the appropriateness of the pity were at issue, it constitutes a fallacy when it is employed under other circumstances. The following request is being made by an MBA student whose grade-point average has dropped below the level of performance required for him to remain in his program:

> I am writing because I understand that I must maintain a grade-point average of 3.0. However, unlike my classmates, whose companies provide financial support, I am paying for my own education. If I am not allowed to continue, I will lose my entire investment to date. This is a substantial sum of money. It will be a great loss not only for me but also for my family and especially my children who will need to enter college shortly.

The situation this student writer describes is certainly an unfortunate one, and the reader is free to sympathize. However, the writer should not expect a change of mind based on the reasons given since the way they are presented above makes them irrelevant to the problem of inadequate academic performance. Presented as the *cause* of this problem as opposed to the consequences, family hardship might have been more relevant.

The appeal to pity is perhaps best seen in the extreme but popular (at least among logicians) story of the young man who was charged with the horrible murder of his parents. After realizing that he had no case based on conventional evidence, he solicited the pity of the court by pointing out that he was an orphan.

Hasty Generalization

Also known as "converse accident," this fallacy is present in attempts that take exceptional cases and generalize from them to a conclusion about nonexceptional cases.

Hasty generalization is reasoning that assumes what is true for the exceptional is true for everyone. For example, one might observe that several employees with a record of heart problems collapsed during a company-sponsored marathon. If one then argued from this that employees in general ought not to participate in company sporting events, this reasoning would be open to the charge of hasty generalization, among other things.

This fallacy may be found routinely in discussions of substance abuse and control. It begins with the recognition that some people have had great misfortune in their lives as a result of narcotics or alcohol. Perhaps one or two dramatic and tragic stories are told of those who have lost everything because of their addiction. Although this *might* be sufficient to establish the possibility of danger to others, it would be both hasty and a generalization to say that these substances should be banned because they are harmful to all. Yet this is a position that has been argued more than once, as have other positions that have been adopted on the relationship between use of substances by some and the similar use by many.

Abuse of the Arguer (argumentum ad hominem)

This infamous directive to the arguer exists in two forms. The first is abusive, and it refers to the attempt to disprove a claim by attacking the person who made the claim, as opposed to the claim itself. Since it is always directed to a person, it can be distinguished from invective, which can be directed at anything or anyone. Below is a mild example from *Smoker's Advocate*, a national newsletter that presents itself as "A Service of Philip Morris, U.S.A."

> 1993 has been a busy year for the millions of smokers who have an interest in protecting the right to choose to smoke. Thousands upon thousands of letters and phone calls to legislators at all levels of government have reinforced the message that smokers are tired of being singled out for additional taxes, will no longer accept unreasonable conditions on when and where they can smoke, and will stick up for themselves when accosted by self-righteous antismokers.[23]

Taken as part of the larger attempt to disprove the danger of ambient smoke, this passage simply attacks the nonsmokers by referring to them as "self-righteous" people who "accost" others who have an interest in protecting their rights.

Circumstance of the Arguer (argumentum ad hominem)

The second form of the *ad hominem*, this directive is not to the person but to the person's circumstances, including beliefs, affiliations, associations, or assumptions. In its circumstantial form, the *ad hominem* characteristically attempts to disprove or support a claim by drawing attention to those circumstances that the arguer assumes should compel the reader or listener to agree. For example, in the fiction of the following example, the speaker attempts to persuade someone to stop smoking:

> I simply cannot understand why you continue to smoke. It is a self-destructive habit. You are a good Christian in all other respects and a good member of your community, but what you are doing is simply not consistent with your faith, which celebrates life. You, on the other hand, are destroying it.

The arguer could argue many things here to support the contention that smoking is self-destructive and should be stopped. However, showing (or claiming) that smoking is inconsistent with one's religious views proves nothing about the habit itself. It only appeals to the special circumstance of the listener.

Reduction to the Absurd (reductio ad absurdum)

As a form of reasoning, the "reduction to the absurd" may not be fallacious at all if it is used to show that a statement will lead to a conclusion that is inevitably absurd. However, if it is used to disprove that statement or to speculate on absurd consequences, it will be fallacious. For example, one does not disprove the statement "Honesty is the best policy" simply by showing that adopting such a policy will lead to the absurd consequence of offending so many people that one would have nobody with whom to be honest. The following comments show how a position can be reduced to the absurd through simple speculation:

> I was sorry to hear that Jones is against our telecommuting project simply because he feels we need direct supervision. Perhaps he also feels he needs to check in with us on the weekend. Maybe he should join us when we go to the health club or to the men's room. Never can tell what we might try to do if he doesn't keep an eye on us.

Nothing here really disputes Jones's position on the inadvisability of telecommuting or his concern with supervision. All the speaker has done is consider supervision in the extreme, in its absurd form.

Fallacies in Combination

We have thus far considered the fallacies individually. However, we might expect them to appear in a variety of combinations, particularly in longer arguments. The following passage contains several fallacies, including assumed authority (*argumentum ad verecundiam*), invective (*argumentum ad invidiam*), and question begging (*petitio principii* from Chapter 3). The writer is attempting to show that the telecommunications company, Pacific Telecom, will be dishonest in its obligation to the covenants of a legal contract. Here is the lead paragraph:

> After a month of secret negotiations, Mayor Tom Fink signed a contract Wednesday to sell the Anchorage Telephone Utility for $412 million and a bundle of promises some of which promise more than they deliver.[24]

What the reporter has referred to as "promises" are actually covenants listed in a legally binding contract, which is enforceable in a court of law. In an ironic sense, the reporter is literally correct in the headline (PROMISES AREN'T QUITE WHAT THEY AP-PEAR TO BE), but this is a joke that will be lost on the reader, who cannot tell what the writer is referring to. By referring to specific contract covenants as a "bundle of promises," the reporter begs the question and prepares the reader for the spurious inductive reasoning of subsequent paragraphs, where "promises" only momentarily becomes "commitments":

> Not all those commitments will deliver in practice what they suggest, however.
>
> For example, PTI's promise not to lay off employees for five years is a response to charges that the utility sale will cost jobs. But, while the no-layoff promise may protect individual employees, it does nothing to protect the city's economy from a potentially sharp cut in the number of jobs provided by ATU.
>
> While the contract prevents PTI from laying off workers, it doesn't require the company to replace those who quit voluntarily. ATU officers say about 10 percent of the workforce quits or retires every year; over a five-year period, that could reduce ATU's present 680-person workforce to about 400, or a 40 percent reduction.
>
> And while PTI promises no new rate increases, a five-year utility budget plan already calls for boosting rates by 25 percent in 1991 and 9 percent in 1993; PTI would be allowed to ask the APUC to grant those. ATU was granted a 9.4 percent increase earlier this year.

The reporter's presentation of his reasoning is extraordinarily clear: the opening one-sentence paragraph contains a highly controversial statement that will then be supported with premises in the three longer paragraphs that follow. But if the reasoning is clear, it is clearly defective. This can be seen most easily by inserting a "because," a standard logical cue word, before each of the supporting paragraphs. The result is a series of hidden assumptions that even the reporter, if pressed, would probably not accept. The assumptions are presented below, according to the paragraphs that contain them.

Paragraph 6
When a company responds to charges that a sale will cost jobs, it will not, in practice, deliver on its promises.

When a company's promise involves no assurance that the city's economy will be protected from a potentially sharp cut in the number of jobs, it will not, in practice, deliver on its promises.

Paragraph 7

When a company enters into a contract that doesn't require it to replace workers who quit voluntarily, it will not, in practice, deliver on its promises.

Paragraph 8

When a company is allowed to ask a regulatory agency for a rate increase, that company will not, in practice, deliver on its promises.

Worth special comment is paragraph 7, where the reporter argues for a reduction in the ATU workforce by amplifying a rate quoted by an ATU official. The ATU official's rate is logically unrelated to the percent of workforce resignations or retirements under Pacific Telecom management. Yet this does not prevent the reporter from speculating about the extremely dramatic consequences of the ATU sale to Pacific Telecom. What allows the writer his speculation is the auxiliary verb "could," which is used elsewhere in the article to make the possible appear important. In paragraph 13, the reporter uses it both to characterize negotiations as secret sessions that may deprive the voting public of important information, and to portray Pacific Telecom as the kind of company that negotiates in a setting of nondisclosure:

> But if voters were silent partners in the negotiations, they were also blind and deaf. The talks were conducted in secret, and the contract devotes most of its 74 pages to setting out information that will be kept secret. Those provisions could mean the public will not get important information although everyone involved in the deal says that won't happen.

The use of the word "secret" to describe a perfectly common "closed session" only advertises the lack of the reporter's justification for the public not getting important information. Of course, no justification is needed when one predicts what is *possible*, and that is a point well worth making about this passage and this article. If one accepts the assumption that most anything is possible (and a great many people do), then statements of possibility have little meaning. This should raise the question of why such statements need to be made in the first place, particularly when, in this paragraph, all stated evidence suggests that not even the possible is probable: ". . . everyone involved in the deal says that won't happen." Who then says it will? If the reporter says it *could*, and if that statement means anything, it must have meaning because the reporter is aware of the "important information." Otherwise, how would he be able to call it "important?" Yet the reporter states that the information is secret.

What is disturbing about the passage above, and this article in general, is that most readers will probably not examine the reasoning in any detail. However, they will respond to the more controversial and negative statements about Pacific Telecom, and they will most probably remember them, if they remember anything from the article at all.

▓ Some Consequences

Although this chapter has been devoted to discussing the technical shape of argument that is ethically suspect, the consequences of producing such argument are important enough for a concluding comment, even if some have already become evident. Because argument has such a centrally influential role in the decisions we make about ourselves and others, we might expect problems in argument to result in problems in decision making and judgment. In fact, we should be surprised to find the latter *not* being significantly affected by the former. In practice, this means that ethically suspect argument has a great potential for affecting not simply the quality of rational exchange, but the quality of life itself, in its many dimensions and expressions.

Although the daily newspaper may well supply an account of disasters caused by the kind of confusion that is produced by bad decision making, seldom will the cause be made apparent to the reader, particularly if it is rooted in ethically suspect argument. Nevertheless, several interesting studies are available that concentrate on the connection between unethical argument or persuasion and injury or damage to property or people. One recent work is by Cynthia Crossen, an editor and reporter for *The Wall Street Journal* since 1983. In *Tainted Truth: The Manipulation of Fact in America*, Crossen not only chronicles some of this decade's more newsworthy catastrophes, but she attempts to trace them to their ultimate source: the manipulation of information designed to persuade through argument or other means.[25] Of course, argument is only one element in Crossen's account, but it is an important one, and those who are familiar with it will be better able to protect themselves against some of the disasters Crossen discusses as well as become more circumspect about the role they may play in creating their own.

RELATED READINGS

Many interesting and well-argued writings are available on the general subject of business ethics. However, practitioners interested in reading further may want to begin with the thought-provoking articles and useful bibliographies provided by contributors to *Business Ethics Quarterly*, the Journal of the Society for Business Ethics, which is distributed by the Philosophy Documentation Center, Bowling Green State University, Bowling Green, OH 43403-0189 (800-444-2419).

Nothing has been written specifically on the ethical dimensions of argumentative discourse in management, though some articles exist on the ethics of particular mishaps in management communication, such as those which led to the Exxon *Valdez* oil spill or the Challenger disaster. In lieu of writings specifically in the area of argument, ethics, and management, the following entries are offered as a specialized and very brief list of a wide variety of available readings. Some are considered classics. They are drawn from the work of both academics and practitioners, and many of them have been selected because they discuss ethics in relation to language.

Aristotle. *The Nicomachean Ethics* (Trans. Harris Rackham). Cambridge, MA.: Loeb Classical Library, Harvard University Press, 1975.

Beauchamp, Tom, and Norman E. Bowie, eds. *Ethical Theory and Business.* Englewood Cliffs, NJ: Prentice-Hall, 1979.

Brown, Marvin. *Working Ethics.* San Francisco: Jossey-Bass, 1990.

Bentham, Jeremy. *An Introduction to the Principles of Morals and Legislation.* New York: Hafner, 1948 (original published 1789).

Burke, Kenneth. *Language as Symbolic Action. Essays on Life, Literature, and Method.* Berkeley: University of California Press, 1968.

Burke, Kenneth. *A Grammar of Motives.* Berkeley: University of California Press, 1969.

Diggs, Bernard. "Persuasion and Ethics." *The Quarterly Journal of Speech* 50 (December 1964): 359–73.

Eubanks, Ralph T. "Reflections on the Moral Dimension of Communication." *The Southern Speech Communication Journal* 45 (Spring 1980): 240–48.

Fisher, Roger, and Wayne Ury. *Getting to Yes. Negotiating Agreement Without Giving In.* New York: Penguin Books, 1987.

Gellerman, Saul W. "Why *Good* Managers Make Bad Ethical Choices." *Harvard Business Review* (July–August 1986): 85–90.

Habermas, Jürgen. *The Theory of Communicative Action. Volume I. Reason and the Rationalization of Society* (Trans. T. McCarthy). Boston: Beacon Press, 1984.

Habermas, Jürgen. *The Theory of Communicative Action. Volume II.*

Johannesen, Richard L. "Richard M. Weaver on Standards for Ethical Rhetoric." *Central States Speech Journal* 29 (Summer 1978): 127–37.

Johnstone, Christopher Lyle. "Ethics, Wisdom, and the Mission of Contemporary Rhetoric: The Realization of Human Being." *Central States Speech Journal* 32 (Fall 1981): 177–88.

Johnstone, Christopher Lyle. "An Aristotelian Trilogy: Ethics, Rhetoric, Politics, and the Search for Moral Truth." *Philosophy and Rhetoric* 13 (Winter 1980): 1–24.

Mathison, Donald L. "Business Ethics Cases and Decision Models: A Call for Relevancy in the Classroom." *Journal of Business Ethics* 10 (1988).

Mill, John Stuart. *Utilitarianism.* Indianapolis: Bobbs-Merrill, 1957 (originally published 1863).

Minnick, Wayne C. "A New Look at the Ethics of Persuasion." *Southern Speech Communication Journal* 45 (Summer 1980): 352–62.

Moore, G. E. *Principia Ethica.* New York: Cambridge University Press, 1978 (originally published 1903).

Perelman, Chaim. *The Idea of Justice and the Problem of Argument* (Trans. J. Petrie). New York: Humanities Press, 1971.

Perelman, Chaim, and L. Olbrechts Tyteca. *The New Rhetoric. A Treatise on Argumentation.* Notre Dame, IN: University of Notre Dame Press, 1971.

Stolz, A. "An Exercise in Argumentation." In B. Schildgen, *Foundations in Lifelong Learning* (2nd ed.). Minneapolis, MN: Burgess, 1983.

Toulmin, Stephen. *The Uses of Argument.* New York: Cambridge University Press, 1957.

Toulmin, Stephen et. al. *An Introduction to Reasoning,* (2nd ed.). New York: Macmillan, 1984.

Velasquez, Manuel G. "Why Corporations Are Not Morally Responsible for Anything They Do." *Business and Professional Ethics Journal* (Spring 1983).

Velasquez, Manuel G. *Business Ethics: Concepts and Cases* (2nd ed.). Englewood Cliffs, NJ: Prentice-Hall, 1988.

Weaver, Richard. *The Ethics of Rhetoric*. Southbend, IN: Regnery/Gateway, 1953.

Wieman, Henry Nelson, and Otis M. Walter. "Toward an Analysis of Ethics for Rhetoric." *Quarterly Journal of Speech* (October 1957): 266–70.

NOTES

1. For more on the history of business ethics as a once emerging but now established field, see often-cited R. T. DeGeorge, "The Status of Business Ethics: Past and Future," *Journal of Business Ethics* 6 (April 1987): 201–11. DeGeorge views the study of business ethics in North America in five distinct stages of evolution.

2. For example, see *The Journal of Business and Technical Communication*, 1992–1994; *The Journal of Business Communication*, 1990–1994; and especially *The Bulletin of the Association of Business Communication*, in which conference trends and practitioner concerns are often discussed. See also "Ethical Issues in Business Communication" in *The Bulletin of the Association of Business Communication* 56, 4 (December 1993): 56–63. One might even argue that the relationship between communication and ethics is at present studied as much outside the field of management communication as it is inside of it. As a good example of this, see Michael Bowen and Clark Power, "The Moral Manager: Communicative Ethics and the Exxon *Valdez* Disaster," *Business Ethics Quarterly* 3, no. 2 (April 1993): 103–15.

3. The examples mentioned here are representative, and they are taken from the venerable and enormously popular Himstreet, Baty, and Lehman, *Business Communications*, 10th ed. (Belmont, CA: Wadsworth, 1993), 156. For a recent and representative example of ethics integrated into coverage of business communication concerns, see Vik and Gilsdorf, *Business Communications* (Urbana, IL: Richard D. Irwin, 1994).

4. On the importance of communication, both written and oral, in business, many studies exist. One that is infrequently cited but is both recent and comprehensive is Dan B. Curtis, Jerry L. Winsor, and Ronald D. Stephens, "National Preferences in Business and Communication Education, *Communication Education* 38, no. 1 (January 1989): 6–13. See also Garda W. Bowman, "What Helps or Harms Promotability?" *Harvard Business Review* 42 (January–February 1964): 6–26; Francis J. Connelly, ed., "Accreditation Research Project Report of Phase 1," *AACSB Bulletin* 14 (Winter 1980): 2–15; S. Divita, "The Business School Graduate—Does the Product Fit the Need?" L. Preston, ed., *Business Environment/Public Policy 1979 Conference Papers*, AACSB, St. Louis (1979): 167–68; Alfred G. Edge and Ronald Greenwood, "How Managers Rank Knowledge, Skills and Attributes Possessed by Business Administration Graduates," *AACSB Bulletin* 11 (October 1974): 30–34; J. W. Hildebrandt, F. A. Bond, E. L. Miller, and W. W. Swinyard, "An Executive Appraisal of Courses Which Best Prepare One for General Management," *Journal of Business Communication* 19 (Winter 1982): 5–15.

5. For discussions in which the line between argument and ethics is blurred indeed, see Marvin Brown, *Working Ethics* (San Francisco: Jossey-Bass, 1990) and Joan Vesper and Vincent Ruggiero, *Contemporary Business Communication* (New York: Harper Collins, 1993). For the initial discussion of the more general relationship between rhetoric and ethics, see Plato, *Phaedrus*, trans. W. C. Helmbold and W. G. Rabinowitz (Indianapolis: Library of Liberal Arts, 1956) and the contemporary discussion of *Phaedrus* in Stanley Fish, *Self-Consuming Artifacts* (New York: MacMillan, 1978).

6. See Marvin Brown, *Working Ethics* (San Francisco: Jossey-Bass, 1990), xi: "Although

this may sound odd, the purpose of ethics is not to make people ethical; it is to help people make better decisions."

7. LaRue Tone Hosmer, "Why Be Moral? A Different Rationale for Managers," *Business Ethics Quarterly* 4, no. 2 (April 1994): 191–204. For another treatment of the relationship between ethical action and the development of trust in business, see K. R. Andrews, *Ethics or Practice* (Boston: Harvard Business School Press, 1989). For a collection of other cases tied to the more pragmatic interests of practicing managers, see M. Slayton, *Common Sense and Everyday Ethics* (Washington DC: Ethics Resource Center, 1980).

8. Although these will be recognized by anyone who has done even preliminary reading in the field of business ethics, a particularly clear presentation of them appears in Joan Vesper and Vincent Ruggiero, *Contemporary Business Communication* (New York: HarperCollins, 1993), 39–44.

9. See B. J. Diggs, "Persuasion and Ethics," *Quarterly Journal of Speech* 50, no. 4 (December 1964): 360–73.

10. See Wayne C. Minnick, "A New Look at the Ethics of Persuasion," *Southern Speech Communication Journal* 45 (Summer, 1980): 352–62.

11. Richard Weaver, *The Ethics of Rhetoric* (Chicago: Regnery/Gateway, 1953), 20–21. See also Richard L. Johannesen, "Richard M. Weaver on Standards for Ethical Rhetoric," *Central States Speech Journal* 29 (Summer 1978): 127–37.

12. Henry Nelson Wieman and Otis M. Walter, "Toward an Analysis of Ethics for Rhetoric," *Quarterly Journal of Speech* 43 (October 1967): 266–70.

13. See Irving Copi, *Introduction to Logic* (New York: Macmillan, 1953). The reader will no doubt point out that this comment on general agreement is open to criticism for its reliance on the *ad populum* fallacy.

14. Wayne C. Booth and Marshall W. Gregory, *Rhetoric: Writing as Thinking and Thinking as Writing* (New York: Harper and Row, 1987), 119.

15. Steve Rinehart, "ATU Sale Gains Just Single Bid—Pacific Telecom Inc. offers $400 million," *Anchorage Daily News*, June 23, 1989.

16. Booth and Gregory, *Rhetoric, 122.*

17. This exchange was described in "For the Public," *Newsweek*, July 4, 1994.

18. Don Hunter, "ATU Bidder No Stranger to City Hall," *Anchorage Daily News*, June 23, 1989.

19. Steve Rinehart, "Utility Sale Funds Don't Always Pay Off as Planned," *Anchorage Daily News*, September 8, 1989.

20. George Frost, "City May Owe Old Debt After ATU Sale," *Anchorage Daily News*, August 22, 1989.

21. George Frost, "Pacific Telecom Refuses to Talk About ATU Plans," *Anchorage Daily News*, September 28, 1989.

22. Irving Copi, "Informal Fallacies," in Richard Young, Alton Becker, and Kenneth Pike, *Rhetoric: Discovery and Change* (New York: Harcourt, Brace & World, 1970), 251.

23. *Smokers' Advocate* 4 (September 1993): 2.

24. Don Hunter, "Fink Signs ATU Sale Contract—Promises Aren't Quite What They Appear to Be," *Anchorage Daily News*, August 24, 1989.

25. Cynthia Crossen, *Tainted Truth: The Manipulation of Fact in America* (New York: Simon & Shuster, 1994). See also Michael Wheeler, *Lies, Damn Lies, and Statistics: The Manipulation of Public Opinion in America* (New York: Liveright, 1976). For those interested specifically in ethical discourse and the presentation of statistical analysis, the following should be of interest: Darrell Huff, *How to Lie with Statistics* (New York: Norton, 1954); Francis Ely, *Using Charts to Improve Profits* (Englewood Cliffs, NJ: Prentice-Hall, 1962); Gregory Kimble, *How to Use (and Misuse) Statistics* (Englewood Cliffs, NJ: Prentice-Hall, 1978).

MANAGING ETHOS 7

Argument and Credibility

As man speaks, so is he.

—Seneca, *Thyestes*

The character [ethos] of the speaker is a cause of persuasion when the speech is so uttered as to make him worthy of belief; for as a rule we trust men of probity more, and more quickly, about things in general. When one points outside the realm of exact knowledge, where opinion is divided, we trust them absolutely. This trust, however, should be created by the speech itself, and not left to depend upon an antecedent impression that the speaker is this or that kind of man. It is not true, as some writers on the art maintain, that the probity of the speaker contributes nothing to his persuasiveness; on the contrary, we might almost affirm that his character [ethos] is the most potent of all the means to persuasion.

—Aristotle, *Rhetoric*

■ Ethos in Communication

The quotation from Seneca might not fare well in the modern world of business management simply because it appears so insensitive to that world's expectations concerning inclusive language, language that does not discriminate on the basis of gender or sex.[1] By using language that limits speakers to men, Seneca appears to be sexist, though perhaps not as much as he would were he a modern manager and referred to the receptionist as "the girl at the front desk."[2]

However, once we have allowed for differences between classical and modern norms of language (and have forgiven Seneca for the bias of his world), we can find in his aphorism an important concept of classical rhetoric: *ethos.* Unlike reputation, which one acquires and brings to an act of communication, ethos arises from that very act. Thus one might have a reputation for being honest, trustworthy, or credible, but that is an attribute of character or person that can stand apart from the use of language. Ethos, on the other hand, cannot be separated from the act of communication, just as Seneca's use of the word "man" cannot be separated from his aphorism.

To say that ethos and reputation are independent is not to suggest that they are unrelated. For example, one might well enjoy a reputation—earned through successful efforts as a corporate trainer for being expert in matters of time management—and then undercut that reputation by giving a verbose and disorganized presentation. What is important to notice here is that the ethos of a wordy and disorganized speaker arises from the speaker's use of language itself, whereas the reputation that precedes or follows it is independent of ethos, even though it may be heavily influenced by it. This is consistent with Aristotle's own remarks on ethos, as they introduced this chapter: "This . . . should be created by the speech itself, and not left to depend upon an antecedent impression that the speaker is this or that kind of man."[3] Thus a distinction between ethos and reputation is worth making if one is to be clear about how ethos can be used in argument and communication.[4]

An additional distinction is worth making here, between what one may say about oneself, and what one's use of language may reveal about oneself. An example of the first is the speaker who tells an audience that she has thoroughly examined the issues and has weighed matters carefully. Let's say she states this to her audience, and she does this outright, as a matter of assurance at the beginning of an oral presentation. Of course, whether she has done what she has stated will depend less on what she states she has done and more on the evidence of it in the presentation of her analysis. She might offer such evidence, or her language—with shaky assumptions, hastily drawn conclusions, and no attention to other points of view—might suggest the opposite of a careful examination. This means that analyzing ethos is less about the statements a speaker or writer might make as a matter of *direct* self-reference, and more about the *indirect* evidence language provides about that person. For example, a writer may claim in the following passage that brevity is a goal of an oral presentation:

> In order to achieve brevity in this presentation, I will make a decision about which is the very best of the presentation software that is now presently available to us for our uses here.

However, the ethos here, which we might describe as that of a verbose speaker, is not consistent with the claim. A more consistent ethos would be this:

> To help us present concisely, I will decide on the best software to use.

The revised passage is now more consistent with the claim because it shows *in practice* that the speaker is able to practice what she preaches. Without this, the listener has only the speaker's *pronouncement* that she is able to produce a concise message. Such a pronouncement is then open to the same criticism as other arguments or appeals to a primary authority.[5] This distinction, between pronouncement and practice, is also essential to understanding the character of ethos.

▧ **Ethos and Argument**

Finally, a distinction needs to be drawn between ethos and argumentation, as the following quotation from a modern writer on rhetoric might suggest:

> But ethos is a prerequisite to persuasion; it should not be a means. The line between the two uses of ethos is a fine one, and writers frequently find themselves on the wrong side of it.[6]

When this writer mentions that writers frequently find themselves on the wrong side of a fine line, he is suggesting that ethos, as "an inescapable dimension in argumentation," is not to be confused with other kinds of support, such as the kind of support provided by main reasons. To invest ethos with that kind of support is both to commit the fallacy of *argumentum ad verecundiam*, discussed in the previous chapter, and to honor the assumption behind it.[7] During argument, few speakers or writers can marshal an ethos so invested, though their own convictions and inflated sense of self may not prevent them from trying. For most people, the best strategy is probably one that strives for a *consistent* ethos, one that is in line with the claims of the argument, one that does not distract from or undercut those claims, and one that does not attempt to provide their exclusive support.

▧ **Aristotle's Three Qualities**

This kind of consistency of ethos may well have been in Aristotle's mind when he named three general qualities—intelligence, character, and goodwill—as necessary to creating the kind of ethos that would ease acceptance of most claims. Although this does not assume that the argument of an intelligent person who shows goodwill and good character will always win the day, it does suggest that such an argument is more readily accepted, and less automatically challenged, when a writer or speaker with these qualities is the one making it. Such an ethos is useful because it helps to put the audience in a particular frame of mind, or emotional state, one that is more receptive to the writer's or speaker's point of view.[8]

Keeping in mind the general qualities of ethos Aristotle described, and assuming they will also have appeal in the world of business communication, we might now look to specific and familiar expressions of ethos. One good source for this is a passage we have already seen and considered as part of our discussion of opposition.[9] There we analyzed the persuasiveness of entertaining opposing points in one mail-order distributor's open-letter attempt to overcome the skepticism of consumers who are concerned about mail-order shopping.

We might recall that this distributor did not simply present a point of view and argue for the benefits of ordering through the mail, but instead decided to respond directly to readers who have their *own* concerns about mail-order purchases. The distributor did this by speaking directly to those customers who are concerned about getting a product that does not meet their expectations, as well as those who resist purchasing by mail because of their concerns about slow or poor service. These are also the very concerns this distributor apparently believed the reader had in mind when the original message was crafted. Here they are again but offered now for a different kind of analysis:

> The first fear which consumers apparently have is that they will be defrauded. Actually, this is extremely unlikely in today's society. Principally because of tough mail fraud laws, we feel that you have more legal protection buying from a mail order firm than from any other type of retailer. Since mail order companies depend on the mails for soliciting and receiving their orders, fraudulent sales practices can be easily reported to a local Postal Inspector who can initiate a formal mail fraud investigation. Also, a consumer complaint can be made to the Federal Trade Commission in Washington or the Attorney General's office of the state in which the mail order company operated. Consequently, almost all of the fraudulent mail order schemes are very short lived.[10]

▓ Ethos and Opposition

What might we say about the ethos of this passage? To begin with Aristotle's qualities, we might ask what the language of this passage implies about the intelligence, character, and goodwill of the writer. Of course, part of the answer may already be apparent from the chapter on opposition. By leading with the customer's concern, and even expressing the concern on behalf of the customer, the distributor has demonstrated all three qualities—intelligence, character, and goodwill—Aristotle has mentioned. For example, *intelligence* is demonstrated in several ways, one of which is through the simple act of paying attention to customer interests. Relevant to this version of intelligence are the many contemporary business slogans and affirmations that suggest smart companies listen to their clients. Intelligence is also expressed through the distributor's *knowledge* of retail practices, mail fraud laws, and the consumer resources of the local postal inspector, the Federal Trade Commission, and the state-level attorney general's office.[11] We can also point to signs of intelligence in the distributor's ability to reason, as evidenced by the logical cue word "consequently," even if we do not accept the premises of the reasoning. And finally, the distributor's ability to follow the mechanics of English grammar and usage suggests intelligence in an almost universally respected application. Notice that the distributor does not *state* any of this, even though it could have through a mission statement or letterhead slogan, such as "We place our customers first." Still, to do so would be unconvincing in a letter of this kind; instead, the credible ethos of the distributor becomes apparent from the language.

Also apparent from the language is the *goodwill* of the distributor, which is implied by its willingness to consider the views of others, in this case, the views of the audience. And this is a consideration in depth because the distributor is not simply offering lip service by saying it is attentive to customers' concerns; it is explaining those concerns and the reasons behind them. As we have seen in our earlier discussions of opposition, this helps to avoid creating an image that the reader will interpret as patronizing. Goodwill is also implied by providing the reader with personally beneficial information, in this case, methods for protecting oneself against fraudulent practices.

The *character* of the distributor arises in part from creating an impression of intelligence and goodwill. However, while these may be necessary conditions for establishing character, they are not sufficient to show it in the sense of moral or ethical strength.[12] Here the distributor might be criticized for not fully disclosing information but using the passive voice to diminish the responsibility of the consumer and the effort the consumer must make to be protected. Here are the passages with the agents supplied in brackets:

> Since mail order companies depend on the mails for soliciting and receiving their orders, fraudulent sales practices can be easily reported [by you, the customer] to a local Postal Inspector who can initiate a formal mail fraud investigation. Also, a consumer complaint can be made [by you, the customer] to the Federal Trade Commission in Washington or the Attorney General's office of the state in which the mail order company operated.

We might also point out the shakiness of a suppressed premise, or assumption, that ease of reporting fraud to authorities leads directly to a state of affairs in which "fraudulent mail order schemes are very short lived." Thus we have remarked on all three of Aristotle's qualities in this passage, and we have noticed that one of them might be strengthened.

We are now ready for the second passage in the distributor's open letter, where the three qualities are perhaps just as apparent:

> The second and more justified concern with mail order is the fear of slow and poor service. Fortunately, this is becoming less of a problem as mail order retailers adapt to changes in the public's attitude. In the past, people shopped mail order either for price or because it was the only way in which they could get what they wanted. Therefore, service was not the overriding concern of the seller or buyer. However, people are now shopping mail order for convenience and service as well as price. With the widespread use of credit cards, toll-free WATS lines and UPS shipments, it is now possible for a customer to receive his purchase within a few days after ordering it. Smart mail order merchants recognize this and are finding that fast, efficient service is vital to their business success.

We also find in this passage many of the features we noticed in the previous one: intelligence and knowledge implied by an awareness of modern methods of shipment and changes in shopping practices; goodwill implied by considering at length another concern of the customer, who presumably is reading this document; and character in the form of modesty implied by the third-person reference to "smart mail order merchants." Thus the conclusion that the reader is asked to draw is that this distributor provides "fast, efficient service" which should remove any fear or "justified concern" the reader might otherwise have.

Each of the passages above reveals how one major argumentative feature, the raising of opposition, may influence the reader's impression of the writer's ethos. We may now consider how another feature, the disposition of opposition, can similarly shape ethos. We might even be able to improve the writer's ethos by making a minor change in the first passage, but one that will make a major difference:

> The first fear which consumers apparently have is that they will be defrauded. Fortunately, tough mail fraud laws will give more legal protection buying from a mail order firm than from any other type of retailer. Since mail order companies depend on the mails for soliciting and receiving their orders, fraudulent sales practices can be easily reported to a local Postal Inspector who can initiate a formal mail fraud investigation. Also, a consumer complaint can be made to the Federal Trade Commission in Washington or the Attorney General's office of the state in which the mail order company operated. So, being defrauded is actually extremely unlikely in today's society.

What have we changed here? Aside from several revised transitions, we have moved the concluding sentence from its second place in the original paragraph to the end of the paragraph in the revision. What this does for the writer's ethos is help to enhance the credibility of the writer by allowing time for reasons to be given before a conclusion is drawn. In this way, the writer appears more "reasonable" (literally) because we have prevented any jumping to conclusions. If we were to describe the original writer as "hasty," an element of ethos, the revision removes this hastiness so the reader can draw the conclusion along with the writer. We can do the same for the second passage, and with a similar result:

> The second and more justified concern with mail order is the fear of slow and poor service. Remember, though, that in the past, people shopped mail order either for price or because it was the only way in which they could get what they wanted. At that time, service was not the overriding concern of the seller or buyer. However, people are now shopping mail order for convenience and service as well as price. With the widespread use of credit cards, toll-free WATS lines and UPS shipments, the customer can now receive a purchase within a few days after ordering it. Smart mail order merchants recognize this and are finding that fast, efficient service is vital to their business success. Fortunately, then, slow service is becoming less of a problem as mail order retailers adapt to changes in the public's attitude.

We have again reordered the presentation so the second sentence of the original now stands as the last sentence of the revision. Now, instead of drawing a conclusion ("Slow service is becoming less of a problem") before the reader is able to accept or reject it based on reasons, the writer is able to draw the conclusion at precisely the same point as the reader, and with the same body of evidence or cited "reasons." Thus a minor adjustment to the distributor's order, or disposition of presentation, can have major implications for creating an ethos in which the distributor appears more reasonable and less hasty. Of course, behind our analysis is the assumption that such an ethos will ease acceptance of the claim.

What we have seen thus far are some of the implications two major argumentative features—the treatment of opposition and the disposition of the refutation—may have for the construction of ethos. We might expect that other elements of argument covered in previous chapters would have a similar influence. For example, the commitment to arguing consequences shows that the writer or speaker has vision and is not limited to considering short-term effects. Such a commitment demonstrates intelligence, character, and goodwill if the consequence concerns the welfare of the reader or listener. Similarly, proceeding from an agreed-upon assumption will help to promote an ethos of intelligence and good will. However, chief among the elements of argument already covered in this book is the very act of reason-giving required by the plan of the argument as well as its presentation. What better evidence of intelligence, in the form of a reasoning agent, than the very demonstration of reasoning itself? What better proof of good will than the willingness to provide reasons for discussion and thus challenge? And finally, what better indicator of character than the disclosure of reasons that guard against bias, including the special interests of the writer?

■ Ethos and Fallacies of Argument

Of course, running counter to establishing an ethos of credibility is the presence of any of the fallacies of reasoning, and much of the good work described above can be jeopardized by these. Just as the development of serious reasons will help to give evidence of an intelligent writer or speaker, so will the appearance of *post hoc* reasoning or faulty analogies suggest that the communicator's judgment is not to be trusted. Beyond the suggestion that such reasoning is not expected from an intelligent agent are the additional threats such fallacies would pose to creating goodwill. As we have seen in the chapter on fallacies, the character of the speaker is especially at risk when one employs fallacious reasoning. Thus the fallacies would distract from any serious attempt to establish a persuasive ethos and undercut the strength of any major argumentative feature such as the management of opposition.

■ Ethos and Revision

We have now seen how the major argumentative features covered in previous chapters can contribute to or distract from an ethos of credibility.[13] However, much of what contributes to a communicator's ethos resides not in the message's major argumentative features but in the more minor, far more numerous, elements found at the sentence level. Many of these receive the greatest attention during revision. For example, a simple choice of words (as in Seneca's choice of "man") can communicate a very strong impression of the writer's or speaker's ethos. As we consider some of these sentence-level elements, we will probably find no better example of a writer involved with questions about ethos than in the following passage from a college professor who is struggling with the options for expression in a sentence about French critic Georges Louis Leclerc. Professor John Gage first quotes the sentence he has written and then provides us with rare insight into some of the questions it raised for him.

> In the eighteenth century, a French critic, George Louis Leclerc, comte de Buffon, coined a phrase that is still sometimes quoted as a definition of style: "Le style c'est l'homme, même," he wrote, or "Style is the man, himself."
>
> When I wrote this sentence, I was aware of taking a risk. I faced the stylistic decision of whether to include the full name of the critic and, furthermore, whether to include the French phrase or the English translation, and I knew that my choices might affect the tone of my writing in ways that I might not want. Would I sound pedantic if I gave the critic's full name, or would I sound careless if I called him simply "Buffon"? I could have left his name out altogether—but would I then be insulting my readers by assuming that they wouldn't care who had coined the phrase? Would I seem to be parading my knowledge by including the information at all, rather than saying something like "Perhaps you have heard the phrase 'Style is the man'?" If I left out the English translation, would I be assuming too much about the reader and thereby making my point unintelligible, or would I insult the reader by including the translation? These are the kinds of considerations I faced when I chose to write the sentence in the way in which I did. I am not sure that I chose correctly. The sentence may have distracted you, or it may have insulted you, or it may have caused you to judge me as one who is too picky about details.[14]

Although Gage does not use the term *ethos*, he is most certainly talking about it in several places. For example, when he asks "Would I sound pedantic," he is asking about the kind of ethos—that of a nitpicker or perfectionist—that would be produced by giving Leclerc's full name. He is also concerned about producing an opposite ethos—that of the inattentive or careless—if he does not provide the full name. He is similarly concerned with ethos when he asks whether he would seem to "be parading my knowledge by including the information at all" because he does not wish to appear to be showing off or using language just to impress his readers. Of course, not all of the questions Gage asks are questions about ethos. His concerns about distracting or insulting his readers, or making his point unintelligible, are very good concerns to have, but they are not concerns about ethos because they are not directly related to the way his language is making him appear to his reader.[15]

Questions similar to Gage's might be asked in the less academic environment of business, but they will remain essentially the same questions. For example, ethos can be a major consideration in producing what some writers have called the "you-attitude" in workplace writing. The following two examples, from a workplace writer in an imaginary company, will help to illustrate:

> I have negotiated an agreement with Apex Rent-a-car that gives you a discount on rental cars.
>
> As a Sunstrand employee, you can now get a 20 percent discount when you rent a car from Apex.

One major difference between these two sentences lies in the choice of pronouns. Whereas the first sentence emphasizes the first-person singular "I," the second emphasizes the second-person singular "you." The strategic difference, according to one observer, is this: "The first sentence focuses on the writer. Any sentence that focuses on the writer's work or the writer's generosity lacks you-attitude. Instead of focusing on what we are giving the reader, focus on what the reader can now do."[16] To recast this discussion as a consideration of ethos, we need only ask how the reader's impression of the writer changes as a consequence of the change in word choice. Would our writer appear different to the reader? If so, would that difference contribute to or distract from the argumentative quality of the message? Although various interpretations are possible, one is that the ethos of the writer in the second sentence is more desirable and contributes more to the persuasiveness of the message because it helps to create the kind of goodwill discussed earlier. Thus a simple change in the choice of words, in this case pronouns, can result in a change of ethos.

Another example in which ethos changes, but now as a consequence of word order, may be found in the shift from active to passive voice. Let us say this writer is struggling over choosing from one of the following two constructions:

> Because you did not conduct hardness tests, I find your "degrees rotation" information meaningless.
>
> Because hardness tests were not conducted by you, I find your "degrees rotation" information meaningless.

As the vice president of marketing for a manufacturer of medical products, our imaginary writer decides that the first sentence makes her appear too hard on her research scientist. "I don't want to come across as a bully," she reflects; "after all, we still need to work together." She decides to go with the second sentence, and with the passive construction, which subordinates the scientist and thus makes the writer and her statement appear less accusatory. She then considers whether she might even remove the blame entirely from the sentence by omitting the scientist:

> Because hardness tests were not conducted, I find your "degrees rotation" information meaningless.

This has an advantage, she reasons, because it removes the direct link between the scientist and the necessary tests. By doing this, she could appear much more diplomatic and less threatening. However, after some thought, she decides against this construction and returns to the second version, in which the scientist was mentioned. "I really think he needs to be held accountable. And I want him to know I am holding him accountable. Still, I don't need to be heavy-handed about it." Our writer therefore chooses the passive with the agent stated as the best construction for the job and for her ethos.

To be fair, one might argue that the workplace does not afford the luxury of time to ask questions at the level of detail Gage or our fictional writers have. One committed to his level of questioning might never complete other work, much less the writing task at hand![17] However, asking questions about ethos will be necessary if the writer is to draw on all resources available for easing the reader's acceptance of controversial claims. Although one might not find Gage's scrupulous concern with ethos practical to emulate at the workplace, asking similar questions, in appropriate degree, will only help to insure that an appropriate ethos is created or at least not ignored entirely. Perhaps the best strategy to adopt is one that keeps the importance of ethos constantly in mind. The five chapters that follow—on conciseness, word choice, word order, grammar, and punctuation—are designed to help the writer become mindful of ethos, as well as to provide practical techniques for achieving the kind of ethos that is appropriate to writing in the modern workplace.

RELATED READINGS

In addition to the writings listed in the notes to this chapter, the materials below consist of works that discuss ethos and its function in persuasion or argumentation. In the larger works edited by Murphy and Schiappa, the index will be a helpful guide to discussions of ethos.

Aristotle. *Rhetoric* (Trans. J. H. Freese). Loeb Classical Library. Cambridge, MA.: Harvard University Press, 1982. Any serious study of ethos should probably start here.

Booth, Wayne C., and Marshall W. Gregory. *The Harper & Row Rhetoric: Writing as Thinking/Thinking as Writing.* New York: Harper & Row, 1987. Contains a discussion of writer's persona, a term sometimes used in place of ethos.

Brandt, William. *The Craft of Writing.* Englewood Cliffs, NJ: Prentice-Hall, 1969.

Brandt, William. *The Rhetoric of Argumentation.* Indianapolis: Bobbs-Merrill, 1970. Excellent work on argumentative analysis with an emphasis on ethos. Several extended analyses of ethos are offered.

Corbett, Edward P. J. "What Classical Rhetoric Has to Offer the Teacher and the Student of Business and Professional Writing." In *Writing in the Business Professions*, ed. Myra Kogen. Urbana, IL: National Council of Teachers of English and the Association for Business Communication, 1989.

Gage, John. *The Shape of Reason: Argumentative Writing in College.* New York: Macmillan, 1987. See especially Chapter 6, "Style: Who Are You When You Write?" and Chapter 7, "Revision."

Grimaldi, William M. A. *Aristotle's Rhetoric: A Commentary.* 2 vols. New York: Fordham University Press, 1988.

Murphy, James J., ed. *A Synoptic History of Classical Rhetoric.* Davis, CA: Hermagoras Press, 1983. Books from Hermagoras press are in general an excellent resource for understanding the history, theory, and principles of classical rhetoric.

Schiappa, Edward, ed. *Landmark Essays: On Classical Greek Rhetoric.* Davis, CA: Hermagoras Press, 1994.

NOTES

1. Part of the joy I take in using this passage to introduce ethos comes from the fact that one might well say it demonstrates what it describes. If Seneca appears sexist, it is because of the language he has used; if he is sexist, he is sexist "as he speaks."

2. Example of sexist language quoted in Kitty O. Locker, *Business and Administrative Communication* (Boston: Irwin, 1992), 113.

3. Lane Cooper, trans., *The Rhetoric of Aristotle* (Englewood Cliffs, NJ: Prentice-Hall, 1932), 8–9.

4. An associated distinction that is often made at this point is between nonartistic (also known as inartistic) proofs, or those that are available outside the message, and artistic proofs, or those that are available as part of the message. Ethos is one of the artistic proofs. For more on this distinction, see Joseph Golden, *The Rhetoric of Western Thought* (Dubuque, IA: Kendall Hunt, 1989) and the Lane Cooper translation of *The Rhetoric* (New York: Appleton-Century-Crofts, 1932).

5. Simply claiming to have a quality of personality or presentation style, in this case conciseness, only begs the question and invites evidence, particularly when the speaker's ethos puts the claim in question. Another useful distinction here is between "telling" and "showing." A writer may *tell* a reader he (the writer) is committed to disclosure, but the passive constructions in his writing *show* that he is not.

6. William J. Brandt, *The Rhetoric of Argumentation* (New York: Bobbs-Merrill, 1970), 218.

7. This and other apparent fallacies of reasoning are covered at length in Chapter 6.

8. Considered in this way, ethos can be seen in the service of creating pathos, a point anticipated by Brandt in his discussion of constructing pathetic appeals: "The second way in which a pathetic appeal can be made is by simulating in ourselves the emotion we wish from our readers or hearers. If someone with whom we have some basic sympathy becomes angry, we are very apt to become angry too. This is of course the basis for the pathetic appeal of traditional oratory. But seen from this point of view, traditional pathos is merely a variety of ethos. This fact is apparent in the peroration of almost every traditional speech. The speaker steps forward in a role that is ordinarily a modification of the one assumed to that point, and takes for himself a stance toward the subject which his audience will presumably assume with him." From *The Rhetoric of Argumentation,* 220.

9. Specifically in Chapter 4, as part of the planning process but also in Chapter 5.

10. *Crutchfield's,* July 1984.

11. My reader would be correct in criticizing my apparent inattention to the difference in meanings here. Although "intelligence" generally refers to one's ability (how) to apply "knowledge," and "knowledge" usually refers to the storehouse (what) that is applied, Aristotle's discussions of the quality of intelligence suggest that knowledge might be included in an assessment of this quality.

12. "Character" is a word admitting many meanings, and several of them are supported by Aristotle's discussion in the *Rhetoric*. The one I have used here, which signifies moral or ethical strength, is only one of the several. The point is that intelligence and goodwill are considerably less impressive if the speaker lacks an ethical character. For a discussion which assumes "character" means "moral excellence," see James J. Murphy and Richard Katula, *A Synoptic History of Classical Rhetoric* (Hermagoras Press: 1995), 79: "Since bad advice is given either through lack of sense or lack of integrity or dislike of the auditors, it follows that a speaker will seem trustworthy if he shows good sense, moral excellence, and good will."

13. Although the form of distributed organization covered in Chapter 2 would qualify as an argumentative element of writing, it certainly contributes to the writer's ethos because it helps to create the impression of an organizing and controlling agent. The implications for creating an impression of goodwill and intelligence are probably evident. Without organization in their messages, and all other matters being equal, most communicators would probably seem less credible than those whose messages are organized.

14. John Gage, *The Shape of Reason: Argumentative Writing in College* (New York: Macmillan, 1987), 129–30.

15. I have worked hard to resist the temptation to talk about the extraordinary ethos Gage is able to create by providing the commentary on the passage about Leclerc. By providing this commentary, Gage is able to suggest to the reader that an astonishing degree of careful thought has gone into his writing.

16. Both the examples and the advice are taken from Kitty O. Locker, *Business and Administrative Communication* (Boston: Irwin, 1992), 101.

17. Of course, one could always argue the opposite here and say that writers who expect to be convincing cannot afford to ignore ethos, regardless of the time constraints imposed by the workplace, because such neglect threatens to waste the time they have already invested in a persuasive task.

MANAGING ETHOS 8

Conciseness

I never write "metropolis" for seven cents, because I can get the same money for "city." I never write "policeman," because I can get the same price for "cop." ... I never write "valetudinarian" at all, for not even hunger and wretchedness can humble me to the point where I will do a word like that for seven cents; I wouldn't do it for fifteen.

—Mark Twain, to the Associated Press

Since how a person speaks and writes is a fair reflection of how a person thinks and feels, shoddy language may imply shoddy people—a public whose ideals have been discarded and whose ideas have been distorted.

—Robert Fiske, *Concise Writing*

College graduates who enter business are often surprised by the difference between the kind of writing they did in school and the kind of writing they are expected to do as part of their profession. For the most part, college students do not write in the heavily formatted style that is used to produce memoranda, nor do they usually write to a multiple audience, one that could easily include both an external client with technical expertise and an internal supervisor who has no technical background at all. College students seldom write collaboratively, a practice that is characteristic of business writing.[1] And finally, college students generally do not write for action, for readers who will be expected to implement their ideas. They write instead for appraisal, and for a reader they expect will evaluate their ideas.[2]

One of the more remarkable differences between writing at school and writing at work is that each appears to encourage a different economy of expression. Early academic essays are typified by the two-thousand-word essay, and subsequent assignments frequently have page requirements. Although teachers may defend word and page requirements as a necessary means of forcing students to develop their ideas, those students who do not appreciate this academic intention will simply equate length with quality. Students who write under the assumption that "more is better" will produce writing that is verbose, and when they are rewarded for it, they will produce it again. Produced often enough, and reinforced often enough, this excessive expression soon becomes habitual.[3]

Writers who have developed this habit in college may well be disappointed by the responses of their workplace readers. Supervisors do not give page limits or word requirements primarily because they see no necessary connection between the number of pages produced and the quality of the job completed. Nor do they reward writers who write according to their old economy of expression and produce a supply of words that exceeds the reader's demand. Just as products in a market decrease in value when supply exceeds demand, so do words in a message when readers are given more than they want or need. Writers who produce verbose prose thus cheapen their ideas and introduce unnecessary distraction to the points they are trying to make. Because of this, writers will do well to overcome the bad habit of verbose writing.[4]

For the competitive writer, breaking this habit is critical because a concise writing style offers the reader the promise of low cost, or reduced reading time and effort. Just as a buyer of more conventional goods will be attracted to the low cost of a purchase, so will the reader, the consumer of words, be attracted to concise writing. Concise writing thus competes well against verbose writing for two reasons: first, it promises the reader reduced effort; second, it differentiates itself from verbose writing by offering a difference that has considerable value to the reader. Because of this, writers who break this habit can expect to be rewarded for their efforts at the workplace.

One of the greatest rewards will come from establishing the right ethos. By writing concisely, writers will be creating the impression that they are in control of their material and possess clarity of thought. Verbosity often suggests that writers are unclear about where they are going or are unaware of the point they are trying to make, perhaps because they do not really know their material. Writing concisely will thus help to establish at least an ethos of intelligence, one of Aristotle's three qualities. It should also help to create a sense of goodwill, another of these qualities, because of the respect for the reader's time that is implied by concise expression. Such an ethos is worth creating if the writer wants to do everything possible to ease acceptance of the message, particularly if it is argumentative and contains controversial statements.

Although verbose writing is a bad habit to have at the workplace, it is still just a habit, and it can be broken if the writer makes the effort. Writers do not inherit verbosity from their parents, though they may learn to be verbose from behavior at home or elsewhere. Because wordiness is learned, it can be unlearned. By following a few straightforward principles, a writer can usually reduce the number of words on a page by one third if not by one half.

■ Conciseness and Revision

Many habits of effective writing are encouraged through the activity of revision, the constant changing and refining of written expression. This is certainly true of writing concisely. Although other editorial concerns are very important, writers will probably find the best way to *begin* revising is by editing for conciseness. Several good reasons argue for this.

Conciseness promotes efficiency in editing. If the writer is intent on deleting unnecessary words, many of the problems those words produce will be eliminated, simply because the words that caused the problems will have been eliminated. This, of course, will save time later, when the writer is revising for other things such as word choice, word order, grammar, and punctuation.

Conciseness helps to clarify thought. Revising for conciseness will help the writer to free sentences from the unnecessary clutter that will distract from main ideas. As a consequence, the key ideas the writer wants to convey will become more apparent and available for additional editorial consideration. Decisions about word choice, for example, can now be made more reliably because the writer will have a clearer idea of what the sentence is trying to say.

Conciseness encourages additional improvement. Simply by revising for conciseness, the writer should be able to produce prose that is more easily edited and improved. Just as a garden that has been pruned is easier to maintain or change, so is writing that has had the dead or useless material removed. Concise writing invites further attention and attempts to improve it. Thus, conciseness encourages further editorial effort.

▨ Redundancy

Editing for conciseness begins when writers become committed to removing redundancy, the unnecessary repetition of ideas. Redundancy will occur in two forms: direct and indirect. Direct forms are the easiest to spot because the repeated ideas take similar if not identical form. The following examples illustrate:

> I'll call you if the need for more information becomes necessary.

> The chemist applied the new chemical to several applications.

The writer means:

> I'll call you if I need more information.

> The chemist applied the new chemical in several ways.

These sentences and others like them are probably produced more by inattention and poor memory than by intellectual inability or poor command of the language. Since writing is a form of storage, the writer can easily assume that "stored" words at the beginning of a sentence are safe from loss and can be forgotten toward the end. Unfortunately, this causes a redundancy when the meaning of the sentence is considered as a complete thought. Whatever the reasons for redundancy in these sentences, the general failure to write concisely results from a failure to consider meaning. By considering the meanings of these sentences, the writer can easily remove the direct redundancy.

Indirect redundancy, which is less noticeable in writing, is for that reason much more common and requires greater effort to identify. For example, the writer who says that a certain object is "round in shape" or "tan in color" may well not notice the indirect redundancies for at least two good reasons: first, the words "round" and "shape" and "tan" and "color" have little in common either in sound or sense; second, because these redundancies are less direct, they are not routinely removed by other writers and therefore appear more frequently in the writer's reading experience. Because of this, writers who are learning to edit often remark that a particular redundancy is "one you see all the time."

Of course, frequency of occurrence does not make an expression any less redundant. Simply because one commonly encounters the expression "whether or not" in both speech and writing does not mean it should be left as it is. The expression should be revised to remove the redundancy, as should other expressions that are familiar though redundant. With practice, writers can spot these expressions and others simply by becoming familiar with the more common categories of redundancy. These categories follow but with the reminder that they are far from exhaustive. Writers interested in a more complete study may want to review some of the materials mentioned at the end of this chapter.

Expressions of Time

Redundancy commonly involves expressions of time. For example, the terms "current" and "now in progress" repeat information about the present tense. Whatever is "current" is "now in progress," and vice versa. Because the reader needs only one of these expressions, the writer should provide only one.

This form of redundancy can occur in any one of three familiar verb tenses: past, present, and future. The most common form contains both the main verb, which expresses the tense of the sentence, and an adverb, which renders that tense redundant. In the examples below, the verb is underlined; the adverb or its equivalent is italicized.

Include some of the hospitals from the list I *previously* sent to you.

Assign the same scheduling priority as is *now currently* in effect for regular check processing.

At present, they are purchasing a Baker Edgegard hood.

CMDAR indicated that, *in the future*, all such requests will be routinely reviewed.

Two examples above involve the present tense, and they require a special comment. Some will object to deleting the redundancy in these samples because the adverbs "currently" and "at present" or "presently" can be used to distinguish between what *is* happening and what *will* happen. In sentences where that is the case, the adverb has a function, and it may be used, or the tense itself may simply be underlined (as it is in the previous sentence). Revised, the sentences contain only the verbs:

Include some of the hospitals from the list I sent to you.

Assign the same scheduling priority as used for regular check processing.

They are purchasing a Baker Edgegard hood.

CMDAR indicated that all such requests will be routinely reviewed.

Redundancy in expressions of time can be produced in another way, by using nouns that have the same meaning. For example, "period," "present," "point," "brief," and "length," are redundant with "time" and "duration" in the sentences below.

We understood his request only after a considerable period of time.

At the present time, we are not inclined to bill them for our services.

At that point in time, I managed the best I possibly could.

Fortunately, the final meeting was brief in its duration.

The length of time involved was simply too great for the information received.

Two special examples are worth mentioning here simply because the potential for abuse is so great. Even though they do not fit the model above, they do express time-related ideas. Note that "month" will be redundant with any of the twelve choices and that "year" will be redundant with an even greater number of possibilities.

The transition to Piedmont may be started in the month of June.

In the year 1992, we considered diversifying our investments.

Joined Expressions

Writers who say "first and foremost" may well think that they are saying "first and most important." They are not. They are saying "first and most in the fore," or "first and first," or "foremost and foremost." They are joining two ideas that are the same. The part of speech used for this is the coordinating conjunction, which connects other words, phrases, or clauses. For example, "and" and "or" are coordinating conjunctions in the following examples.

When they order breakfast, it's always steak and eggs.

This information can be presented to the clients by phone or letter.

These examples present no problem because the words that are joined are different, and deleting either of them would change the meaning. The kind of joining that produces redundancy usually involves synonyms, as the following examples from legal writing show:[5]

last will and testament

cease and desist

null and void

Even though lawyers will be quick to defend this practice, the redundancy here is apparent. Less apparent are the more common examples below. Note how the redundant expressions become more extensive with each succeeding example.

We really don't know whether or not we will invest when they want us to.

The Northwestern and the Pacific districts could be included to prevent disturbance or interruptions of sales gain.

Adequate security should be provided to protect inventories from loss through pilferage or theft.

This safe is locked by a key only and does not have a combination lock.

Common to all of these examples is the conjunction "and" or "or." In each case, the writer should choose one item from the joined pairs.

Expressions of Location

Some expressions are redundant when they precede or follow the name of a place with implied information about the place itself.

Oakland is a *place where* housing is depressed.

We will hold the conference in the *city* of *San Francisco.*

The *state* of *California* does not provide enough tax incentives for us to relocate.

Pennsylvania is a *state* that has a 6 percent sales tax.

The *country* of *Brazil* provides us with unique types of coffee.

In none of the sentences above does the writer need to provide both italicized words. Of course, if the place described requires more information to be identified, then the writer should provide it. Not everyone knows Lucinda is a town in Pennsylvania. For that reason, the writer might say, "We may relocate our eastern office to the town of Lucinda, Pennsylvania."

Expressions of Direction

Expressions of direction can be redundant when they are followed by information they already imply. For example, writers who say that a manager has "retreated back to a former position" need not say "back" since that is the only direction one can retreat.

> After all of this talk about empowerment, Jones soon *reverted back* to his autocratic style of management.

> They *advanced* their chip technology much farther *forward* in the industry.

> The mechanical spatula *circled around* the curious compound until it was thoroughly blended.

> Each element was *separated out* until only the pure medium remained.

A form of redundancy that cuts across expressions of location and direction can be identified by giving special attention to the prepositions "of" and "at" when they are used with descriptions of place or movement. Even the word "by" in "close by" and "nearby" can be omitted. In the examples below, the writer should omit the prepositions:

> We need to know *where* the expansion board is *at*.

> They found problems *inside of* the tower case.

> The helicopter lifted *off of* the diving board .

> We will want to keep the guidelines *close by*.

> The OCR software is *nearby* the new color scanner.

Other Expressions

The redundancies above have been catalogued under the assumption that the categories will be easier to remember than unrelated example after example. However, the variety of redundancy is so great that any attempt at a catalogue would be time consuming at best. Nevertheless, the more popular redundancies are provided below. By becoming familiar with and thinking about them, writers can spot them and similar ones more easily. First is a list of sentences with redundancies. Following that is the same list with the redundancies crossed out.

>   1. The exterior of the Chevrolet was orange in color.
>   2. The planted area behind the courtyard was square in shape.
>   3. You will find that talented managers are few in number.

4. The foreman was not consciously aware of any danger.

5. Her supervisor had a bad mental attitude toward her.

6. You should try to fuse these two metals together.

7. These are the contributing factors to drug abuse.

8. Their affirmative action rules are adequate enough for us.

9. An MBA is a necessary requirement for this position.

10. This future effort will require our mutual cooperation.

11. The reason is because you did not get an RMA.

12. These can be ordered as a single unit of memory.

13. We waited for them to disappear from sight.

14. When this was first initiated, management certainly opposed it.

15. Any changes will require some advance planning.

Revised Sentences

1. The exterior of the Chevrolet was orange ~~in color~~.

2. The planted area behind the courtyard was square ~~in shape~~.

3. You will find that talented managers are few ~~in number~~.

4. The foreman was not ~~consciously~~ aware of any danger.

5. Her supervisor had a bad ~~mental~~ attitude toward her.

6. You should try to fuse these two metals ~~together~~.

7. These are the ~~contributing~~ factors to drug abuse.

8. Their affirmative action rules are adequate ~~enough~~ for us.

9. An MBA is a ~~necessary~~ requirement for this position.

10. This future effort will require our ~~mutual~~ cooperation.

11. The reason is ~~because~~ you did not get an RMA.

12. These can be ordered as a ~~single~~ unit of memory.

13. We waited for them to disappear ~~from sight~~.

14. When this was ~~first~~ initiated, management certainly opposed it.

15. Any changes will require some ~~advance~~ planning.

▧ Hidden Verbs

With the hidden verb, we leave the realm of the redundant and enter the domain of the dilute. Unlike redundancy, dilution does not repeat ideas, but it does weaken or water them down. Unfortunately, the consequence is the same: the writer produces more words than the reader needs. Harriet Tichy, one of several who have written about this, provides a particularly clear description of the hidden verb and follows it with an apt analogy:

> Common in functional prose is the weakened or dilute verb. Some writers avoid a specific verb like *consider*; they choose instead a general verb of little meaning like *take* or *give* and add the noun *consideration* with the necessary prepositions, as in *take into consideration* and *give consideration to*, *devote consideration to*, and *expend consideration on*. Thus they not only use three words to do the work of one, but also take the meaning from the strongest word in the sentence, the verb, and place the meaning in the noun that has a subordinate position. . . . Weak as a jigger of Scotch in a pitcher of water, this is neither good liquor nor good water.[6]

Also called "nominalizations," or "smothered verbs," the grammatical feature is always the same: a verb is hidden in another part of speech. For example, the writer who tells readers to "give careful consideration to" a proposal is really trying to say "consider carefully." The one-word verb was "hidden" in the longer phrase. As a consequence of the hidden verb, the writer's ideas must fight to get through an inherently weak construction because the writer is attempting to express action through a part of speech that is not a verb. This is similar to using scissors to mow the lawn: it takes longer, does a poorer job, and as anyone will tell you, it's the wrong tool for the job.

The number of hidden verbs is as great as the number of verbs to be hidden. However, these nine "helping" verbs commonly produce long, verb-suppressed constructions: "have," "give," "perform," "make," "produce," "accomplish," "achieve," "experience," and "conduct." Compare the hidden verbs in the sentence pairs below. In each case, the second example contains a verb that has surfaced.

The new law will have an influence on future building.
The new law will *influence* future building.

We will need to perform an analysis of traffic volumes at this intersection.
We will need to *analyze* traffic volumes at this intersection.

We are experiencing a slow-down in production of 486 chips.
We are *producing* 486 chips more slowly.

I shall perform an analysis of the system.
I shall *analyze* the system.

Socialists want to accomplish income equalization.
Socialists want to *equalize* incomes.

The new policy produced benefits for employees.
The new policy *benefited* employees.

We can conduct a survey of this lot.
We can *survey* this lot.

Too many nouns will achieve the dilution of writing.
Too many nouns will *dilute* writing.

Looking for the helping verbs above is one good way to identify potential verbs. Another is looking for the following noun endings because the full nouns will often contain hidden verbs.

-tion   (e.g., connection, consideration, correction)

-sion   (e.g., decision, conclusion, revision)

-ment   (e.g., agreement, experiment, measurement)

-ance or -ence   (e.g., assistance, resistance, dependence)

Here are some sample sentences with revisions.

An adequate reconciliation of garage charges is not being performed.
Garage charges are not being adequately reconciled.

The client group must make its own decision about what to do with the investment.
The client group must decide what to do with the investment.

It is our belief that his method would make an improvement in the process.
We believe his method would improve the process.

Manufacturing Documentation will provide any assistance if needed.
Manufacturing Documentation will assist if needed.

By noticing the particular helping verbs and noun endings above, writers can spot a great many constructions from which verbs may be extracted. However, writers will eventually want to free themselves from these indicators because many hidden verbs cannot be spotted by using these indicators alone. For example, while the following two sentences contain helping verbs and familiar noun endings, editing them for those features alone would still produce wordy writing.

Cutter has achieved success in winning a bid for 150,000 vials of Bacteriostatic Water.

If a U.S. firm anticipates a devaluation in currency, it may make the decision to hedge in order to protect its investment.

On first revision, the writer produces these sentences:

Cutter has succeeded in winning a bid for 150,000 vials of Bacteriostatic Water.

If a U.S. firm anticipates a devaluation in currency, it may decide to hedge in order to protect its investment.

On second revision, the writer does better:

> Cutter has won a bid for 150,000 vials of Bacteriostatic Water.

> If a U. S. firm anticipates a devaluation in currency, it may hedge its investment.

The final version here is the best because it is the most concise. While the usual indicators helped in the first revision, the final revision was possible only when the writer started to look for words that could be converted to verbs. Writers who approach revision with the importance of verbs in mind will produce better revisions than those who restrict their efforts to revising constructions with particular helping verbs and noun endings. However, by starting with these constructions, writers can eventually move beyond them.

■ Hidden Adverbs

Just as verbs can hide, so can adverbs, words that are often identified by their "-ly" ending. For example, the writer who says, "proceed with caution" can save words and the reader's time by writing, "proceed cautiously." Hidden adverbs frequently disappear into prepositional phrases. Sometimes they involve combinations with "with." Compare:

> Cars enter this area with great frequency.
> Cars enter this area very frequently.

> This must be monitored with some diligence.
> This must be monitored diligently.

More often, though, they can be found as the variable in the following constant expressions: "in a _____ manner," "in a _____ way," "in a _____ fashion," and "on a _____ basis." The last item is particularly popular with expressions of frequency, as in the last two examples below.

> The contractor always acted in a professional fashion.
> The contractor always acted professionally.

> This area can be accessed on a regular basis.
> This area can be accessed regularly.

> Have the medication checked on an annual basis.
> Have the medication checked annually.

Note that the last example also applies to the expressions "hourly," "daily," "weekly," and "monthly." In each case, the expressions can be reduced from four words to one.

Of course, editing for hidden adverbs assumes that the writer needs the adverb in the first place. Unfortunately, even the writer may not realize that the adverb itself is redundant or useless until it stands clearly as an adverb. However, once it is brought out of hiding, the writer will want to be sure that it is really needed. For example, when the following sentence is revised, the adverb will no longer be hidden:

On occasion, personnel occupying positions other than those authorized for access may enter the premises of the computer center because of emergency reasons.

Occasionally, unauthorized personnel may enter the computer center in an emergency.

Once this is done, the writer will be in the best position to see that the adverb is not needed:

Unauthorized personnel may enter the computer center in an emergency.

Other adverbs that writers can often omit entirely include these: "basically," "fundamentally," "essentially," and "primarily." Here are some typical examples:

Basically, I am on your side with this issue.

He is sorry to report that the committee is fundamentally opposed to your recommendations.

This is essentially the reason you were asked.

The staff was primarily concerned about the future hirings in this area.

Omitting these words will probably not change the meanings of these sentences. Of course, the writer can always contrast the thought of any one of these sentences with those that might follow. For example, after writing "Basically, I am on your side," the writer might say, "However, I have some reservations." If the writer chooses to do this, then the adverb is redundant. If the writer chooses not to, then the adverb provides only incomplete meaning about why the writer would not be on the reader's side.

▓ Prepositional Chains

Related to hidden adverbs are simple prepositions or conjunctions that have turned into long prepositional strings. A writer can write "with regard to" a freeway off-ramp, only to realize on proofreading that talking "about" a freeway off-ramp says the same thing more concisely. Many simple prepositions and conjunctions are needlessly expanded this way. The more common ones are "about," "before," "because," and "to." The expression "in order to" is probably the most common prepositional chain, one that can be condensed to the simple preposition "to." Note below the longer expressions most simple prepositions can replace.

about	(will replace)	with regard to
		with response to
		with respect to
		in relation to
		as regards
		with reference to
before	(will replace)	prior to
		in advance of
		previous to
		at an earlier time than
		at a time preceding
because	(will replace)	on account of
		due to the fact that
		seeing as how
		for the reason that
		by reason of
to	(will replace)	in order to
		for the purpose of
		with a view to

■ Expletives

"It is" and "there is" and the related constructions "it seems" and "there appear" are *expletives* when the words "it" or "there" do not refer to anything. They are always meaningless and roundabout. Writing "There is a tendency among our respondents to believe the system is safe" is simply the long and tedious way of saying "Our respondents tend to believe the system is safe." The difference here is between engaging the reader by delivering information quickly and fatiguing the reader by forcing delay.

The expletive is especially unfortunate not simply because it is (note that the preceding "it is" is not an expletive because the "it" refers to something) wordy in its own right, but also because it usually sets off a chain reaction of wordiness. "There is" constructions almost always lead to hidden verbs and other problems that have been covered in this chapter. Fortunately, by removing the expletive, writers will be better able to spot and remove other problems. Compare:

It is important for us to conduct an investigation of this problem in the month of July.

We need to investigate this problem in July.

From Table 5.1, it has become apparent that the normal slope information does not apply.

Table 5.1 shows that the normal slope information does not apply.

If investors are in the state, then there is a chance that problems for this group can be avoided with the SEC.

If investors are in the state, then they can probably avoid problems with the SEC.

It appears that (with the exception of the coffee shop deficit) this department will have sufficient funds to cover expenses.

This department should have funds to cover these expenses, except the coffee shop deficit.

The revised passages above are more concise and more readable, even though they were not very long to begin with. With longer passages, such as the one below, the revision will be even more remarkable.

Original Passage

There is an indication in this table that there appears to be some justification for the city establishing crosswalks on an as-needed basis across the northern and southern legs in order to insure safety and reduce hazards.

Revised

This table indicates that the city might insure safety by establishing crosswalks across the northern and southern legs.

True, the writer has done more here than simply remove expletives. The writer has also removed hidden verbs ("indication," "justification"), the hidden adverb ("on an as-needed basis"), the prepositional chain ("in order to"), and the redundancy ("safety" and "hazard"). In short, the writer has applied all of the principles mentioned in this section. The result? Roughly a 50 percent cut in the number of words and a correspondingly dramatic increase in readability and the quality of the writer's ethos.

Of course, what holds for the sentence also holds for the paragraph, the section, and the entire document. This means that editing for conciseness is not limited simply to considerations of how words may overlap in meaning or dilute each other's sense. Editing of this sort should extend from local-level concerns to the level of concerns about global redundancy or dilution. For example, writers who provide information in one sentence should avoid providing the same information elsewhere, unless they have a compelling reason to do so. Similarly, material expressed in one paragraph or chapter ought not to appear elsewhere unless the writer has a reason to include it again. Sometimes this more global redundancy may be avoided simply by providing the reader with the ease of reference (by parenthetic note, perhaps) if the writer has cause to believe that reference to an earlier section might serve the reader.

By editing for conciseness both locally and globally, the writer will take the most critical step toward insuring that the reader will receive only the necessary information presented in a form that is fundamentally readable. The favorable impression, the ethos, this creates can only ease the reader's acceptance of the writer's ideas, especially if they are controversial. By editing for other matters—word choice, word order, grammar, punctuation—the writer can extend this ethos and produce documents that are engaging, competitive, and highly readable. The following chapters of this book are devoted to describing these remaining matters of editorial technique.

RELATED READINGS

Most discussions of conciseness occur in one of three forms: comprehensive studies of discourse, textbook presentation of editorial technique, and usage manuals or dictionary lists. The short list of selected readings below is representative and recommended.

Aristotle. *"Art" of Rhetoric.* Trans. J. H. Freese. Loeb Classical Library. Cambridge, MA: Harvard University Press, 1982. Conciseness is considered as part of a systematic approach to discovering the means of persuasion. See Book III for a specific treatment of conciseness and persuasion.

Fiske, Robert Hartwell. *Webster's New World Guide to Concise Writing.* Englewood Cliffs, NJ: New York Prentice-Hall, 1990. An extensive alphabetical listing of verbose expressions and their concise counterparts. Very good for reference. Very bad for recreational reading.

Lanham, Richard. *Revising Business Prose*, 2d ed. New York: Macmillan, 1987. Conciseness is considered as part of a practical system of editing.

Munter, Mary. *Guide to Managerial Communication.* 2d ed. Englewood Cliffs, NJ: Prentice-Hall, 1987. Conciseness is considered as part of a larger concern with both writing and speaking.

Tichy, Harriet. *Effective Writing for Engineers, Managers, Scientists.* New York: Wiley, 1966. Conciseness is covered in list form with special attention to translations of problem expressions.

NOTES

1. Attention to this feature of business writing is beginning to increase in the academic community. Those interested in this may want to see Andrea Lunsford, "The Case for Collaboration—in Theory, Research, and Practice" in Donald A. Daiker and Max Morenberg, eds., *The Writing Teacher as Researcher: Essays in the Theory and Practice of Class-Based Research* (Portsmouth, NH: Boynton/Cook, 1990).

2. For a very recent and interesting discussion of professional writing and its place in the traditional liberal arts curriculum, see Margaret Mansfield, "Real World Writing and the English Curriculum," *College Composition and Communication* 44 (February 1993): 97–118.

3. This is most true of the academic professional. For an excellent discussion of this, see

Dan Dietrich, "Writing by Academic Professionals," *Writing in the Business Professions*, Myra Kogen, ed. (NCTE, 1989), 174–84.

4. For an opposing point of view, see Lewis Foley, "Brevity Isn't Everything," *Journal of Business Communication* 12, no. 1 (Fall 1974): 30–35.

5. Richard C. Wydick, "Plain English for Lawyers," *California Law Review* 66, no. 4 (1978): 733.

6. Harriet Tichy, *Effective Writing for Engineers, Managers, Scientists* (New York: Wiley, 1966), 122.

MANAGING ETHOS 9

Word Choice

"When I use a word," Humpty Dumpty said in rather a scornful tone, "it means just what I choose it to mean—neither more nor less."

"The question is," said Alice, "whether you can make words mean so many different things."

"The question is," said Humpty Dumpty, "which is to be master—that's all."

—Lewis Carroll, *Through the Looking Glass*

Writers who give special attention to their choice of words have an opportunity to provide their readers with the kind of writing that is both distinctive and engaging. It is also the kind of writing that will compete well for the reader's attention when the choices the writer makes result in increased familiarity, clarity, and ease of reading. Considered alone, word choice will contribute greatly to creating the kind of ethos the writer desires because the words one chooses communicate important information about intelligence, character, and goodwill. Combined with conciseness, careful word choice can produce writing that promises readers the most return in meaning for the least investment in time and effort.

Following conciseness with word choice makes particularly good sense: the writer who has determined which words to leave out must now decide what to do with the words that remain. This is a consideration separate from conciseness in both complexity and procedure since it involves replacing words instead of simply omitting them. Nevertheless, conciseness and word choice are causally related in editorial practice because engaging in the first almost always influences the necessity of choice in the second. For example, in the following sentence, the writer may choose different words for "matter" and "made."

To put this matter simply, projection to fiscal year-end is made on the following assumptions:

The writer may choose instead to say:

To put this situation simply, projection to fiscal year-end is calculated according to the following assumptions:

However, the writer who edits *first* for conciseness will spot the redundant opening "To put this matter simply" and the hidden verb in "assumptions." Consequently, the choices among words will be fewer:

Projection to fiscal year-end assumes:

Editing for conciseness is thus sensibly done before turning to word choice because it will help to avoid changing words that would only be deleted later. Once this is completed, the writer can turn full attention to selecting the best words to convey a particular message to a particular reader. How difficult this can be is well expressed by the *New Yorker* cartoon in which a writer sitting at a table has to his left a thesaurus and to his right a loaded revolver.

Although word choice is not as dangerous as the cartoon would suggest, it is still not easy. Particularly in business, where increasing diversity and multiple readers simply increase the chances that one will be misunderstood, word choice is a matter that must be managed with great care. However, these chances can be reduced if writers become familiar with four kinds of problems that are prevalent in the writing of working professionals: jargon, cliché, abstraction, and euphemism.

▤ Jargon

Usually described as the specialized or technical language of a specific profession or group, jargon becomes problematic when it is used *outside* of its particular community of writers or speakers. Because jargon is the language of the specialist, it can usually be identified by its source, particularly when it is imported from easily recognized professions or fields. For example, the word "interface" qualifies as jargon since it can be easily traced to a particular field of specialization: computing. Used outside this field, "interface" can cause considerable confusion because it has no agreed-upon meaning. Here is a good example of not very good usage:

You will have many responsibilities in your new position as supervisor, but probably your greatest task will be to interface with our clients from the business marketing organization.

Even good guesses may not reveal what the writer intended here. The more popular responses—"meet," "discuss," "have contact with," and even "tolerate" and "put up with"—all show that this word can mean many different things, particularly outside the world of computing. Unfortunately, even in that world, the word suffers from lack of a generally agreed-upon meaning. For example, its original use as a noun is ambiguous since it can refer to both hardware and software, to items such as SCSI (small computer system interface) adapters and to operating environments such as Digital Research's DOS, Microsoft's Windows, or IBM's OS2. Writers will do well to avoid "interface" by using the more specific word it almost always stands for. The following illustrates both the original misuse and the revision.

> After considerable discussion, they decided that each must interface with the district manager at least during the first stages of the project.

> After considerable discussion, they decided that each must report the project status to the district manager at least during the first stages of the project.

Here the more specific idea is simply lost in the original. While clear, perhaps, in the mind of the writer, it simply did not arrive at the reader's page.

"Interface" is just one of many terms of jargon that the world of personal computing has produced. Others that have been around for some time and cause similar difficulty are "input" and "output." Used to describe computer operations or results, these are ambiguous at best. For example, the writer who is impressed by the quality of type produced by a laser printer may well describe it as "excellent output." Unfortunately, this doesn't account for "output" meaning something quite different when describing these printers: pages per minute. Used to describe matters that are unrelated to computers, these terms are even more baffling. For example, what does one really want when asking for another person's "input"? A comment, criticism, written response, oral response, agreement, support, analysis, or what? Any one of these guesses would be more specific and consistent with agreed-upon meanings.

Computer jargon is worth the business writer's special attention because it is the most inescapable source of new and rapidly multiplying words. Those who are committed to keeping current will probably have to monitor the linguistic changes much more often than dictionaries or usage manuals are revised. In fact, monthly checks with popular publications will show that instances of computer jargon are increasing almost as quickly as products in this rapidly expanding industry. The following is from the back pages of *PC Magazine*, one publication that includes jargon as a matter of reader interest if not alert:

Buzzword Watch

crossgrade   To move from a DOS to a Windows version of the same product. First heard: *Jackie Brinker, Symantec Corp.*

picon   A visual element in a multimedia application. First heard: *Microsoft Multimedia Publishing Group, talking about the new Encarta Encyclopedia.*

context-sensitive modality   An intuitive interface. First heard: *Mark Zimmer, president, Fractal Design Corp.*[1]

Although personal computing as an industry is probably the greatest producer of jargon in the world of modern business, it is not the only producer. Other major sources of jargon are law, engineering, finance, and accounting. Whatever the source, the writer's use of jargon, particularly when it is used in the more general community of nonspecialists, will impede understanding and communication.

▓ Clichés

If jargon is specialized language that is *underused* in the more general community of writers or speakers, clichéd language is *overused*, both in business and elsewhere. George Orwell, among others, has written about clichés. His *Politics and the English Language*, written in 1946, is still relevant today, particularly in the comments he offers on clichés. Here is one of them:

> As I have tried to show, modern writing at its worst does not consist in picking out words for the sake of their meaning and inventing images in order to make the meaning clearer. It consists in gumming together long strips of words which have already been set in order by someone else. . . . The attraction of this way of writing is that it is easy.[2]

Clichés *are* attractive most probably for the very reason Orwell gives. Writers who want to avoid thinking through their own ideas can simply find borrowing the ideas of others easier. This is no doubt obvious about some clichés, and most readers will probably regard expressions like "you hit the nail on the head" and "let's do lunch" as no more than the borrowing of expressions that have been popular for probably too long. Other expressions may be more difficult to see as clichés. "Per," for example, is a word that continues to open many memoranda, yet it is as much of a cliché as "have a nice day." Writers who use it will open their writing in the least distinctive way.

Writers who want their writing to suggest independence of thought, or at least distinctiveness of expression, will do well to avoid clichés. Noting the frequency with which words occur in speech and writing is a good way to begin to develop a sensitivity to clichés. Trying hard to omit or replace them is a good second step.

▓ Abstraction

Like clichés, abstract words are overused, but unlike clichés, abstract words are always nonspecific. The best way to understand the problems abstraction produces is by understanding abstract language. The ladder of abstraction is a wonderful device linguists use to describe and explain abstract language, or language that refers to more things than the writer intends. The ladder below was first developed by S.I. Hayakawa.[3] Note how the terms on the ladder gain reference as they succeed one another on the ladder's rungs.

Wealth

Farm Assets

Farm Animals

Livestock

Cattle

Cow

Bessie

One might even insert a picture of Bessie below the bottom rung simply to indicate that the first term, "Bessie," is itself an abstraction since it *refers* to the *one* "real" thing, the object of reality, Bessie the cow. In this sense, names are always abstractions of things. As abstractions, names allow us to talk about things in their absence. Once past the object of reality, writers begin their climb on the ladder at the rung with "Bessie" on it. Note that every rung above this one still includes "Bessie," though every rung also includes (refers to) more than Bessie. "Cow," for example, refers to Bessie as well as other cows. Similarly, "cattle" refers to "Bessie," "cow," and then some. By the time the writer reaches "farm animals," the phrase refers not only to "Bessie," "cow," "livestock," and "cattle" but also to animals that are not raised for consumption, such as dogs and cats.

The ladder above provides an explanation of abstraction that should be clear to anyone. However, it may not have much relevance to people in business, unless they spend their time exclusively on small farms. For that reason, another ladder may be helpful, one that draws from an area of business that should be familiar to many, though not always in a way that is pleasant: internal audit.

Item

Finding

Performance Finding

Performance Violation

Misplaced Records

Burned Receipts

Once again, the higher one goes on the ladder, the greater the reference of the terms. Writers who wish to have their ideas understood will want to keep them low on the ladder of abstraction. Although few writers would say "wealth" when they mean "Bessie," many writers will routinely use words that are higher on the ladder of abstraction than they need to be. For example, the ladder above was assembled from over fifty internal audit reports in which the terms "item" and "finding" stood as substitutes either for the terms below them in the ladder or terms that were similarly specific. Although the writer may be more diplomatic by using "finding" instead of "burned receipts," the writer will certainly not be as well understood.

The words discussed below—"address," "deal with," and "handle"—are common and representative abstractions. Becoming familiar with them and the problems they create (their range of reference) should help writers to avoid abstract language or at least use it with an awareness of its potential for damage.

The verb "address" is both abstract and avoidable as an abstract term. Probably the best way to understand the danger of this abstract term is by understanding that what it does mean is simply a part of what it can mean. Although "address" does have a perfectly concrete meaning (i.e., "to address an envelope"), this is not one of its many senses when it is used abstractly.

> I want to *address* your proposal on the new affirmative action policy.

This could mean that the writer wants to describe the proposal, but it could just as easily mean that he wants to question it, modify it, clarify it, oppose it, defend it, extend it, or suggest an alternative to it. The following is another option, yet it is just as specific:

> I want to support your proposal on the new affirmative action policy.

"Deal with" and "handle" are similarly abstract and are unfortunate replacements for "address." They, too, have concrete meanings, but these meanings—of distributing cards and touching with the hand—are not the ones that cause problems.

> Our programming team will have to *deal with* our client's change to Microsoft Windows.
>
> We had no idea how to *handle* the new manufacturing safety standards.

Does the first sentence mean we will have to change as well? Or not change but accept it? Get them to change back? Does the second sentence mean follow the safety standards? Find a way around them? Follow them without losing too much productivity?

"Handle," in particular, can be both abstract and embarrassing in its implications. The following passage is from a job advertisement placed by a major bank in the office of career planning and placement at a major California university:

> We have a position available for someone who can handle our clients personally. This position has an opportunity for rapid growth.

Pointing out the comic implications, one student wrote above this ad: "Glad to see the bank is finally diversifying."

"Address," "deal with," and "handle," are not the only abstract terms writers will encounter, but they are probably the most common except for expressions of frequency, words that indicate how often an event occurs. The following are especially worth watching: "sometimes," "usually," "often," "frequently," "occasionally," "seldom," and "regularly." These terms can mean dramatically different things to different people, and while "occasionally" may suggest "frequent" to one person, it may suggest "infrequent" to another. Writers will do well to consider whether a quantitative expression is available. For example, if the writer can say "three times a week" or even "about three times a week," the idea will be better understood than in its abstract form of "regularly." Of course, quantitative expressions will not always be available, but the writer who attempts them will at least have considered how adequate the expression of frequency is.

■ Euphemisms

Euphemisms are usually described as the substitution of an inoffensive term for one that would otherwise be considered offensively explicit. Several that are commonly offered as examples are "perspire" for "sweat" and "seniors" for "old people." One consultant and writer on business communication offers the euphemisms below for the word "die." She claims that the "word *die* . . . is simple and dignified. It is far better than many of the substitutes for it."[4] Her examples follow. Note that she missed "buy the farm."

> to cash in one's chips, to pass away, to pass over, to pass to one's reward, to go beyond, to depart this world, to expire, to enter the valley of the shadow, to come to an untimely end, to perish, to be taken, to resign one's breath, to give up the ghost, to end one's days, to breathe one's last, to depart this life, to join the great majority, to kick the bucket.

Euphemisms differ from jargon, cliché, and abstraction because of the more deliberate intention of the writers who use them. Probably very few writers think about using jargon for an intended effect; even fewer consider the rhetorical uses of abstract terms or clichés. However, most writers probably think carefully at least about the impression, the ethos, they are attempting to create by using euphemisms. H. L. Mencken certainly believed this. In discussing euphemisms and the American worker, he wrote:

> The American, probably more than any other man, is prone to be apologetic about the trade he follows. He seldom believes that it is quite worthy of his virtues and talents; almost always he thinks that he would have adorned something far gaudier. Unfortunately, it is not always possible for him to escape, or even for him to dream plausibly of escaping, so he soothes himself by assuring himself that he belongs to a superior section of his craft, and very often he invents a sonorous name to set himself off from the herd.[5]

The consequence of this, according to Mencken, are titles that make the job appear more important than it really is. Older examples of this kind of euphemism are "mortician" for "undertaker," "aisle manager" for "floor-walker," and "beautician" for "hairdresser." More modern versions are "fashion consultant" for "sales clerk," "automotive technician" for "mechanic," and "telemarketer" for "annoying person who calls you at dinner time to sell you a subscription to a newspaper you already receive." A version of the euphemistic title was applied to the victims of the 1991 hills fire in Oakland, California. They probably did not feel much better when local columnist Herb Caen reported that they had been referred to as the "residentially disadvantaged." This is similar to television character Doogie Howser's short friend Vinnie calling himself "vertically challenged."

Similar to euphemistic titles are euphemistic words for actions. Probably the most popular in contemporary business describes the act of firing employees. However, it is a euphemism that has developed over time. Its linguistic history began with the phrase "to fire," which became "to lay off," which became "to downsize." More recently, "to downsize" lost its negative connotation by becoming "to reorganize." Only in the past two years has it acquired a positive connotation in "to rightsize." However, people are still being fired.

Although this and the preceding examples would suggest that euphemism is something writers ought to avoid, most usage specialists concede that euphemism has an occasional and acceptable use when it is employed to avoid causing others pain or embarrassment. Writers will do well to avoid euphemisms at all other times.

The four problem areas—jargon, cliché, abstraction, and euphemism—present mistakes made in effectiveness. In addition to these are mistakes of correctness. Mistakes of correctness are really misapplications of information contained in "good" dictionaries and "authoritative" usage manuals. Because of this, a few words about dictionaries and usage manuals should help in understanding the misapplications that will follow.

▨ Dictionaries

Although one commonly hears "look it up in the dictionary," no such book "the dictionary" exists. Instead, many do, and some are better than others. The list below contains good ones. Arranged alphabetically, it offers a representative sampling of dictionaries with the minimum that writers in the professions should expect: information on denotation, parts of speech, derivation. *The American Heritage Dictionary of the English Language* is especially useful since it has wide acceptance in the academic community, contains many words used in the professions, and provides the adult reader with information about problematic usage. Its usage panel, chaired by Edwin Newman, includes a broad cross section of people whose opinions about language are considered authoritative or at least important. Among those who have served: Russell Baker, Pulitzer Prize–winning columnist; Jacques Barzun, writer and Columbia University professor; Julian Bond, author and legislator; William F. Buckley, Jr., editor in chief, *National Review*; the late Charles Kuralt, CBS news correspondent; Dorothy Fey, executive director, the United States Trademark Association; Joan Manley, chairman of the board, Time-Life Books; Jessica Mitford, writer; Neil Simon, playwright and screenwriter; and Gloria Steinem, writer and editor, *Ms.* magazine.

The American Heritage Dictionary of the English Language
The Random House College Dictionary

Webster's New Collegiate Dictionary
Webster's New World Dictionary

▨ **Usage Manuals**

Writers will be disappointed if they rely solely on dictionaries to help them determine whether they are using words correctly. Although dictionaries will help, they are not designed for this as their primary purpose. For example, any dictionary will provide information about the meaning of the word "anxious," but it may not tell you that people often confuse it with "eager." Nor will a dictionary provide reasons to distinguish "who" from "whom" and "which" from "that."

For information about these confusions and distinctions, writers will want to turn to a good usage manual. As with dictionaries, usage manuals are many. However, the ones below have gained wide acceptance over time. Particularly helpful is Nicholson's *Dictionary of American-English Usage* since it is derived from the highly respected version written by H. W. Fowler, but it concentrates on the concerns and linguistic norms of American writers.

H. W. Fowler, *A Dictionary of Modern English Usage*

H. W. Horwill, *A Dictionary of Modern American Usage*

Margaret Nicholson, *A Dictionary of American-English Usage*

The only problem with these usage manuals, one that they share with dictionaries, is their lack of currency and their inability to respond quickly to additions. They are simply not published often enough to represent the more rapid changes in language. New words, particularly words used to describe products or services, will not appear until the next edition, if they appear at all. Because of this, writers should have a copy of the *Associated Press Style Book and Libel Manual,* which provides this more current information, and as the title suggests, offers guidance on an important matter in which the language and the law overlap.

The following collection of texts would serve as a good example of a basic library of reference works for working professionals who want to write well. Several of the works listed, for example, *The American Heritage Dictionary* and the *Associated Press Style Book and Libel Manual*, are also available in electronic versions for DOS computers and the MS Windows operating environment.

The American Heritage Dictionary of the English Language

Margaret Nicholson, *A Dictionary of American-English Usage*

Associated Press Style Book and Libel Manual

Armed with these works, or another similar collection, the writer in business has a good chance of becoming an informed consumer and producer of words. However, everyone must start somewhere, and a good place to begin is with words that are already known to cause problems in the professions.[6] The list below contains many of these words, and writers who become familiar with them will be able to avoid some of the problems they can create. They will also become more sensitive to their use of other words.

■ Frequently Misused Words

Affect and Effect

"Affect" and "effect" are frequently confused. As verbs, "affect" means to influence, and "effect" means to bring about or cause to happen:

> Bad publicity *affected* public reaction to our product (the publicity influenced the public's previous reaction).

> The salesman *effected* the sale (the salesman brought about the sale).

Note that choosing the wrong word in these cases would change completely the meanings of the sentences:

> Bad publicity effected public reaction to our product (the public had no reaction before, and the publicity brought one about).

> The salesman affected the sale (the salesman influenced a sale already made).

The noun meaning *an* influence is invariably "effect," and the adjective is invariably "effective":

> He had an effect on company policy but was not effective as an administrator.

Aggravated and Irritated

Most usage specialists agree that these words are worth keeping distinct because of the useful difference between them. They also agree that the difference is one that speakers and writers observe less in casual communication than they do in more formal exchanges. The difference is this: "irritate" means to annoy or make something worse; "aggravate" means to make *an already bad* condition worse than it is. The following sentences may describe the same behavior, but one provides different information about the circumstances within which the behavior occurred:

> This vice president was irritated by the general manager's implementation of the new policy.

This vice president was aggravated by the general manager's implementation of the new policy.

In the first sentence, the reader has no information about the vice president before the general manager's actions; in the second sentence, the word "aggravate" indicates that the vice president was already in some way upset before the general manager's actions.

Anxious and Eager

A recent survey of misused words in business ranked these two at the top. Be careful to choose carefully between them according to the sense you are trying to convey. You may be able to distinguish between the two by remembering that "anxious" is related to "anxiety." Because of this, you probably don't want to say any of the following:

I am *anxious* to attend the Friday manager's meeting.

Our team is *anxious* to begin working with your clients.

We are *anxious* to receive our upgrade of Lotus 123.

These could make sense, of course, if you expected the agenda to include news of your dismissal, if you had heard that the clients were difficult to work with, and if the upgrade had advertised bugs. In each case, "eager" or "looking forward" is probably the best choice:

I am *eager* to attend the Friday manager's meeting.

Our team is *looking forward* to working with your clients.

We are *eager* to receive our upgrade of Lotus 123.

Assure and Insure

Many distinctions in English depend on the further distinction between people and things. "Insure" means "to protect against risk or loss with insurance" and "to make certain or guarantee." Although it *can* be used with *people* (e.g., "to insure persons or property against risk"), it is most often used with *things*. "Assure," which means "to declare confidently," "to cause to feel sure," is most often used with *people* as the *American Heritage* usage notes suggest: "*Assure, ensure,* and *insure* all mean 'to make secure or certain.' Only *assure,* however, is used with reference to a person in the sense of 'to set the mind at rest.' " Writers will do well to reserve "assure" for people and "insure" for things. The following sentences follow this reservation:

The general manager assured them that the new pay scale would not hurt anyone now considering early retirement.

You will all want to insure your properties even though the structures no longer exist. Doing so should assure you that you are protected.

Because and Since

These words are often confused, and this is unfortunate because they have quite different meanings to readers. "Because" alone does not cause the problem; most people use it to suggest a reason. Consequently, the only danger is usually one of redundancy: "The reason is because . . ." needs only "reason" or "because." The problem occurs when "since" as a conjunction is used with the meaning of "as a result of the fact that." Consider these sentences:

Since Wilson joined this division, marketing has become much less cooperative.

Because Wilson joined this division, marketing has become much less cooperative.

The first sentence may carry the same meaning as the second, but the reader will have no way of knowing that. Perhaps the writer simply means "since the time." If that is the case, then marketing's lack of cooperation is chronological and not causal. Perhaps the best solution here is the one just given: use "because" to express causal connections; use "since" with a time word (e.g., "since then," or "since that time") to express temporal connections. See also "Although and While."

Between and Among

The distinction between these words concerns the number of people or things being discussed. Writers will do well to use "between" when discussing two items and "among" when discussing three or more. However, the distinction blurs when "between" is used to distinguish between sets, since the total number of items will be three or more: "Conflict existed between the four partners." This makes sense if two partners disagreed with the other two. The following sentences are correct:

The return on investment was divided equally between Betsy and Nicole.

The return on investment was divided equally among Betsy, Nicole, and Alicia.

Bring and Take

Both of these words express information about the conduct of people or things, but they differ in the *direction* the writer wishes to communicate to the reader. "Bring" expresses movement *toward* a place; "take" expresses motion *away* from a place. The following examples show the difference between these two words. Note the use of "come" and "leave."

> When you come to the meeting, please bring the portfolio with you.

> When you leave the meeting, please take the portfolio with you.

Generally, these words will be paired in the following ways: "bring" with "come," "take" with "leave," and "take" with "go." Because of that, writers and speakers who are puzzled about which word to use can ask themselves which additional word, "leave" or "come," they would use if they *had* to use one of them. The answer should help to decide whether "bring" or "take" is the best word to select.

Comprise and Compose

These words express either inclusion or composition. However, they have individual meanings that are useful to keep distinct. For example, "comprise" means "contain" or "include". Because of that, a writer might sensibly say:

> This department comprises many management and secretarial services.

> Our software line comprises database programs and spreadsheet utilities.

In the first case, the writer is saying that the department includes these services; in the second, the writer states that the software contains database and spreadsheet programs. While often confused with "comprise," "compose" means instead "to make up." For that reason, the following sentence would make more sense if the words were switched:

> Computer chips comprise our most profitable product line.

The computer chips do not *include* the most profitable product line; they *make up* that product line. "Compose" or even "constitute" would be the right word here.

Continually and Continuously

These words are confused probably because they look and sound similar. However, a useful distinction exists since the adverb "continually" means "recurring frequently." The adverb "continuously" means in an "incessant" or "uninterrupted way." A writer might use both of these to describe a meeting that was held, without interruption, from 9:00 to 11:00 a.m. and the behavior of a sales representative who many times proposed taking a break:

Although the meeting was held continuously from 9:00 to 11:00, Jones continually proposed taking short breaks.

Had the writer written the following, the time would have been filled with Jones's proposals with occasional breaks:

Although the meeting was held continually from 9:00 to 11:00, Jones continuously proposed taking short breaks.

The distinction that exists between the adverbs "continuously" and "continually" also exists between their adjective forms "continuous" and "continual."

Disinterested and Uninterested

"Disinterested" means "free of bias and self-interest, impartial." The writer who uses "disinterested" to describe a worker's attitude toward a new pilot project is saying something good about that worker. A "disinterested party," then, is one who has no particular stake in the matter at hand.

"Uninterested" is the word often confused with "disinterested." This is unfortunate because "uninterested" means "indifferent" or "unconcerned." The sentences below exemplify the confusion this can cause:

We are seeking an uninterested person to evaluate the performance of new managers in this department.

We are seeking a disinterested person to evaluate the performance of new managers in this department.

Although neither expresses the writer's ideas very clearly, at least the second provides sensible meaning, if one assumes that interest in evaluation makes sense in a way that bias does not. Although "disinterested" and "uninterested" are often confused, one can see why a majority of the *American Heritage* Usage Panel believes that the two words should not be used interchangeably.

E.g. and Other Abbreviations

Writers commonly confuse several abbreviations for Latin terms. The abbreviation "e.g." means "for example" and should not be used interchangeably with "i.e.," which means "that is," which in turn is shorthand for "that is to say." Writers should reserve "e.g." for listing one or more incomplete thoughts or items; "i.e.," can then be used to provide complete rephrases of the writer's ideas.

Our company sells several good modems, e.g., Zoltrix, Zoom, and Zytel.

Usually we do well in the interview, i.e., we win nine out of ten times.

"Etc.," which means "and other things" should be distinguished from "et al.," which means "and other *people*." The following two sentences are correct because the first is about things, and the second is about people.

> They checked prices for the usual camping items: dried food, propane, matches, etc.

> The book you want was written by Schmader, Vogelbacher, Carroll, et al.

Note that redundancy is tempting with two of the abbreviations in this group. By saying "i.e.," writers are signaling a restatement that is usually clearer than the expression it restates. For that reason, using only the restatement will avoid redundancy. Also, because "etc." already means "*and* other things," saying "and etc." would be redundant.

Enormity and Enormous

Well worth keeping distinct are "enormity," which means a crime or atrocity, and "enormous," which means large. Because the first word is a noun and the second an adjective, one might expect that the two would not be confused that often. However, writers and speakers alike will routinely use "enormity" to mean the enormousness of an action or thing. Unfortunately, the writers who do this will produce nonsense:

> We hope the visitors will be impressed with the enormity of our activities in the Pacific rim.

What the writer probably has in mind here is "size," "extensiveness," or "diversity" and not "extreme wickedness," "monstrous offense," or "evil," though any one of those would also be impressive.

Fail and Neglect

This is a particularly important distinction to remember when describing or evaluating the efforts or performance of others. "Fail" implies trying and not succeeding, but "neglect" means to "ignore" or "disregard." At best, writers who confuse these terms will produce ambiguity:

> We are concerned because our programmer failed to produce the kind of code the client expected.

> The architect failed to let us know about the need for additional soundproofing.

Does this mean that the programmer made an effort but did not succeed, or does it mean that the programmer ignored or disregarded the client's expectations? Did the architect try to contact us and not succeed, or was the architect simply not trying to inform the writer of this need?

Fewer and Less

An advertisement tells us that a frozen dinner contains "less calories." While this may be true, the word "less" should be replaced with "fewer" if the writer wants to communicate that calories can be counted. "Fewer," "few," and "number" are words used to describe quantities that can be counted. In contrast, "less," "little," and "amount" are used to describe quantities that cannot be counted. The following sentences are correct, if we agree that bulk copper is not countable in the way that memory modules are:

> We sell a large *amount* of copper to the primary contractor, but we sell *less* than our primary competitor does. Our secondary competitor sells only a *little*.

> We have in inventory a large *number* of memory modules but only a *few* with more than two megabytes. Fortunately, we compete with Arizona Supply, which stocks even *fewer*.

The writer will usually be able to determine which word to use by noticing whether the noun that is modified is singular (not countable) or plural (countable). For example since the word "tires" is plural, it will take "few," "fewer," and "number"; however, the "air" used to inflate the tires is singular, so it will take "less," "amount," and "little."

Further and Farther

Both of these words express distance, but they differ in the *kinds* of distance they express. "Farther" is used to express a distance that is physical or literal. In most cases, this distance can be measured, counted, or estimated. When, for example, the writer says, "You need to go farther down the road," the distance is intended to be real. However, when the writer says, "This problem will have to be looked into farther," the distance is "not real," at least not in the sense that it can be measured or traveled in conventional ways. The appropriate word in that case is "further" because it expresses nonphysical or figurative distance. "Further" is often used to express intellectual distance or distance in conversational depth. It is also used in the sense of "additional" in sentences like "We hope there will be no further problems" and "Further work on this project would be useless." The following are correct uses of both "further" and "farther."

Our products are available no farther than Pittsburgh, Pennsylvania.

This should have been investigated much further than it was.

We will need to extend the retaining wall twelve feet farther.

The problems they face are only the result of further delay.

Healthy and Healthful

These terms are used increasingly in business because of their figurative application, product descriptions, and the increased attention that is being given to physical well-being. The distinction between the two, while not always observed, is nevertheless simple and useful. "Healthy" means to be in good health or to *possess* health. "Healthful" means to *promote* or *produce* good health. Because of this, writers will want to reserve "healthy" for things that can be healthy (e.g., people and animals) and use "healthful" to describe things or activities that yield or foster health (e.g., foods, diets, exercise programs). The following sentences observe this distinction:

Amway is only one company that produces a complete line of very healthful foods and vitamins.

According to the AMA, people do not need to consume special vitamins and foods to be healthy, but it probably wouldn't hurt.

Infer and Imply

"Infer" means to *read* between the lines, though it is often and easily confused with "imply," which means to *suggest* between the lines. The following sentence will probably not be understood in the way the writer intended:

The president's speech *inferred* that we were in serious financial trouble.

This sentence should be:

The president's speech *implied* that we were in serious financial trouble.

or

I *inferred* from the president's speech that we were in serious financial trouble.

Finally, these two words are like "bring" and "take" because they distinguish direction: "imply" expresses an outward direction; "infer" expresses direction inward. In practice, writers and speakers *imply* while readers and listeners *infer*.

Lie and Lay

Even people who don't often recline, place things, or fib find the "lie" and "lay" distinction troublesome. Keeping them clear is frustrating for at least two reasons: first, both words have forms (present, present perfect, or past) that are spelled the same; second, another distinct verb, "to lie" (to tell an untruth), complicates the matter. However, the following table should help:

To Recline (lie)

Present	I lie in bed.
Past	I lay in bed all day.
Present Perfect	I have lain in bed for a week.

To Place (lay)

Present	I lay bricks.
Past	I laid bricks all day.
Present Perfect	I have laid bricks all week.

To Tell a Lie (lie)

Present	I lie as I speak.
Past	I lied all day.
Present Perfect	I have lied all week.

Some usage specialists believe additional help comes from noticing that "lie" (to recline) is never followed by a grammatical object while "lay" always needs one to be complete. For example, "I lay sick all day" but "I laid the book by my bed."

Likely and Probably

"Likely" usually causes the problem in selecting between these two because it ends in "ly," as do many adverbs. For that reason, writer and speakers alike will use it even though the adverb "probably" is the word for the job. "Likely" is an adjective, which means that it is used to modify nouns, not verbs. Consider the following sentences, in which "likely" is used to modify the nouns "candidate" and "appointment":

Michaels is a very likely candidate for the position of vice president.

His appointment to the board is likely in the very near future.

Note the same sentences with the addition of "probably" used as an adverb to modify the verbs "succeed" and "last":

Michaels is a very likely candidate, one who will probably succeed.

His appointment to the board is likely, though he probably won't last long in the position.

By observing the functional distinction between the words, writers will be able to avoid saying things like "He will likely win the new account for us."

Related to "likely" is "liable," which is best reserved for actions that are not favorable. For example, writers will do well to change "He is liable to win" to "He is likely to win," or "He may win," depending on the meaning. However, saying "He is liable to sue us," while providing unpleasant news, makes perfectly good sense.

Oral and Verbal

Misuse here can cause considerable confusion. "Verbal" means pertaining to words, but it does not *necessarily* mean that these words are spoken. These words could be spoken, but they could instead be in written or even electronic form. "Oral" means spoken *only*.

Most people who confuse these words will use "verbal" when they have "oral" in mind. For example, businesspeople who say that their communication involves many "verbal presentations" probably mean that they give many "oral presentations" or speeches in professional settings.

The distinction between "verbal" and "oral" is especially important to remember when describing contracts and agreements. A transaction that is made on a "verbal agreement" may sound as if it involved only a handshake and a few spoken words. However, if this is the meaning the writer wants to convey, the meaning should be limited to avoid confusion. The expression for this is "oral agreement."

Writers may want to avoid "verbal" entirely and use only "written" and "oral." By doing this, they will be able to avoid much of the potential confusion, particularly at a time when words are transmitted through such a great variety of media.

Principal and Principle

"Principal" means *chief*, whether it is used as a noun to refer to the principal of a consulting business or school or as an adjective to modify a noun: "This is the *principal* reason for investing in this company." "Principle" is used only as a noun (though the adjective form "principled" exists) to mean "a basic truth, law, or assumption," or "a rule or standard of personal conduct, natural phenomena, or mechanical processes." The key word with "principle" is "rule"; the key word with "principal" is "chief." The following sentences show correct uses of these words:

This design will be revised by the project principal and technical consultants in engineering. The general principle we will follow is simplicity of arrangement.

Reticent and Reluctant

"Reticent" means unwilling to speak, and "reluctant" means unwilling in a much less specific way. Writers will do well to avoid using "reticent" to express more general forms of hesitancy or resistance. They will also do well to avoid using "reticent" to express a more general unwillingness. The following sentences are not correct:

> He was reticent to take on more responsibility.

> Although others participated fully, he was reluctant at the monthly managers' meetings.

These should be rewritten:

> He was reluctant to take on more responsibility.

> Although others participated fully, he was reticent at the monthly managers' meetings.

While and Although

The distinction here is similar to the distinction between "because" and "since." However, the ambiguity here is not between causal and temporal connections but between connections that are corrective and temporal. The following sentences will illustrate:

> While she has been in this position, we have seen no deterioration in our relationships with vendors.

> Although she has been in this position, we have seen no deterioration in our relationships with vendors.

The first sentence may carry the same meaning as the second, but the reader will have no way of knowing that. Perhaps the writer simply means "during the time." If that is the case, then the lack of deterioration in the relationship with the vendor is simply coincidental, and the writer should use "while." The second sentence is quite different because "although" tells the reader that deterioration might well be expected from her being in this position. To preserve the distinction between these words, writers should make sure that "while" is understood as an expression of time. See also "because" and "since."

Who and Whom

Confusion here comes from two areas: the first, not knowing the difference between subject and object pronouns; the second, not knowing how to judge which is called for in the sentence. Settling the first is relatively easy. Subject pronouns stand for nouns that act. Object pronouns stand for nouns that receive action. The following abbreviated table provides the usual selection of each.

Subject Pronouns	Object Pronouns
I	Me
You	You
He/She/It	Him/Her/It
We	Us
You	You
They	Them
Who	Whom

Writers who also have difficulty choosing between "I" and "me" will do well to remember this table because it will help them to distinguish between the two. In practice, this means being able to understand the difference in meaning between the following two sentences:

My supervisor likes the new trainer better than I.

My supervisor likes the new trainer better than me.

Either sentence could be correct, depending on meaning, and that, of course, is the point here. The first sentence says that the supervisor likes the new trainer better than I do; in the second, the supervisor likes the new trainer better than the supervisor likes me. Because the sentences are quite different in meaning, the distinction between subject and object pronouns is well worth observing.

A similar distinction between subject and object pronouns exists with "whom" and "who," though writers will generally have a more difficult time determining whether the sentence calls for the subject pronoun "who" or the object pronoun "whom." The sentence below presents just such a difficulty.

She is the one (who/whom) I would like to see direct the marketing meeting.

Some writers might guess "who" because it would match "she," the subject pronoun; others might say "whom" since it would match "her," the unspoken object of "to see"; still others might say "who" since it would match as the subject of "direct." To avoid this confusion of choices, writers can follow these three steps:[7]

1. Pay attention *only* to the words *after* "who" or "whom." This will always produce an incomplete sentence. For example:

I would like to see _____ direct the marketing meeting.

2. Complete the sentence by filling the blank with either "he" ("she") or "him" ("her"):

   I'd like to see *her* direct the marketing meeting.

3. Translate using the following equation: he or she = who; him or her = whom:

   She is the one whom I would like to see direct the marketing meeting.

These steps should help writers almost all of the time, even with sentences that contain prepositions. For example, the sentence "He is the one for who/whom new responsibilities are always an unwelcome challenge" becomes "new responsibilities are always an unwelcome challenge for ____." Few writers would have difficulty choosing "him" instead of "he" for the blank. Therefore, the choice in the sentence above is whom.

RELATED READINGS

On Usage and Correctness

Bolinger, Dwight, and William Buckley. "Usage and Acceptability in Language," *The American Heritage Dictionary, Second College Edition.* Boston: Houghton Mifflin, 1991, 30–32. This article and two others from *American Heritage* listed below provide a brief but good overview of the issues surrounding modern usage.

Freeman, Morton S. *Words to the Wise: The Wordwatcher's Guide to Contemporary Style and Usage.* New York: Penguin, 1991.

Kucera, Henry. "The Mathematics of Language," *The American Heritage Dictionary, Second College Edition.* Boston: Houghton Mifflin, 1991, 37–41.

Paxon, William C. *The New American Dictionary of Confusing Words.* New York: Signet, 1990. Yet another of several good dictionaries of misused words. Contains an interesting discussion of authorities.

Landau, Sidney. *Dictionaries: The Art and Craft of Lexicography.* Cambridge, MA: Cambridge University Press, 1989. This is a very interesting book overall, and its fifth chapter contains a particularly good discussion of usage.

Maggio, Rosalie. *Nonsexist Word Finder: A Dictionary of Gender-Free Usage.* Phoenix, AZ: Oryx Press, 1987.

Miller, Casey, and Kate Swift. *Handbook of Nonsexist Writing.* 2d ed. New York: Harper & Row, 1988.

Nunberg, Geoffrey. "English and Good English." *The American Heritage Dictionary, Second College Edition.* Boston: Houghton Mifflin, 1991, 34–35.

Pinckert, Robert C. *The Truth About English.* Englewood Cliffs, NJ: Prentice-Hall, 1990. Interesting and amusing treatment of usage as a trivial game played well by those who know the rules.

Urdang, Laurence. *The Dictionary of Confusable Words.* New York: Ballantine, 1988. One of several good dictionaries of misused words.

Authoritative Works on Usage

The Associated Press Stylebook and Libel Manual. Ed. Norman Goldstein. New York: Addison-Wesley, 1992.

Copperud, Roy H. *American Usage and Style: The Consensus.* New York: Van Nostrand Reinhold, 1980.

Follett, Wilson. *Modern American Usage: A Guide.* Ed. and comp. Jacques Barzun et al. New York: Hill and Wang, 1966.

Fowler, H.W. *A Dictionary of Modern English Usage.* 2d ed. Rev. by Sir Ernest Gowers. Oxford: Clarendon Press, 1965.

Morris, William, and Mary Morris. *Harper Dictionary of Contemporary Usage.* 2d ed. New York: Harper & Row, 1985.

Nicholson, Margaret. *A Dictionary of American-English Usage.* Oxford: Oxford University Press, 1957.

Dictionaries

The entries that follow are divided into general language and business oriented. In addition, the reader with a strong interest in this section may want to read Sidney Landau's *Dictionaries: The Art and Craft of Lexicography* (see full listing above).

General Language

Flexner, Stuart Berg, ed. *Random House Dictionary of the English Language.* 2d ed., unabridged. New York: Random House, 1998.

Gove, Philip Babcock, ed. *Webster's Third New International Dictionary of the English Language.* Unabridged. Springfield, MA: G. & C. Merriam, 1993.

Morris, William, ed. *American Heritage Dictionary of the English Language.* 3rd ed. Boston: Houghton Mifflin, 1992.

Neufeldt, Victoria, ed. *Webster's New World Dictionary of American English.* 3d college ed. New York: Simon & Schuster, 1998.

Simpson, J. A., and E. S. C. Weiner, eds. *Oxford English Dictionary.* 2d ed. 20 vols. Oxford, England: Oxford University Press, 1989.

Webster's Tenth New Collegiate Dictionary. Springfield, MA: Merriam Webster, 1992.

Business and Professions

American Psychiatric Association. *Diagnostic and Statistical Manual of Mental Disorders.* 4th ed., rev. Washington, D.C.: American Psychiatric Association, 1994.

Berkow, Robert, ed. *Merck Manual of Diagnosis and Therapy.* 16th ed. Rahway, NJ: Merck & Co., 1993.

Black's Law Dictionary. 6th ed. St. Paul, MN: West Publishing Company, 1991.

Cowan, Henry J. and Peter R Smith. *Dictionary of Architectural and Building Technology.* New York: Elsevier Applied Science Publishers, 1998.

Edmunds, Robert A. *Prentice-Hall Standard Glossary of Computer Terminology.* Englewood Cliffs, NJ: Prentice-Hall, 1984.

Glenn, J. A., and G. H. Littler. *Dictionary of Mathematics.* San Francisco: Harper & Row, 1996.

Harris, Cyril M., ed. *Dictionary of Architecture and Construction.* 2d ed. New York: McGraw-Hill, 1993.

Lapedes, Daniel N., ed. *McGraw-Hill Dictionary of Physics and Mathematics.* New York: McGraw-Hill, 1978.

McGraw-Hill Dictionary of Scientific and Technical Terms. 5th ed. New York: McGraw-Hill, 1994.

Rice, Michael Downey. *Prentice-Hall Dictionary of Business, Finance, and Law.* Englewood Cliffs, NJ: Prentice-Hall, 1983.

Rosenberg, Jerry M. *Dictionary of Business and Management.* New York: Wiley, 1993.

Dictionary of Computers, Data Processing, and Telecommunications. New York: Wiley, 1991.

Spencer, Donald D. *Illustrated Computer Dictionary.* Rev. ed. Columbus, OH: C. E. Merrill, 1995.

Timmreck, Thomas, ed. *Dictionary of Health Services Management.* 2d ed. Owings Mills, MD: National Health Publishing, 1986.

NOTES

1. "Buzzword Watch," *PC Magazine* (June 29, 1993): 432.

2. George Orwell, "Politics and the English Language," in *Essays on Language and Usage*, eds. Leonard F. Dean and Kenneth G.Wilson, 2d ed. (New York: Oxford University Press, 1963), 331.

3. S. I. Hayakawa and Alan R. Hayakawa, *Language in Thought and Action*, 5th ed. (New York: Harcourt, 1990), 85.

4. Harriet Tichy, *Effective Writing for Engineers, Managers, Scientists* (New York: Wiley, 1966), 212.

5. H. L. Mencken, "Euphemisms," in *Essays on Language and Usage*, eds. Leonard F. Dean and Kenneth G.Wilson, 2d ed. (New York: Oxford University Press, 1963), 40.

6. Paula Williams, Jolene Scriven, and Stan Wayne, "A Ranking of the Top 75 Misused Similar Words That Business Communication Students Confuse Most Often," *The ABCA Bulletin* (December 1991): 19–25.

7. See Maxwell Nurnberg, *Questions You Always Wanted to Ask about English* (New York: Simon & Shuster, 1972), 33. The steps proposed here are a revision of Nurnberg's.

MANAGING ETHOS 10

Syntax

Meaning . . . involves an analysis of the developing responses of the reader in relation to the words as they succeed one another in time. . . . A reader's response to the fifth word in a line or sentence is to a large extent the product of his responses to words one, two, three, and four.

—Stanley Fish, *Self-Consuming Artifacts*

Writers who have edited for conciseness and word choice will have determined which words to leave out and roughly what to do with the words that remain. They can now turn their attention to casting these concise and well-chosen words into the best possible order. This is important because the order or *syntax* of words can help the writer compete for the reader's attention just as much as the choice, punctuation, or grammar of words.[1] Syntax will also communicate information about the writer's ethos by creating the impression of someone who is in control of the material and whose meaning may be grasped without unreasonable effort. Writers who produce sentences in which the words are poorly ordered run the risk of appearing confused themselves. As we shall see, poor word order also has a way of producing unintended meanings, and thus the implications of a sentence might be comic and at the writer's expense. Neither confusion nor comic implication will inspire confidence in a reader who is being asked to accept a writer's controversial ideas.

Unfortunately, writers do not think as seriously about word order as they do about other matters of effective writing. One reason for this is that writers form their own impressions of meaning, and these impressions will overpower the meaning produced by the order of words. As a consequence, they leave their readers either puzzled or forced to recast their words into an order that makes better sense in context. A good example of this is the following sentence:

> The survey confirmed that the landlords have established a firm practice of requiring renters to paint and refurbish the unit upon departure.

Unless the writer is talking about a mobile home, the unit cannot be moving. Of course, the writer never intended to suggest that the unit is moving, and that's the point here. As writers write sentences, they develop their own impressions—of people painting apartments, of people departing premises, etc. They may assume that the word order will convey these impressions, but they have no assurance unless they check the order of their words and follow the rules in English that govern word order.

Happily, managing word order is a relatively simple matter because the options for expression here are limited, the rules are few, and the more general principles of effective word order can be practiced with little effort and much advantage. In fact, following only the principles and few rules discussed in this section will help most writers to increase readability through effective word order.

■ Placement of Main Clauses

In revising word order, the most dramatic improvement the writer can make is also the easiest and fastest. It requires that when writers construct a sentence of significant length (three or more typed lines), they write it so that the main clause occurs before any subordinate clauses or phrases. What this means in simple terms is that the part of the sentence that can stand on its own should precede the part that cannot. This way, the reader will be able to secure a complete thought that will allow the rest of the sentence to be more readily understood. Below are three examples of sentences that are revised in this way. The first example in each case is in its original form; the second, in italics, has been revised to place the main clause first. Notice how much more immediately readable the revisions are.

> In order to incorporate a safety factor for future planning, and to remain consistent with capacity ratings used in other communities in the San Remalda region, the conservative values are used in this study.

> *The conservative values are used in this study to incorporate a safety factor for future planning, and to remain consistent with capacity ratings used in other communities in the San Remalda region.*

> Because the trip-generation rates do not take into account vehicles making more than one stop during the course of a single trip (for instance, a person driving from work to home stopping at the store or the bank), double-counted trips were removed.

> *Double-counted trips were removed because the trip-generation rates do not take into account vehicles making more than one stop during the course of a single trip (for instance, a person driving from work to home stopping at the store or the bank).*

> With the input data provided by Lantrans (i.e., freeway mainline and ramp volumes, existing lane configurations, and vehicle occupancy data), existing conditions were simulated.

> *Existing conditions were simulated with the input data provided by Lantrans (i.e., freeway mainline and ramp volumes, existing lane configurations, and vehicle occupancy data).*

In each of the revisions, the core sense of the sentence is immediately understood, and in each case, revision on a word processor took *fewer than ten seconds*. Nevertheless, most writers would not make these changes unless they were made aware of this problem. Their original versions would probably look fine to them. Even during their revisions, writers will enter the sentence *already knowing* at least the sense of the forthcoming main clause. For example, the *writer* who starts to read the last sentence already knows that "existing conditions were simulated." Of course, the *reader* has no way of knowing this. The reader will have to wait until the end of the sentence and then return to the beginning for complete sense. When this happens, the reader will be forced to edit for the writer.

The examples above show the problems that can result from placing the main clause last. Nevertheless, some have argued for the rhetorical effectiveness of this sentence form, once called the "periodic" sentence because the main clause is offered just before the period. The argument is based on the way in which the sentence delays the reader's ability to understand until the final clause is produced. When the final clause appears, the argument goes, the reader will be especially impressed by its content and more compelled to pay attention to it. The problem with this argument is that it assumes the reader is patient and willing to juggle ideas until the writer is ready to make sense of them.[2]

■ Active and Passive Constructions

Active constructions are those in which the sentence presents the subject first, followed by verb, followed by the object. In active constructions, the subject acts on the object. For example, "Norman fired the assistant" is active because "Norman" is the subject, "fired" is the verb, and "assistant" is the object. In this sentence, Norman "acts" on the object, his assistant. In its passive form, the sentence becomes "The assistant was fired by Norman." Norman is still acting on the assistant, but the assistant is presented first.

Both active and passive constructions are available to writers, even though the basic textbook advice is overwhelmingly against using passive constructions. Computer programs, in particular, have taken a strong stand against passives, perhaps because identifying them is one of the few text operations these programs can reliably perform. Nevertheless, no rule of grammar or usage prohibits writers from using the passive construction. The best policy here is to choose wisely when to do so.

Choosing wisely requires understanding the strengths of each construction. The two sentences below will illustrate the commonly inherent advantages of the active construction over the passive. Each active construction, in italics, is preceded by its original, passive version.

Four-hour traffic counts were conducted by the client and Traffic Monitoring Service at several locations in this study area.

The client and Traffic Monitoring Service conducted four-hour traffic counts at several locations in this study area.

Few traffic or parking needs would be generated by the Eugene Office if it were closed, as planned, on Saturdays and Sundays.

If it were closed as planned, on Saturdays and Sundays, the Eugene Office would generate few traffic or parking needs.

If the revisions are more readable, they are so because no advantage was to be gained from subordinating the subject of the sentence in the original (in the first, "The client and Traffic Monitoring Service"; in the second, "the Eugene Office"). Most of the time, this will be the case, and writers will probably do well to try to write primarily in the active, particularly when they want to emphasize the subjects of their sentences.

However, no rule governs the use of passive and active constructions, and some sentences will call for passive expression, either because the writer will want to emphasize the object of the sentence, subordinate the subject, or take advantage of the placement of the subject, all of which are illustrated by the following example:[3]

Additional recommendations were made by the San Remalda Study Advisory Committee, which includes representatives from Lantrans, Wemberly County, and the AAGA member cities.

Here, the fact that "additional recommendations" were made is presumably more important than the committee that made them, and the dependent clause that begins with "which" is able to modify the subject, "the San Remalda Study Advisory Committee" because the passive places the subject next to the clause. While this last point might have been possible in an active construction, it probably would strike the reader as awkward and difficult to read. So, while passive constructions are permissible, they will probably be exceptions to a more effective, predominantly active style.

▨ Placement of Subjects and Verbs

Keeping the subject and verb close together is another way to insure readability through word order because the two combined provide the core sense of the sentence. If writers prefer active constructions in general, it will help with this because the logical subject and verb will at least be stated. However, this does not mean that the subject and verb will fall into any naturally effective or even readable order. That is still the writer's responsibility. For example, the subject and verb, which are italicized below, are in a sentence that is both active and ineffective:

Our day *foreman*, after taking enough abuse from Bill Smith, the new project supervisor, finally *filed* the complaint.

This could be revised in at least two ways to bring the subject and verb closer together. Note that only the word order is changed:

> Our day *foreman* finally *filed* the complaint after taking enough abuse from Bill Smith, the new project supervisor.

> After taking enough abuse from Bill Smith, the new project supervisor, our day *foreman* finally *filed* the complaint.

▪ Introductory Modifiers

If the subject and verb are closely linked, the sentence is framed, and the writer can then check for the next feature of clear word order: modifiers that occur either at the beginning of the sentence or at the end. The ones that occur at the beginning are sometimes called "dangling modifiers" when they are not carefully managed, and they are a common problem in word order. To avoid these, writers will want to be sure the phrases that open many of their sentences are modifying the first noun in those sentences.

This rule is one of many that make very good sense. Because the reader will attach meaning to the first noun anyway, the rule simply makes this an understanding shared by writers and readers alike. The three sentences below are correct because each introductory expression modifies the first noun that follows. Notice that the reader cannot make sense of the sentence until that noun is provided. Notice also that each introductory expression is followed by a comma.

> Flying to New Mexico, the foreman had a chance to think about what he would say at the mines.

> To understand this industry, people should read *The Bechtel Story*.

> In the training session, new employees had many questions.

"Flying to New Mexico," modifies "foreman"; "To understand this industry" modifies "people"; and "In the training session" modifies "new employees." By being careful to have the introductory material modify the noun, writers can avoid problems similar to those in the sentences below.

> Having worked hard at Comdex, a vacation from everything technological seemed in order.

> To resolve the conflict, the software manual must be read carefully.

> In reprimanding staff members, great concern should be demonstrated for future working relationships.

The problems here should be apparent: a vacation can't have worked hard at Comdex; the software manual can't resolve the conflict (only the user can); and great concern can't reprimand staff members. Because the modifiers do not modify these words, they may be characterized as "dangling" without words to modify. However, revision is easy once the writer decides to follow the rule:

> Having worked hard at Comdex, Johnson felt he needed a vacation from everything technological.

> To resolve the conflict, you need to read the software manual carefully.

> In reprimanding staff members, supervisors should be greatly concerned about future working relationships.

The importance of following this rule can be demonstrated by the consequences of not adhering to it. The sentence that follows attempts to describe something about managerial competence and drug problems at work:

> With a serious personal drug problem, only a competent manager will be able to give sensible advice.

By not following the rule, the writer has seriously distorted the very thing he is attempting to describe. Not only has the agent of the problem been omitted from the sentence, but the agent of solution has been mischaracterized as having the problem.

■ Concluding Modifiers

Just as introductory information can cause problems if the first noun that follows is not the right one, so concluding information will cause trouble if the noun that most closely precedes it is not the right one. Most often these concluding modifiers will take the form of "which" or "that" clauses. The following two examples are correct because the information in each sentence modifies the respective nouns "Pennsylvania" and "printer":

> Our trainers occasionally visit Pennsylvania, which is freezing in December.

> They appreciate having the new printer that has the expanded paper capacity.

Writers who make mistakes here can easily produce sentences in which the word that should be modified is either the wrong one or is not present at all. For example, the writer of the following was attempting to describe a worker who returned from sick leave only to rerupture a hernia by lifting a toolbox:

> The worker picked up the heavy tool kit, which required further hospitalization.

This should be rewritten to avoid the implication that the tool kit is going to the hospital:

By picking up the heavy tool kit, the worker required further hospitalization.

The sentence below shows how nonsensical a sentence with this error can become. Unfortunately, the nonsense is at the writer's expense:

His death leaves a void in the community which will be hard to replace.[4]

■ Misplaced Modifiers

Unlike the introductory and concluding modifiers in the previous section, misplaced modifiers always modify some word in the sentence, and that word is always the wrong one. Writers can avoid these if they remember that much of what makes word order effective is really a matter of proximity or placing certain words next to certain other words. In this way, modification is allowed to work, not simply for the writer, who presumably knows the sense of the sentence, but for the reader, who may or may not.

Examples of misplaced modifiers abound and contribute to the amusement of many readers. For example, the sign that says "All items not on sale" says that nothing is on sale, a notion that is silly for someone to advertise. Placing the modifier next to the words it modifies produces "Not all items on sale." Although less amusing or odd, this sentence is much clearer.

Several commonly misplaced modifiers are worth special mention not only because of their frequency but also because of their importance. The first is the word "only." It is often misplaced, and it will dramatically change the writer's meaning depending upon its placement in the sentence. Once the problems with this misplaced modifier are apparent, others will be noticed more readily.

Only we need to count the number of cars at this intersection.

We *only* need to count the number of cars at this intersection.

We need to count *only* the number of cars at this intersection.

We need to count the number of cars *only* at this intersection.

The first sentence restricts people; the second, requirement; the third, number of cars; and the fourth, the number of intersections.

Related to "only" are two other commonly misplaced modifiers: "even" and "nearly." Notice how the meanings of the sentences change when the words are reordered:

The speech even bothered seasoned managers (i.e., it bothered as well as dismayed them, challenged them, etc.)

The speech bothered even seasoned managers (i.e., it bothered seasoned managers as well as others).

The chairman nearly fired seven vice presidents.

The chairman fired nearly seven vice presidents.

In the third sentence above, the chairman almost fired seven vice presidents, but he didn't quite fire any. In the fourth, he fired almost all of them but not quite. Writers who are unclear about where to place these modifiers will probably be misunderstood.

Another commonly misplaced modifier is "however," an important word used to signal correction or change. Most writers use this word, but not all place it where it will make the most sense to readers. The following are common misplacements:

It is important for him to know, however, that his division and his department are favored by our laboratory.

A.R.M. will record volunteer injuries within a special classification code and publish this on a periodic basis, however.

Note that "however" does not correct anything in the first sentence. We might find, if we could read the sentence in context, that it corrects something that came before it. If it doesn't, a much bigger problem exists. The same is true in greater extreme with the second sentence, which offers the correction at the very end. In each case, the "however" ought to be placed at the *beginning* of the sentence, and that is where it ought to go in most sentences. The only exception is where the word actually corrects within the sentence; however, that does not happen often.

The final commonly misplaced modifier represents the entire group of words we call adverbs. Words like "regularly," "monthly," "quickly," and "fairly" describe manner or frequency, how or how often something is done. These words modify verbs, among other things, but nothing insures that they will be placed near the verb they modify. For example, the following sentence places the adverb "enthusiastically" away from the verb "endorse":

We will want to endorse their new upgrade enthusiastically.

The sentence above may not cause the reader great distress, but such practice can easily lead to a sentence that can:

We will want to endorse their new spreadsheet upgrade enthusiastically.

or

We will want to endorse the Windows version of their new spreadsheet upgrade enthusiastically.

By keeping the verbs and adverbs close, the writer will be able to avoid both awkwardness and misreading:

We will want to endorse enthusiastically the Windows version of their new spreadsheet upgrade.

The danger of a misreading is stronger when a sentence has more than one verb because adverbs can modify many different verbs:

We should process requests when the member makes them quickly.

The adverb "quickly" *can* modify either "process" or "makes." It *will* modify the verb it is nearest. If the writer had in mind quick processing, the sentence should have been revised to say:

We should quickly process requests when the member makes them.

RELATED READINGS

Word choice, or syntax, is usually treated as part of a larger concern in composition. For that reason, only a few book-length treatments of it are available. However, the works below either give unusually lengthy attention to the role of syntax in effective writing or offer an especially effective treatment of it as a topic of composition.

Cook, Claire Kehrwald. *Line by Line: How to Edit Your Own Writing*. Boston: Houghton Mifflin, 1985.

Lanham, Richard. *Revising Business Prose*. 3d ed. New York: Macmillan, 1992. Word order is considered as part of a practical system of editing.

Olson, Gary A. *Style and Readability in Business Writing*. New York: Random House, 1985.

Smith, Charles K. *Styles and Structures: Alternative Approaches to College Writing*. New York: Norton, 1974.

White, Edward M. *The Writer's Control of Tone*. New York: Norton, 1970.

Williams, Joseph M. *Style: Ten Lessons in Clarity and Grace*. 2d ed. Glenview, IL: Scott, Foresman, 1985.

NOTES

1. A number of writers have attempted to make a case for the importance of word order in business writing. See, for one, Louis Foley, "For Smooth Word-Order and Easy Transition," *The ABCA Bulletin*. 33, no. 2 (September 1987): 26–40. For an interesting study of how word

order, among other stylistic concerns, might affect readers, see Stanley Fish, "Affective Stylistics," in *Self-Consuming Artifacts* (New York: Wiley, 1979).

2. For an opposing view on periodic sentences, see Harriet Tichy, *Effective Writing for Engineers, Managers, Scientists* (New York: Wiley, 1966), 246–47.

3. Although passives are not prohibited by any rule of usage, they appear to be just that by "default" in the growing world of computer-assisted text analyzers. Both of the two major programs, *Grammatik V* (Reference software) and *Rightwriter 4.0* (Rightsoft), continue to flag passives as errors. For an interesting and recent study of these programs, see Richard Mende, "Grammatic 5 for Windows: Random Thoughts from a White, Male, Middle-Class German Canadian," *The ABCA Bulletin.* 57, no. 3 (September 1994): 9–11.

4. Quoted in Richard Lederer, *Anguished English* (Charleston, SC: Wyrick, 1987), 54.

MANAGING ETHOS 11

Punctuation

My attitude toward punctuation is that it ought to be as conventional as possible. *The game of golf would lose a good deal if croquet mallets and billiard cues were allowed on the putting green. You ought to be able to show that you can do it a good deal better than anyone else with the regular tools before you have a license to bring in your own improvements.*

—Ernest Hemingway, *Selected Letters*

Punctuation is an area of writing that is not always taken seriously, even by those who are experts on it. It is not a particularly glamorous or even interesting part of composition. No debates rage over it. No journals devote much attention to it. No working professionals spend their time wishing they could master it. In short, it is usually treated in the way Harry Shaw suggests in his foreword to one of the few book-length treatments of modern punctuation:

> Punctuation and spelling apparently cause more people more trouble than any other aspect of writing with the possible exception of what is loosely known as "grammar." Both are somewhat mechanical and superficial phases of writing, not nearly so important as having something significant to say and a genuine interest in saying that something, whatever it is.[1]

Yes, punctuation does cause people trouble. And it is mechanical. However, it is not superficial. Effective punctuation powerfully affects what the writer says, and questions about punctuation are almost always questions about the writer's meaning.

Effective punctuation also contributes to the writer's construction of ethos in several ways. First, it promotes the clarity of the writer's ideas, and this will help to show that the writer is in control of the material and able to communicate. Second, it demonstrates that the writer is familiar with literary conventions taught as part of a formal education. Third, it shows that the writer is willing to follow these conventions, as one might follow other conventions in our society, in the interest of providing the reader with shared meaning.

Unlike other areas of editing, such as conciseness, much of punctuation is governed by rules, good rules. Ignoring them will lead to two consequences, neither of them good. First, writing that is not properly punctuated can easily make the writer appear careless or uneducated. Whether the writer is, is another matter, but the reader's most compelling and available evidence is the text itself. Second, poor punctuation can easily cause misreadings, which will frustrate and annoy the reader even under the best circumstances. The reader will often be able to puzzle through a misreading, but no reader has reported enjoying it.

With both of these problems, the writer either leaves the reader helplessly confused or in a position to select one meaning, perhaps the very one that makes the writer look the worst, from the several meanings that poor punctuation has made possible. Writers will do well to remember that both problems—impressions of carelessness and misreadings—will compete directly for the reader's attention. The writer who wishes to compete against them will do so most effectively by removing them entirely. Becoming familiar with the rules will help writers do just that.

Familiarity with the rules of punctuation becomes much easier when writers can free themselves from a pervasive myth about punctuation and editorial technique in general: that the sound and rhythm of the voice should serve as the writer's best guide to proper punctuation. No standard for sound exists in usage manuals or dictionaries. No general or even particular agreement exists on what sounds might translate into what kind of punctuation. Consequently, writers who punctuate according to what they believe are the "natural" pauses of their voices can produce nonsense just as easily as sense. If, in fact, writers seriously take sound as a guideline, then they must be prepared for the absurd, such as a sentence that has a comma after every word because the writer has the hiccups or is hyperventilating at the keyboard. The safest and most sensible approach to proper punctuation requires knowing the rules.

Although writers should know the rules and avoid sound as a guideline for punctuation, they will still benefit from thinking about punctuation in other than literary terms. Two analogies to matters outside of writing are particularly useful. Each should help writers think productively about punctuation, not simply as a set of rules but as a system of sensible and familiar principles.

The first analogy compares punctuation and nonverbal communication. Here writers are asked to think about the nonverbal signs that help us to understand messages in interpersonal exchanges. We certainly use words to communicate our ideas in conversations, but we also rely heavily on signals that have little to do with our words. We might smile, frown, gasp, lean forward or backward, roll our eyes toward the ceiling, or maintain a constant gaze. Although those who study these extraverbal signs do not always agree on their specific meanings, few would dispute that they powerfully influence how the speaker's words are understood by another.[2] Similarly, punctuation affects the way readers interpret the writer's meaning in sentences. For example, the speaker of the following sentence appears to be asking one simple question:

Are you driving into San Francisco this afternoon?

The listener might be tempted to answer "No, I am not." However, that answer assumes that the question was asked in a monotone. As soon as the speaker provides emphasis, either through volume of voice or gesture, perhaps by pointing, the meaning of the question changes. The only way the writer can represent this is through punctuation or additional words.

Are *you* driving into San Francisco this afternoon?

This is the punctuated equivalent of "Are you and not somebody else driving to San Francisco this afternoon?" Of course, depending on the speaker's or writer's intended meaning, the voice emphasis or italics will change:

Are *you* driving into San Francisco this afternoon?

Are you *driving* into San Francisco this afternoon?

Are you driving into *San Francisco* this afternoon?

Are you driving into San Francisco *this* afternoon?

Are you driving into San Francisco this *afternoon*?

Reading these orally will help to demonstrate the differences among them. In each case, the question is different, and in each case, the listener or speaker may give a different answer. This does not mean that writers should punctuate according to the emphasis they would provide if they were speaking the sentence. It means only that the analogy to nonverbal communication is a useful way to think about punctuation, as a method of clarifying the meaning of written words.

The second analogy compares punctuation and directional markers. This analogy makes particularly good sense because both are systems of agreed-upon signs, and both work well when the agreement is observed in practice. One writer has even suggested a direct analogy between punctuation and specific traffic signs.[3] The "stop" sign, as a mark of termination, is thus comparable to periods, exclamation marks, and question marks. The "slow" sign is comparable to commas, semicolons, and colons. And the "detour" sign suggests redirection of the type indicated by double dashes, parentheses, and brackets. What is important about this analogy is not how similar punctuation and traffic signs really are, but that both direct the movement of others in ways that are predictable if everyone agrees to their meaning. In this sense, a stop sign and a period work in the same way. The driver and reader will both stop: the first because it insures safety; the second because it insures clarity. Not following the signs in either case usually gets one into trouble.

The following rules of punctuation will help writers to avoid trouble. In each case, the rule is described, explained, and applied. For reasons mentioned earlier in this book, these rules are not exhaustive. However, they are representative of the kinds of practical problems working professionals encounter with punctuation. For additional and exhaustive treatments, the reader may want to review some of the materials listed at the end of this chapter.

■ Commas and Introductory Clauses

Introductory clauses and phrases require a comma to separate them from the main clause of the sentence. This is a longstanding rule, and it is an important one. Not paying attention to it can easily result in confusion because the reader will have no way to separate the information in the main clause from the information that introduces it. However, because this confusion is usually not evident to the writer, who has a privileged sense of the sentence's meaning, the importance of the comma can easily be overlooked. Sometimes, even the reader may not notice its absence:

> To determine the traffic volumes we used the trip-generation rates in Table B.

> In this analysis we have reached the following conclusions and findings.

If readers objected to these sentences, they would probably report only a minor awkwardness in the sense and not any pronounced confusion. However, the following sentence is another matter:

> As you pointed out in a few instances failures were due to environmental testing.

The reader can guess but has no way of being sure what the writer intends here. Inserting a comma after "out" will produce one meaning; inserting one after "instances" will produce another. Of course, the reader might place commas after each of these words, but that would only restore the sentence to its original ambiguity. Note that with each guess, the reader is attempting something only the writer can do successfully because only the writer knows what the sentence should say.

Running introductory information into the main clause does not always produce this kind of extreme confusion, but it will often produce a misreading. Each of the following sentences invites misreadings because the writer has omitted this comma:

> In response to this request Persoft is making available a professional team for on-site lectures.

> When you have finally identified the alternative request a review of it by the managers.

Sometimes these misreadings cause amusement at the writer's expense. For example, the writer of the following sentence probably did not mean to suggest that the diner is a cannibal:

If you are now ready to eat the host can seat you.

All of these problems can be avoided simply by placing the comma after the introductory material. This will also help to avoid similar problems with introductory phrases, though here the rule is less agreed on. Some authorities allow the writer to determine whether a comma is needed if the introduction to the sentence is in the form of a phrase instead of a clause.[4] However, even a phrase can cause trouble, and the writer who routinely punctuates these sentence openings will greatly reduce the risk of producing the following kind of sentence:

To date employees have been satisfied with the program.

Notice that the *opposite* is usually true when the introductory material is no longer introductory but follows the main clause. For example, if the sentence above were revised to place the main clause first, it would *not* take a comma:

Employees have been satisfied with the program to date.

■ Commas and Compound Sentences

Writers should punctuate compound sentences for the same reason they punctuate introductory clauses and phrases: to avoid combining separate ideas. Compound sentences have two or more independent clauses. These clauses are joined by one of only seven conjunctions that are called "coordinating": "and," "but," "or," "nor," "for," "so," and "yet." Determining whether a sentence is compound is easy. Simply strike the conjunction and ask whether the remaining words can stand on their own as two complete sentences. For example, the following is a compound sentence. The conjunction is "and."

The openings on top of the tanks permit easy access to the gasoline supplies, and gasoline removed through these openings will not be recorded on the meters.

The comma before the "and" is required for a very good reason. Without it, the object of the first clause and the subject of the second would be joined. Although compound sentences do join ideas, they do not join these. For a compound sentence to make sense, its two halves need to be clearly separate. The sentences below will show what happens when they are not. In each case, a comma should be inserted before the coordinating conjunction.

Tax and internal audit will benefit since they will receive more accurate data and many of the cumbersome old manual procedures required to process information will thereby be limited.

Each of you should be prepared to spend no more than one-half hour discussing your area and handouts outlining your presentation are strongly encouraged.

The review remarked on the poor performance of the film graphics department and its new chairman has agreed to correct it even though he was not responsible.

The last sentence is a particularly good example of what happens when a comma is not used to separate the halves of the sentence. Without the comma, the chairman is grouped with the poor performance of the graphics department.

■ Commas and Series

Writers punctuate a series for the same reason they punctuate introductory clauses and compound sentences. Punctuating a series communicates to the reader which ideas go with others. A series is often introduced by a colon, though sometimes it will occur without any introductory punctuation. Here is an example before the series is punctuated:

> Let's be certain that the budget is sufficient for training facility rental and educational materials.

Almost everyone can see the need for punctuation here, once the writer explains that "training facility rental" is not one unit. Here it is again but now expressing not just the writer's ideas but also the way the writer intends them to be grouped:

> Let's be certain that the budget is sufficient for training, facility rental, and educational materials.

In this version, all items are separated so that "training," "facility rental," and "educational materials" receive equal attention. This is the standard punctuation for a series unless the writer wants to communicate that some items in the series are to stand with others. For example, if budget dollars go into a separate account for training (services) but into the same account for facility rental and educational materials (physical resources), then the writer might want to group the last two by omitting the final comma:

> Let's be certain that the budget is sufficient for training, facility rental and educational materials.

Although one would never use parentheses to group these, it is a good device to understand the grouping in the sentence above:

> Let's be certain that the budget is sufficient for (training) (facility rental and educational materials).

The comma or lack of it before the last item is not optional. It is called for or not by the sense the writer is trying to make. However, if the writer does use it, the "and" *is* optional, though writers will want to be consistent from sentence to sentence.

■ Commas and Restrictive Clauses

Of all rules of punctuation, this one is the most difficult to explain and understand; consequently, it is the most difficult to apply. Unfortunately, it is also the one that most dramatically affects the meaning of a sentence. Without an understanding of the writer's intention, an editor has about a 50 percent chance of properly punctuating a sentence that is a candidate. This will become evident from the sentence below. Let us say that we know the writer, and the writer intends to say that *all* of the trainers are familiar with interactive video.

Example A

Our trainers, who are familiar with interactive video, should be able to help you with program design.

This sentence is nonrestrictive because the subject, "trainers," is not *restricted* only to those "who are familiar with interactive video." If it were, then the commas (*both* of them) would be removed, and the sentence would appear:

Example B

Our trainers who are familiar with interactive video should be able to help you with program design.

The sentence now *restricts* the meaning of trainers to those who are familiar with interactive video. This is important, of course, because the change in meaning is significant. In example A, *all* of the trainers are familiar with interactive video; in sentence B, only *some* of them are.

One way to test for restriction (assuming the intended meaning is known) is to ask whether the information that follows the subject is necessary to understand the sentence or whether it might be omitted without any serious misunderstanding. For example, the following sentence should be relatively easy to edit:

A floppy diskette, which has had coffee spilled on it, should not be inserted into a drive.

Most editors would say that the commas need to be removed here simply because leaving them would produce nonsense. For the sentence to make sense, then, the clause would have to be restrictive. Otherwise, it would have this meaning:

> A floppy diskette should not be inserted into a drive.

This makes no sense or at least the sense it makes is paradoxical. Therefore, to convey the meaning in the way the writer intended, the sentence would have to be:

> A floppy diskette that has had coffee spilled on it should not be inserted into a drive.

Note the use of the word "that," the relative pronoun used to signal restrictive clauses. This sentence means that a "floppy diskette" *of the kind that is contaminated by coffee* should not be inserted into a drive. The opposite would be true of the following sentence:

> A floppy diskette, which is included free, can be used to back up your data.

The commas are appropriate here because the information the reader gets from "which is included free" is not necessary to identify the floppy disk the writer is talking about. To use a contemporary expression, we can say that this information is provided because it is "nice to know" and not because it is "needed to know."

■ Semicolons

Writers who understand the rules governing commas are better prepared to use other marks of punctuation and to see these marks as options for expression. The semicolon in particular serves the writer well when revising compound sentences. It may take the place of both the comma and the conjunction in the compound sentence. For example, instead of writing

> She reprimanded the vendor, and her boss supported her fully.

the writer may say

> She reprimanded the vendor; her boss supported her fully.

 The semicolon thus takes the place of the comma and the coordinating conjunction, and this is one of its functions: *to separate independent clauses in a compound sentence*. However, the writer should be careful here to supply the appropriate transition word so the connection between the clauses will be apparent to the reader. For example, the writer might have in mind any one of the following:

> She reprimanded the vendor; nevertheless, her boss supported her fully.

> She reprimanded the vendor; happily, her boss supported her fully.

She reprimanded the vendor; however, her boss supported her fully.

She reprimanded the vendor; fortunately, her boss supported her fully.

Each one of these conveys important information that the original could not convey with the semicolon alone.

A semicolon has another function: to separate items in a series if those items have commas within them or if they are lengthy enough to require more separation than a comma can provide. Writers using semicolons in this way may think of them as marks that provide greater division than commas. For example:

> Your contact people are Michael Carroll, president; Derrel Triplett, vice president; Mary Williams, treasurer; and Tim Conley, secretary.

Although this information could probably be presented with commas only, the semicolons help the commas do their work and lend additional separation to names and positions. In more complex lists, where the items listed are more varied, the semicolon would be essential. For example, readers will have difficulty understanding this sentence without its semicolons:

> Your contact people are Michael Carroll, who will serve as the project principal; Derrel Triplett, engineering consultant for AMCO; Mary Williams, our CAD expert; and Tim Conley, whose former company still does business with Delco.

■ Colons

after a noun   *list of 3 or more*

Sometimes sentences promise additional information in the form of enumeration, explanation, or illustration. Colons serve to "make good" on this promise by introducing the information. The following are good examples of each promise:

> When you go to Comdex, make sure you visit the following booths: Borland, Lotus, Wordperfect, and Symantec.
>
> *, or semi colon*
>
> I hope you will understand the reason we refused your application: you bounced ten checks in the last ten days and you are wanted in six different states.
>
> Everyone who wants to submit vouchers should do so according to our three-step process: first, fill out the form; second, get the proper signature; third, turn it in.

The colon is one of the easier marks to work with. Nevertheless, two cautions are worth keeping in mind. Writers should avoid using the colon to separate prepositions and their objects. Similarly, they should not use the colon to divide a verb from its object. Here are examples of what to avoid:

after a complete thought

I am very interested in: participative management, the global economy, and small business planning. *[preposition]*

Our supervisor likes to see: people in their offices, working lunches, and teams meeting after hours.

Neither sentence requires a colon or any other mark of punctuation in place of the colon. Note that in addition to being unnecessary, the colons above interrupt ideas that the grammatical parts of the sentence are attempting to connect.

▪ Quotation Marks

When working with quotation marks, writers need to remember that conventions govern their combination with other marks of punctuation. In the United States, the following holds: periods and commas always go *inside* quotation marks; semicolons and colons go *outside* the quotations; question marks (also exclamation marks and dashes) go *outside* the quotation marks unless they are part of the quotation.[5] The following are examples:

3 rules —

Periods and Commas—Place Inside PCI

His performance was rated "far exceeds," but his first supervisor rated it only "very good."

The advertisement for our product states, "Our diet bread has fewer calories per slice." The word "diet," which is vague here, has caused us problems.

Colons and Semicolons—Place Outside LSO

Take a look at the following topics in "Policy and Procedures": EEO, Affirmative Action, and Comparable Worth.

They asked us to read the section "Escape Codes"; after we did, though, we were more confused than we had been before.

Question Marks—Place by Meaning QM

Did the chairman really say, "We need to finish reorganizing before hiring even one contract consultant"? Or did he ask, "What do we need to do before we can hire contract consultants?"

▪ Dashes *—sparingly & only for dramatics / can be substituted for other proper punctuation*

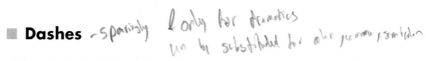

Although the dash is used routinely in business writing, most authorities on punctuation have advised that it should be used sparingly and with an understanding that it can always be replaced with another, often more expressive mark. This advice makes some sense when one considers that dashes are often used to indicate an interruption of thought. Instead, the authorities suggest, look for ways to work this material into the sentence proper. Still, the dash does have its uses, primarily as a more dramatic application of other marks. For example, here it is used in place of a colon:

Although he was careful to conceal it, only one thing interested him—profits.

The delay here is probably worth using the dash that produces it. However, if the writer cannot substitute for the dash either a period, a comma, or a colon, then the dash should probably be reconsidered. This will prevent writers from using dashes to string only loosely associated thoughts:

We need to consider upgrading here—later on we will have much more trouble—so now is the time to do it.

The writer will do better to say:

We need to consider upgrading now; if we don't, we will have much more trouble later.

■ Punctuation and Numbers

what is accepted?

Writers who must present numbers sometimes wonder whether numerical or alphabetical expressions are appropriate. Although agreement on this particular convention is far from universal, some reliable guidelines exist, and the authorities generally agree on at least three helpful points. First, writers should never begin a sentence with a numerical expression. Second, they should use words for numbers between (and including) one and ninety-nine. Third, they should use numbers for words above ninety-nine. The sentences below follow these guidelines.[6]

Seventy-five dollars is the amount you owe each of the participants. *3 rules*

The total for these components is twenty-five dollars.

We have been able to place 265 technicians this quarter alone.

RELATED READINGS

The reader may want to pay particular attention to two publications below: *The Chicago Manual of Style* and *Style Manual of the United States Government Printing Office*. In matters of dispute, agreement between these two authorities may be used to persuade with success. Other sources below provide a sometimes less authoritative but broader range of readings on the subject of punctuation.

Ball, Alice Morton. *The Compounding and Hyphenation of English Words.* New York: Funk & Wagnalls, 1951.

Collins, F. Howard. *Authors' and Printers' Dictionary.* 10th ed. London: Oxford University Press, 1956.

The Chicago Manual of Style. 14th ed. Chicago: The University of Chicago Press, 1993.

Nurnberg, Maxwell. *Questions You Always Wanted to Ask about English.* New York: Simon & Schuster, 1972.

The MLA Style Sheet. Revised edition. New York: The Modern Language Association of America, 1970.

The New York Times Style Book. Edited and revised by Lewis Jordan. New York: McGraw-Hill Book Company, 1976.

Shaw, Harry. *Punctuate It Right!* 2d. ed. New York: Harper Perennial, 1994.

Skillin, Marjorie, et al. *Words into Type.* 3d ed. Englewood Cliffs, NJ: Prentice-Hall, 1974.

Style Manual of the United States Government Printing Office. Revised edition. Washington, D.C.: U.S. Government Printing Office, 1984.

NOTES

1. Harry Shaw, *Punctuate It Right!* (New York: Harper & Row, 1963), xi.

2. For an extended discussion of this, see Loretta A. Malandro and Larry Barker, *Nonverbal Communication* (New York: Addison-Wesley, 1983), 6–10.

3. Maxwell Nurnberg, *Questions You Always Wanted to Ask about English* (New York: Simon & Schuster, 1972), 168–241.

4. For the more liberal approach that is argued against here, see *The Associated Press Stylebook and Libel Manual,* ed. Norman Goldstein (New York: Addison-Wesley, 1992), 266–74.

5. In two cases will the writer put the period or comma goes *outside* the quotation marks: with alphabetical figures and with in-text citations. Here is an example of the first: The new font causes problems with the letter "L", but they were very happy with the "M". Here is an example of the second: Melville begins *Moby Dick* with the sentence "Call me Ishmael" (11).

6. For a complete discussion of numbers in text and a comment on the difficulty of providing reliable guidelines, see *The Chicago Manual of Style,* 14th ed. (Chicago: The University of Chicago Press, 1993), 294–312.

MANAGING ETHOS 12

Grammar

This category of editing often elicits groans and winces from business writers because it summons images of painful schoolroom exercises, unreasonable entrance examinations, and other unpleasant academic events that many would like to forget. It also elicits groans and winces from business readers because writing that is grammatically incorrect will cause misreadings, misunderstandings, and embarrassment. Of course, these problems will interfere with the writer's attempts at engaging and maintaining the readers' attention. Grammatical problems present readers with a form of competition that is similar to noise on an audio recording: just as one competes for the listener's attention to the music, so the other competes for the reader's attention to the message. Fortunately, grammar is a relatively simple matter, at least to the extent that it is primarily concerned with the formation and agreement of words. It is also an important matter, with strong implications for establishing an ethos of credibility and professionalism.[1]

Although writers can inspect their writing for correct grammar at any time during composition, they will probably do well to wait until they have edited for conciseness, word choice, word order, and punctuation. Checking for grammatical problems earlier than this can easily result in a wasted effort, in correcting expressions that will either be deleted, reordered, or substituted. However, once these matters have been settled, writers are ready to turn their attention to grammar, and to the practical points that follow.

■ Subject and Verb Agreement

Readers expect consistency and care in the writing they read. They expect writers to be consistent with matters of meaning and careful about changing meaning without cause. Because of this, writers who violate rules of agreement appear to their readers in a variety of unflattering ways—as uneducated, uncaring, or unable, to name only a few.

Happily, the principle behind grammatical agreement is easy enough to understand, although it is violated in practice even by the most careful writers. The principal rule of agreement requires a match between associated words. For example, the first sample sentence below shows normal agreement between the subject and verb of a sentence. Meaning does not change here because the subject remains plural throughout the sentence.

Several fingers are required for the signal.

111 ...   111 ... *[main] subject [verb] are in agreement*

Several fingers   are   *both are singular or plural*

When agreement is violated, the sentence appears in this way:

Several fingers is required for the signal.

111 ...   1

Several fingers   is

The sentence above is offered as an obvious example of disagreement, one that most writers would be able to avoid. However, it is useful because it shows two things: first, the reader's impression of the number of fingers changes as the sentence progresses; second, the reader's confusion (one or more fingers?) cannot be resolved by the sentence. To prevent this experience for the reader, the writer will need to make sure that associated parts of the sentence agree. This does not happen in the sentences below. They represent less obvious but more common examples of this grammatical problem. Corrected sentences follow the example and contain subjects and verbs in italics.

[is = singular are = plural]

The overcrossings in that area is a concern to us all.

The tables on the next page indicates that the city needs to study the matter.

An understanding of the data file copy commands are not required to operate this confidently.

The funding for these two programs have not been increased for a number of years.

The *overcrossings* in that area *are* a concern to us all.

The *tables* on the next page *indicate* that the city needs to study the matter.

An *understanding* of the data file copy commands *is* not required to operate this confidently.

The *funding* for these two programs *has* not been increased for a number of years.

Most writers will notice the problems in the original sentences, and they will probably have little trouble making the corrections above. However, fewer writers will notice that all of these problems result from the same error: the writer tries to force agreement between the verb and the *closest noun* instead of between the verb and the *subject of the sentence*. The result is lack of agreement between the associated parts of the sentence. This is unfortunate because this grammatical problem prevents the reader from making the connections the writer would expect. It is also avoidable for those writers who take the time to review their writing. Repairing this grammatical error has little to do with skill, though it will require effort.

In fact, making such repairs will probably require considerable effort from everyone, particularly if Theodore Bernstein is correct. Bernstein was assistant manager of *The New York Times,* after which he became director of the New York Times Book Division. While at the *Times*, he was responsible for *W & S*, the bulletin *Winners & Sinners*. He said this about agreement between subjects and verbs:

> After some twenty years of lint picking, *W & S* is in a position to say the grammatical error that crops up most often is disagreement between subject and verb. This sort of thing: "More independence and initiative in agricultural planning was given today to the farmers. . . ." Or this sort: ". . . the Egyptian version of his remarks were published.[2]

■ Noun and Pronoun Agreement

Agreement between subjects and verbs is one of two major rules governing grammatical agreement. The other is agreement between nouns and pronouns. Just as verbs have to agree with their subjects, so do pronouns with their nouns. Although mistakes here may take many forms, the most common by far is lack of agreement between the subject form of the third-person plural ("they") and the singular noun it stands for:

> Our customer is the most important concern we should have. They are very important to us.

> Each partner should evaluate their performance in relation to their agreements.

Sometimes writers will make this mistake in their attempt to avoid problems with exclusive language, language that many believe discriminates on the basis of gender. This intention is well worth promoting. However, most writers can avoid the problem when it is caused by noun and pronoun agreement. For example, rewriting the sentence

> Each partner should evaluate their performance.

need not become

> Each partner should evaluate his performance.

One could just as easily cast the entire sentence into the plural, and this would produce a grammatically correct *and* rhetorically inclusive passage:

Partners should evaluate their performance.

Note that this also allows the writer to avoid the awkward "he/she" and "him/her" constructions. Most writers will be able to solve most problems of this type in this way.[3]

Agreement and Company Names

The two major agreement problems covered above should be easy enough to understand and correct: once writers see the difficulty that they create and become sensitive to these problems in their own writing, they should have no problem editing for them. However, other problems of agreement are less easy to grasp. For example, agreement involving company names may not make logical sense to many writers because it would appear to run counter to the principle of grammatical agreement. Nevertheless, *company names take singular verbs*, even though the companies themselves are made up of many people. This is true even if the company name appears plural:

[DeMartini and Associates] offer their services to California businesses that seek an alternative to conventional networks.

We have studied Johnson & Johnson and their management of the Tylenol problem.

Corrected, these sentences should read:

[DeMartini and Associates] offers its services to California businesses that seek an alternative to conventional networks.

We have studied Johnson & Johnson and its management of the Tylenol problem.

Agreement and Collective Nouns

The rule governing company names applies more generally to other collectives that are usually viewed as a unit. For example, nouns like "government," "administration," "public," "management," "committee," and "team" are all collective nouns and take a singular verb when they are viewed as singular units:

Some believe our government is responsible for national health care.

The public is an important source of information about this product.

The committee is willing to reconsider your submission.

By contrast, if the writer wishes to emphasize that individuals within these collections are functioning *as individuals*, then the collective noun will take a plural verb. The following sentences are technically correct, even though they will probably appear awkward to writers and readers alike:

Now that the session is over, the committee are all going their separate ways.

The orchestra are not cooperating with Maestro Maazel today.

After our representative finished speaking, she noticed that the audience were mixed in their reactions.

Of course, the writer who is concerned about this apparent awkwardness can always recast the sentences to show a more fully expressed plurality:

Now that the session is over, the committee members are all going their separate ways.

The musicians are not cooperating with Maestro Maazel today.

After our representative finished speaking, she noticed that the members of the audience were mixed in their reactions.

The writer has at least these options for presenting collective nouns. Yet whatever option appeals most, the writer should still feel obligated to be consistent. This means that a noun initially presented as plural cannot change later in the sentence:

The faculty here is very proud of the campus and especially proud of their library.

Although "faculty" can be presented as a singular or a plural, it should be presented consistently as one or the other.

▨ Agreement and Compound Subjects

The agreement of compound subjects is related to grammar and collective nouns because the writer again has to determine the number of agents and whether the verb will be plural or singular. However, the solution is easier here. All the writer needs to do is consider the joining word or words. For example, two or more subjects joined by "and" will take a plural verb:

The client and the vendor understand the need for updates.

Other joining expressions may appear to be interchangeable with "and," but they are not. These include "along with," "as well as," and "in addition to." Here, the rule is this: the main verb should agree with the subject of the sentence.

The user's manual, as well as the software, is kept in the sysop's office.

The manager, along with her staff members, is available.

The financial studies, in addition to their interpretation, are the subject of careful scrutiny.

◼ Agreement and Correlatives

Correlative conjunctions are those of the form "either . . . or" and "neither . . . nor." The agreement is made between the main verb and the part of the subject that is closest to it. In the first sentence below, the main verb is "considers" because "Nelson," the part of the subject that is closest, is singular. In the second sentence, the main verb is "consider" because "others" is plural. In the third sentence, the verb is "is" because "table" is singular.

Subject always closest to verb

Neither Stanley nor Nelson considers General Counsel's opinion to be appropriate.

Neither Stanley nor the others consider General Counsel's opinion to be appropriate.

Either the worksheet or the table is sufficient for the final calculation.

◼ Agreement and Problem Expressions

Other matters of agreement cause writers problems because one expression (e.g., "the number") may sound like another (e.g. "a number"), but each will take a different verb. Probably the best approach here is to remember the problem expressions and the rules that normally govern them. Here are the more popular expressions on the left and the rules that govern them on the right:

A number ~~of~~ *usually*	takes a ~~plural~~ verb
The number	takes a ~~singular~~ verb
None	takes a singular verb
Each	takes a singular verb
Everyone	takes a singular verb
Everybody	takes a singular verb
Nobody	takes a singular verb
Neither	takes a singular verb

Here are some examples of correct agreement:

> We are well aware that a number of variables have attracted his attention.
>
> Unfortunately, we have found that the number of variables increases with each passing hour.
>
> Are you saying that neither of these facilities is worth considering?

Case

Grammatical agreement involves insuring an appropriate "fit" between the word or words selected and other words and the sentence as a whole. Grammatical case also involves making an appropriate fit by determining which form of a word to use according to its function in the sentence. The cases that are available in English are subject (I), object (me), and possessive (mine).

An example of a common case problem is the three-letter combination "its." This word can take two grammatical forms: it can be a contraction, "it's," which means "it is," and it can be a possessive pronoun, "its," which means that it will own the noun that follows it. These two forms need to be kept distinct to avoid making the grammatical error. They also need to be kept separate to avoid an error in meaning.

> A very good management team acknowledges its superior.
>
> A very good management team acknowledges it's superior.

The difference between these sentences is this: one has an apostrophe and one doesn't. It is also this: the first sentence says that a good management team acknowledges a person who is superior to it; the second sentence says that a good management team acknowledges that it is superior. For this very reason, that the difference between the two is a difference in meaning, case is important to the careful writer.

Many other case problems also involve pronouns. For example, choosing the appropriate pronoun for the following comparisons involves a consideration of case:

> Everyone is aware that his supervisor is smarter than (he or him?). *finish the sentence*
>
> I am sorry that my client is more interested in discounts than (I or me?).
>
> You have already told us you like his manager better than (he or him?).
>
> My assistant works harder for her than (I or me?).
>
> You like off-site meetings more than (they or them?).

In some of the examples above, the word the writer chooses will be determined by the meaning the writer wants to express; in others, the writer will choose the word according to its required case. In the first sentence, the writer's only choice is to use "he," because completing the sentence with "him" would produce:

Everyone is aware that his supervisor is smarter than him is.

Few writers would allow this sentence to stand after it has been completed in this way, yet many would have no problem writing it in its incomplete form. For this reason, completing the sentence by including the second verb provides the best way to determine which word to use. This will work even with the second sentence in the group of sentences above, though its ambiguity could mean either of the following, and either would be grammatically correct:

I am sorry that my client is more interested in discounts than I.

I am sorry that my client is more interested in discounts than me.

Once they are completed, the sentences offer a clear choice of meanings.

I am sorry to say that my client is more interested in discounts than I am.

I am sorry to say that my client is more interested in discounts than she is in me.

Whether the writer chooses the first or the second depends entirely on the meaning the writer wants to convey to the reader. Because the intended meaning will be communicated by the appropriate case, the table of pronouns introduced earlier, in the chapter on word choice, may be worth recalling here:

Singular Subject	*Singular Object*
I	Me
You	You
He/She/It	Him/Her/It

Plural Subject	*Plural Object*
We	Us
You	You
They	Them

Of all of these pronouns, "I" and "me" probably cause the most problems for writers and speakers alike. However, writers will be able to choose correctly if they keep three points in mind. First, sentences similar to those above need only be completed to determine which word is best. Second, combinations of these pronouns with the verb "to be" ("is," "are," "was," "were," "will be," etc.) require the subject pronoun in almost every case. This means that the following are correct, even though they may seem stilted:

It is he who is responsible for these problems.

It is we who are to blame for this loss of revenue.

Is that she in the office next to the board room?

If I were she, I would be more careful about this.

The third point to remember is that expressions involving the use of "between" or "among" will invariably take the object case. Even though the following may "sound" correct, they are not:

We should keep his sensitive matter just between you and I.   *You & I buying*

This should be discussed among Jones, Reynolds, you, and I.   *You drue not the end object of a preposition pronoun*

These should be revised to use "me" instead of "I":

We should keep this just between you and me.

This should be discussed among Jones, Reynolds, you, and me.

Writers who wonder which pronoun to use here can also ask themselves whether they would use "we" or "us" if they were the *only* choices. "Us" will need to be the word of choice, if writers are to avoid saying:

This should be discussed among we.

Since "us" readily fits and is simply a more familiar object pronoun, the choice for the singular would have to be "me" or another appropriate object pronoun.

▨ Parallelism

Of all the rules of grammar, this one has special relevance to writing in the professions, where listing devices are used frequently as a quick and convenient way to express ideas that share important elements or features. Parallelism insures the success of this transfer by requiring writers to use similar form to express similar content. By insuring that their lists and series are parallel, writers will be able to increase the readability of their writing.

Lists appear in many forms but can be divided into the two types that readers in the professions most commonly encounter. The first is the text series, an itemization of things or actions, and it is usually introduced by a colon or the word "following." Here is an example:

The control group will be responsible for the following: insuring that reports are available, balancing the output with receipt of the input, and distributing the output to the various departments.

Lists take another form, particularly in business writing, which relies heavily on enumeration. This form is tabular, and it is set off from the text. Usually, writers will provide lists in tabular form when the items listed are more than three. The items of the list may be marked with numbers, letters, or a variety of typesetter's marks, which range from bullets to pointing fingers. Here is an example of a simple list in text form, followed by the same list in tabular form:

Please do the following: send in the review, include a copy of the diskette, enclose your check, and call to confirm our receipt.

Please do the following:

1. Send in the review.
2. Include a copy of the diskette.
3. Enclose your check.
4. Call to confirm our receipt.

The lists immediately above have two things in common: first, they both present items with shared features; second, they present these items *in parallel form*. This means that the *initial words* in each listed item *have the same grammatical form*. Here are the text list and the tabular list, and this time with the beginnings of each item italicized:

The control group will be responsible for the following: *insuring* that output reports are available, *balancing* the final output with receipt of the input, and *distributing* the output to the various departments.

Please do the following:

1. *Send in* the review.
2. *Include* a copy of the diskette.
3. *Enclose* your check.
4. *Call* to confirm our receipt.

The items in both lists are parallel: in the first list, they are all gerunds or "-ing" words; in the second list, they are all verbs. Because the lists are parallel, the reader will be able to absorb the information quickly. In contrast, note what happens when the same lists are not parallel:

The control group will be responsible for the following: insuring that output reports are available, a balance of the final output with receipt of the input, and the distribution of the output to the various departments.

Please do the following:

1. Send in the review.
2. Include a copy of the diskette.
3. Your check should be enclosed.
4. Call to confirm our receipt.

Although these lists provide the same information as their parallel originals, they do not provide that information in the most readable fashion. Of course, this is the main point behind using parallel structures: they increase readability by relying on the form of a message to convey features of the content. Two good examples of this are the nonparallel passages below, each of which is followed by its italicized revision. Note how readable the revision is. Note also that neither of these uses the usual colon to introduce the lists:

All managers feel their understanding could be enhanced by attending division meetings, the discussion of matters with the division leaders, and involving themselves in writing bimonthly reports.

All managers feel their understanding could be enhanced by attending division meetings, discussing issues with division leaders, and involving themselves in writing bimonthly reports.

This will help department management in planning for future audit work, the comparison of budgets to actual time expenditures, and to review the distribution of total time for each staff member.

This will help department management to plan future audit work, compare budgets to actual time expenditures, and review the distribution of total time for each staff member.

Although parallelism applies to lists, it is not limited to them. Other structures benefit from being parallel. For example, any expression in which words are joined by the simple conjunctions "or" and "and" will be a candidate for parallel expression. This is particularly true of the first example below and of others that involve adverbs:

The program performed the calculations quickly and with accuracy.

The program performed the calculations quickly and accurately.

A preoccupation with sales will seldom result in the formation of a resource policy or how better formats for work can be developed.

A preoccupation with sales will seldom result in the formation of a resource policy or the development of better formats for work.

An extension of this joining structure, the correlative conjunction discussed earlier, is made much more readable by insuring that the material following the "either" (or "neither") is grammatically the same as the material following the "or" (or "nor"):

A transportation expert has volunteered free consultant time either in writing up the study proposal or with a draft of the bid.

A transportation expert has volunteered free consultant time either in writing up the study proposal or in drafting the bid.

During first quarter, he neither attended Comdex nor the San Francisco Computer Show.

During first quarter, he attended neither Comdex nor the San Franciso Computer Show.

Writers should strive to provide parallel structures any time they are available. Such structures can only complement earlier efforts in editing and help to produce a final impression of credibility and professionalism.

RELATED READINGS

Comprehensive discussions of grammar are available in abundance, and some of them are quite good. However, few are directed primarily toward the needs of the working professional. The listings below represent good works that give at least some attention to the use of grammar in the professions.

The Associated Press Stylebook and Libel Manual. Ed. Norman Goldstein. New York: Addison-Wesley, 1992.

Brusaw, C., et al. *The Business Writer's Handbook.* 3d ed. New York: St. Martin's Press, 1987.

Copperud, Roy H. *American Usage and Style: The Consensus.* New York: Van Nostrand Reinhold, 1980.

Lanham, Richard. *Revising Business Prose.* 3d ed. New York: Macmillan, 1992.

Munter, Mary. *Guide to Managerial Communication.* 2d ed. Englewood Cliffs, NJ: Prentice-Hall, 1987.

Nicholson, Margaret. *A Dictionary of American-English Usage.* Oxford: Oxford University Press, 1957.

Tichy, Harriet. *Effective Writing for Engineers, Managers, Scientists.* New York: Wiley, 1987.

NOTES

1. The relation between grammatical correctness, similar conventions of writing, and professionalism has been discussed in several interesting studies. See, for example, Alfred G. Edge and Ronald Greenwood, "How Managers Rank Knowledge, Skills, and Attributes Possessed by Business Administration Graduates," *AACSB Bulletin* 11 (October 1974): 30–34; Garda Bowman, "What Helps or Harms Promotability," *Harvard Business Review* 42 (January–February 1964): 6–26.

2. Quoted in Maxwell Nurnberg, *Questions You Always Wanted to Ask about English* (New York: Simon & Shuster, 1972), 18.

3. For a more extensive treatment of grammatical and other solutions to gender-exclusive language, see Rosalie Maggio, *Nonsexist Word Finder: A Dictionary of Gender-Free Usage* (Phoenix, AZ: Oryx Press, 1987); Casey Miller and Kate Swift, *Handbook of Nonsexist Writing,* 2d ed. (New York: Harper & Row, 1988).

ELECTRONIC ETHOS 13

Computer Revision

Businesses have long relied on computers and word processing to produce documents that are acceptable by most standards of professional appearance. Although initial offerings consisted of little more than electronic versions of the more familiar hardcopy typewriter, more recent programs offer features rivaling those of dedicated desktop-publishing systems. Employing automatic formatting, designer style sheets, full graphics capabilities, and on-line layout assistance, the current market's major word processors now insure that the appearance of the final product will be acceptable.[1] Produced on even a low-resolution laser printer, most documents can easily acquire the look of a commercial typesetter. The quality of appearance is thus insured. However, the quality of the writing is relatively unaffected.

Or is it? Some researchers in the field of computer-assisted composition have suggested that the quality of writing can be improved, if only indirectly, by the use of word processing.[2] A study conducted at UCLA revealed, perhaps not surprisingly, that students found electronic revision faster and easier when compared to the more traditional precursors of type and handwriting.[3] Researchers reasoned that such speed and ease can only make the otherwise burdensome tasks of composition much more pleasant, or at least less tedious, and thus the probability of producing quality prose can be increased. A similar study concluded that the "computer provided incentive to spend more time making revisions, and that it allowed more attention for developing content by deemphasizing correctness on the initial draft."[4] From this point of view, the kind of revision that is promoted by computer-assisted composition results in better writing.

These studies, as well as others, suggest that word processing can contribute to the quality of writing, as long as one assumes that ease, speed, and incentive to revise will of necessity result in better prose.[5] How safely one might assume this is another matter. But even if such an assumption were safe, the word processor's contribution would still only be incidental to improving the quality of writing, and better writing would at best still be a byproduct of the computer's assistance. The primary benefits of word processors are thus the same now as they were when such programs were first offered: convenience and speed.

However, much of this may be changing. Recently, manufacturers of major word processors have begun to market their programs with extended claims.[6] They no longer claim increases only in ease, speed, and the quality of the document's appearance, but now also in the quality of the writing, and in the quality of the writer's ethos. They are able to make these claims because of a new feature they have bundled with their software. This feature is the electronic "grammar checker," an auxiliary program that goes well beyond the on-line spelling checker, thesaurus, and dictionary.

Unlike these more traditional reference-work programs, the electronic grammar checker offers comment on the *sense* of the writer's expression—with clear implications for the impression, or ethos, the writer is creating—and it may also include an explanation of the advice it offers. Accessed from the appropriate menu or icon, the "grammar checker" promises writers a new road to improved readability.[7] Given the predominance of word processing as a business application, such a promise could have considerable consequences. Given the critical importance of effective writing in business, which is documented in every major survey of management practice, such a promise is not to be taken lightly.[8]

▓ The Early Development of Computer-Assisted Error Detection

Although computer-assisted grammar checkers are relatively new to desktop computers and personal computing, they are programs of record in the world of mainframe and minicomputers. In that environment, they were first developed in 1981 at Bell Laboratories in Murray Hill, New Jersey, when Lorinda Cherry, a Bell Laboratories computer scientist, created a suite of programs that would identify several stylistic weaknesses in texts composed in English.[9]

Cherry's original collection of programs was relatively limited by contemporary standards and concentrated primarily on diction and style. Initially presented as a program for computer-assisted error detection, her work was extended by colleagues within Bell Laboratories, until the now famous UNIX Writer's Workbench was produced as a larger collection of programs.[10] In its more fully developed form, Workbench consisted of three categories of programs. The first was devoted to "textual analysis," and it offered a wide-ranging list of items that might be "checked," including punctuation, sexist phrases, contiguous appearance of the same word, and incidence of the verb "to be." The second category was called "explanatory" because it provided explanations of some rules of grammar and punctuation. It also housed and allowed for printing of the standards that were used to evaluate documents. The third category concerned "environmental tailoring," and it provided a way of expanding existing diction and spelling dictionaries and offered the user the opportunity to create standards for evaluation from model texts. In addition to these three was one other, a personal program that allowed the user to draw on personalized lists of phrases and spellings.

At about the same time as Workbench was being extended, similar efforts were underway at IBM, where programming teams were at work on Epistle, a software suite that had uses similar to those of Workbench, and like Workbench, also ran under the UNIX operating system.[11] According to early research published in *IBM Sys-*

tems Journal, the long-term objectives of Epistle were "to provide office workers, particularly middle-level managers, with a variety of application packages to help them interact with natural language texts."[12] However, Epistle never moved beyond its initial and experimental form, and the program's limits soon became those of its primary tasks: "the Epistle system addresses only the tasks of grammar and style checking of texts written in English. Grammar checking deals with such errors as lack of number agreement between subject and verb; style checking points out such problems as overly complex sentences."

Like Workbench, Epistle relied on a general language-processing system, in this case NLP, which is responsible for analyzing the text to which it is applied.[13] Text management involves reading the text from its point of entry, converting the text into a form that NLP can analyze, and then presenting the results through the Epistle interface, an early form of overlapping windows.[14] Epistle's NLP functions consisted of a sentence parser and a grammar checker. The parser converted English sentences into sentence outlines or "parse trees," which provide templates that may be used in the program's diagnostic work. The grammar checker employed algorithms similar to those that would eventually be used in more modern programs. To insure that the grammatical problems identified were consistent with prevailing authorities on matters of style, the authors sought direction from both academic and business sources. For the academic contribution, they turned to the very popular *Elements of Style* by Strunk and White and the less popular but more established and academically respectable *English Grammar and Composition* by Warriner and Griffith.[15] To provide the professional complement, authors turned to "reading real business correspondence and watching for stigmatized constructions."

Bell Laboratories' Workbench and IBM's Epistle represented the primary efforts of business and industry to produce programs that would improve the quality of workplace prose through error detection and correction. Immediately following these efforts in business, studies of computer-assisted writing had begun in the academic community, though the emphasis there was less on error detection in workplace writing and more on the use of these programs in educational environments. At UCLA, a Workbench-like program, HOMER, was produced, and it led to a more refined version, WANDAH, which is now generally regarded as having been "the first comprehensive package covering the writing process from beginning to end."[16] While Workbench and Epistle were almost exclusively concerned with sentence-level error detection, HOMER and WANDAH had more comprehensive concerns and considered the multiple dimensions of writing as a process.[17] In fact, grammatical and sentence-level analysis was only one of the three components in the WANDAH program, which included a word processor, a set of prewriting aids, and a system for revising written material. WANDAH's offerings in grammatical analysis and error detection at the sentence level would be found in this last section, which also included several of the prewriting aids now revisited for application in revising prose. With these three levels representing a process-based approach to writing, WANDAH served as the appropriate choice for teaching composition to university students.[18]

Probably the most extensive examination of computer-assisted grammar checkers in either business or academic application was conducted at Colorado State University's Center for Computer-Assisted Writing. Begun in 1981 as a project on textual analysis, it was eventually adapted to more educational needs as Writer's Workbench software was revised and tested in the composition classroom.[19] The evaluation was positive and indicated that not only students but also instructors benefited from using the programs.[20] A journal review of this project concluded by indicating both a level of satisfaction with current use and the expectation of continued development: "Such programs, we believe, offer a potent weapon against insensitivity to diction and style and against further decline in editing skills. . . . As research continues, we can expect even more comprehensive and accurate programs as well as packages adapted to the needs of different writers, whether professional or developmental."[21] As more recent developments will show, these writers were certainly accurate in their prediction.

▓ Grammar Comes to the Desktop: DOS and Windows

Just as other business software applications migrated from mainframe and minicomputer to the desktop microcomputer during the middle and late 1980s, so did programs designed to analyze text and identify sentence errors. One important development in the early part of the decade made such a migration especially easy: the increased size of stationary hard drives. Before this time, the most common desktop configuration, found in the IBM PC or its equivalent clone, consisted of a single or double floppy drive. This meant that storage was severely limited, and such a limitation effectively excluded programs that depended on large information databases. Grammar checkers, which relied on extensive "linguabases," the linguistic equivalent of stored quantitative data, simply could not function under such limitations. The introduction of large hard drives, even the initial ten-megabyte Winchester drives found on the IBM PC, made the use of grammar checkers and other linguabase-intensive programs possible on the personal computer.

The first programs to reach the desktop were all "stand-alone" programs, though manufacturers at times claimed they were "integrated" because they would work from within the user's word-processing program of choice.[22] Although many programs were released, only a handful were competitive in the marketplace.[23] These included Rightwriter, developed by Decisionware; Grammatik, which was created by Reference Software; CorrectText, the production of Houghton-Mifflin's electronic publishing group; Punctuation and Style, the development of Oasis Systems; and Poweredit, which was developed by Artificial Linguistics, Inc.[24] An early review of an early (1.1) version of Rightwriter provides a representative picture of the features offered by its competitors as well:

> Like other automatic writing analyzers, Rightwriter looks through a word-processed document for phrases that match its dictionary of trite, murky, pompous, redundant and otherwise infelicitous language. It also flags passive voice, complex sentence

structure, and overlong sentences and paragraphs. It marks these anomalies on a backup copy, adding a summary page that measures readability and stylistic strength according to average sentence length, the proportion of active to passive verbs, and of adjectives and adverbs to nouns and verbs. To help spot misspellings, slang or words that might confuse an audience, Rightwriter ends the summary with a list of uncommon words in the document.[25]

From this general description of Rightwriter's features, other programs departed in only minor ways. Each relied heavily on a linguabase for matching words, phrases, or clauses, though none of the programs was able to distinguish between these categories. Each program was able to distinguish between active and passive constructions, and each contained a default bias against the latter. Finally, each program provided a quantitative evaluation of writing quality by employing one of several formulas based on the relationship between some combination of sentence length, number of words, or number of syllables in a word. True, Reference Software's Grammatik was normally regarded as being more thorough, primarily because it employed the largest linguabase of these programs. It also attempted to distinguish itself on other grounds, such as being the most "user friendly" offering. It was the only program to include a writing guide, and it was the first program to become available for Microsoft's Windows interface. Thus, if any program appeared to stand apart from the others, it was Grammatik.

Still, these programs all offered many of the same features, and a reviewer's summary of Rightwriter, in its early version, could be applied to others. After offering a list of errors that the program missed, the reviewer commented:

> Rightwriter's inability to find these anomalies suggests that its phrase dictionary is too small, even for routine office application. The program didn't hold the line against the two 500-word freshman themes either, missing tackles made by one or both of the other programs. It didn't suggest avoiding "basically" or "hopefully" or point out that "of" in "inside of" is unnecessary and that "with out" should be one word. It didn't remark that "many" is preferable to "a lot of" or that "different than" can be improved by "different from," "other than," or "unlike."[26]

■ The Second Wave: A Difference in Degree

The next wave of desktop grammar checkers differed from their predecessors more in degree than in kind. However, this difference was significant and went some distance toward diminishing the concerns voiced about Rightwriter in its earlier version (1.1) This difference was also noticed by reviewers, and a review of Rightwriter in a later version (3.1) was accordingly much more positive than the earlier review of its 1.1 predecessor. It was also more optimistic about the future of grammar checkers in general:

> The great potential of style-checking programs to assist young college students in their revision may be realized in the next generation of software. Then, perhaps, pro-

fessors will be able to review and adjust the style-checking algorithms. The programs will be more thorough in detecting errors of style and usage and more circumspect in suggesting improvements. On the basis of Rightwriter's many fine features and its many reflections of quality control in design and documentation, it may well be the first to reach this next plateau.[27]

Several changes help to explain the optimism of this review. First, *all* programs introduced during this second wave, from roughly 1990 (the release of Rightwriter 3.1) to 1995 (the release of the integrated suites below), were offered as part of dramatically improved versions of Microsoft's graphical Windows interface. This means that all of the programs benefited from the improved ease of use that accompanied this interface, including the enhanced graphical capabilities, extended use of color, and ability to cut and paste text between different applications. Consistency of design was also improved, and this accounted for a friendlier interaction and code compatibility between programs that ran under Windows as opposed to those which ran under MS DOS.

Other changes went well beyond the more cosmetic developments that accompanied programs running under the Windows environment, and the author of the Rightwriter 3.1 review hints at some of them when he mentions "style-checking algorithms." That these programs used algorithms at all marks an important departure from programs that relied on exact matches of words, either alone or in combination. The use of algorithms thus allows the programmers to write instructions based on patterns as opposed to vocabulary lists. This dramatically increases speed, which in turn makes possible searches that would have been too slow to consider under other conditions. It also allows for greater comprehension in analysis because searching by pattern is more likely to yield even rare linguistic occurrences, occurrences that would quickly fill a linguabase if each instance required entry. The second-generation releases—Rightwriter, Grammatik, and Correct Grammar—all relied heavily on algorithms for their analysis.

The use of algorithms was an important development, and along with the enhanced interaction and compatibility provided by Windows, it marked a period of progress in grammar checkers, one that made the use of these programs both more inviting and productive. This was a time of optimism, as indicated by the tone of the Rightwriter 3.1 review, even if the content of the review made clear that development here was a matter of degree and not kind. Few changes were made in these programs until the very recent introduction of the integrated programs.

▮ The Current Market: Integrated Programs

Grammar checkers are today found as an integrated feature of the current market's major word processors. This is significant, since it means users will have unprecedented ease of access to these programs. Prior to the integrated offering, a writer needed to purchase the grammar checker as a stand-alone program, start it as a stand-alone program, and then load into the grammar checker a file from the word processor used to generate text. These steps, and the compatibility conflicts that might result from using different programs from different manufacturers, combined to reduce the likelihood of using the program as well as the success in gaining access to it. By offering the grammar checker as an integrated feature, as easily accessed as the spell checker or the thesaurus, manufacturers will now increase dramatically the probability of use by those who use their word processors. Each of the three major manufacturers of word processors offers an integrated grammar checker. Word for Windows 6.0 ships with a built-in version of the Houghton Mifflin CorrecText Grammar Correction System, with underlying technology by Language Systems, Inc. Though a competitor, Lotus's Ami Pro 3.1 relies on the same system, which it will also integrate into its long-awaited next incarnation—Lotus Word Pro. WordPerfect relies on different technology, developed by Reference Software, the company that pioneered Grammatik as a stand-alone program in the DOS days. It is now fully integrated into WordPerfect for Windows 6.1, and it is offered as part of PerfectSense, a "new technology" Novell claims "helps users write better by understanding the meaning of words in context."[28]

Although each of these companies can be expected to advertise the "distinctive" features of its own offering, the programs themselves are more alike than not. For example, they all share a remarkable misnomer: they are really not "grammar" checkers at all, a fact that more than one linguist has pointed out. These programs have very little to do with grammatical correctness, even though their advertisements would suggest otherwise. What, then, do these programs check? Something they call "style," and what constitutes style is a rather remarkable list of items or "options," from which the user can choose. For example, in Ami Pro and Word, the options button in CorrecText provides a dual menu of choices from "rules" of style and grammar. Under "Grammar rules," the writer will find a list of linguistic concerns, including jargon words, passive verb, pronoun errors, double negatives, and format errors (see Figure 13.1).[29]

Under "Style rules" appears an equally diverse list and some overlap: jargon expressions, multiple negation, misused words, and wordy expressions (see Figure 13.2). This overlap among rules suggests that less is being examined *in practice* than the large number of rules might suggest. Finally, in Ami Pro, an additional option, "Word Order Rules" is offered, yet it adds little to the options from which the user might select and could easily have been integrated into either rules of style or rules of grammar.

Although few of these "rules" are rules in any traditional or accepted sense, they nevertheless appear as such. They also appear with an option that allows the writer to adjust the degree of thoroughness, from extreme strictness, in which all rules are applied, to a more casual application, in which fewer rules are brought into play. Finally, all of the grammar checkers provide "readability statistics," an ominous-sounding phrase that refers to the supposed level at which the writing may be comprehended. Using one of several simple scales based on a ratio between the number of syllables in a word, and the number of words in a sentence, these statistics promise

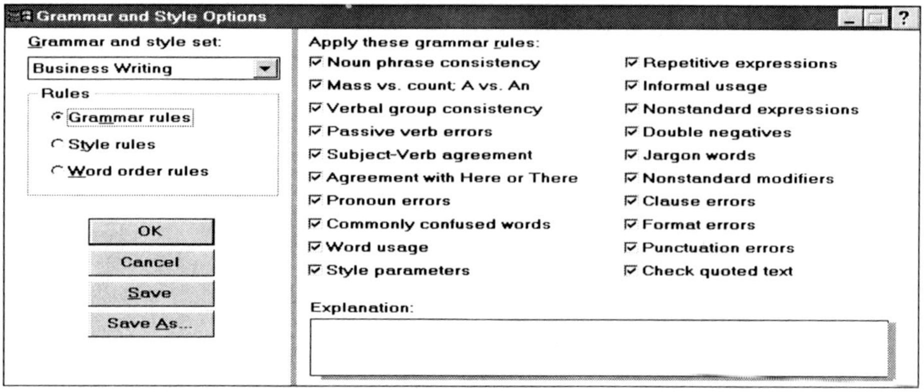

FIGURE 13.1

a numerical representation of reading ease or difficulty. Ami Pro is typical in this respect. It offers four representations, which turn out to be two scales with several variations of the second. The first is Gunning's Fog Index, which the program on-line documentation claims "indicates how difficult the document is to read, based on the averages for sentence lengths and the number of multi-syllable words in sentences. The higher the index, the more difficult the document is to read."[30] The other is several variations of the readability diagnostic developed by Rudolph Flesch for use in analyzing government documents. The Flesch-Kincaid Score indicates the Fog Index as a grade level. The higher the score, the more difficult the document is to read. The

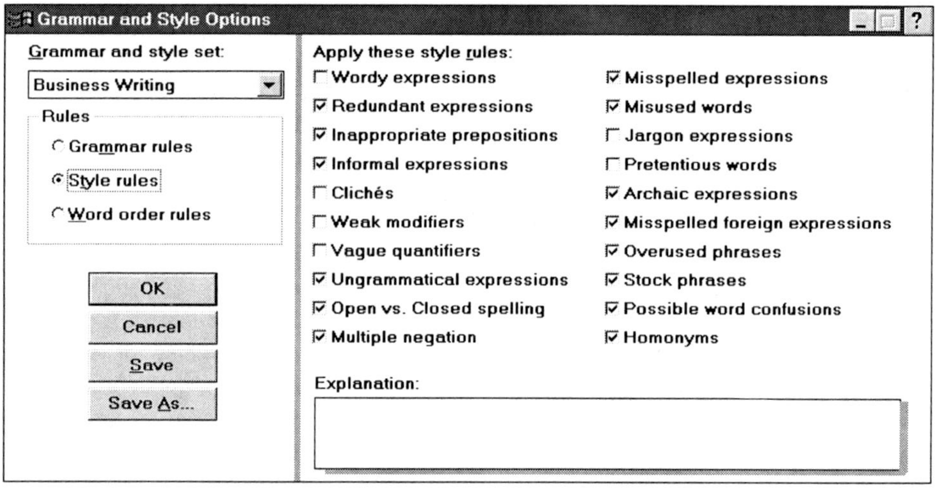

FIGURE 13.2

Flesch Reading Ease Score claims to indicate the ease of reading and understanding a document, based on the average number of words per sentence and the average number of syllables per 100 words. The higher the score, the easier the document is to read and understand. According to the on-line documentation, "the highest score is 100, which indicates the document is very easy to read and understand. An average score is between 60 and 70. A low score is between 0 and 30, which indicates the document is very difficult to read and understand." Finally, the Flesch Reading Ease Grade Level is offered to show the Flesch Reading Ease Score as a grade level. A fourth-grade level corresponds to a score between 90 and 100. An eighth-grade level corresponds to a score between 60 and 70. A college education corresponds to a score between 0 and 30.

■ Parsing and Pattern Matching

Like their mainframe predecessors, these grammar checkers work in general by employing "pattern matching" and "parsing," both of which are methods derived from recent work on the computational analysis of natural language, machine translation, and other large, text-processing projects. Pattern matching, which is the faster of the two, employs algorithms (similar to those used in spelling checkers and earlier versions of the grammar checkers) to analyze the semantics of short word forms as well as the way word forms are combined into larger units. Parsing requires more processing time because it proceeds by analyzing the structure of the sentence, its grammatical form and syntax or word order. The efficiency and sophistication of the parser is critical to the effectiveness of the program. In the early days of text analysis, these parsers were available only through the UNIX-based programs, such as Bell Labs' Writers Workbench, IBM's Epistle, and others mentioned earlier. Now parsers are readily available and run acceptably on the average desktop PC. One of the programs above, Novell's Grammatik, even permits the user a peek at the parsing tree, which is the closest most users will probably get to the internal workings of the program. During most normal operations, most users will encounter a series of dialogue boxes, a description of which (to be given in the next section) will also provide a description of the program's offerings and some indication of the value of the analysis the programs provide.

■ The Value of Analysis

Although the technical operation of the grammar checker will probably be of greatest interest to computational linguists and pioneers in machine translation, and the dialogues boxes will be of interest to those unfamiliar with the programs' basic operations, the practicing manager will want to know whether the programs are any good. Will these programs, as Novell's product information claims, "help users to write better"? A resounding yes, according to the manufacturers. In fact, Novell is so confident about Grammatik's benefits that it goes beyond the normal claims made by others to assert a new distinction: Grammatik in WordPerfect for Windows 6.0 "is the first grammar checker to actually rewrite sentences."[31] However, as enthusiastic as the manufacturers are, the results of actual text analysis suggest that skepticism would be an appropriate stance for users to adopt in the face of manufacturer confidence.

Such skepticism is certainly the result of having each grammar checker analyze the following passage, which was chosen for examination for two reasons. First, it has at its core a realistic sample of business writing, one that is typical of the troublesome prose one often encounters at the workplace. Second, it has additional and commonly recognized business-writing errors inserted as a way of testing the comprehensiveness of each program.[32]

(**1**) SUBJECT: Current Status of Field Trial Evaluation

(**2**) It appears that we are currently encountering more than usual difficulty in obtaining the necessary number of hospitals that are required to complete the field trial evaluation of our Extension Set 806-01, RE-0487 with the plastic slide clamp.

(**3**) To date, only seven hospitals have now made the decision to perform an evaluation of this product and approximately nine or ten evaluation hospitals are required in order to make an assessment of the new plastic slide clamp. (**4**) Delay on this project is attributed to the apathy and lack of interest on the part of the hospitals.

(**5**) We have given consideration to this problem, however, and it is our belief that we may be able to deal with it by offering an incentive in the form of a small stipend to provide them with more motivation.

(**6**) There is another problem in that there is no clamp on our existing 20" Extension Set and many of the hospitals are currently making use of this set without the addition of the clamp on a satisfactory basis.

(**7**) We have concerns about this but we are of the opinion that hospitals will show a greater interest once we have had an opportunity to make it clear that the clamp offers an advantage. (**8**) Several hospitals we have contacted have even objected to making use of the set with the clamp and they have made the decision not to perform an evaluation of the product.

(**9**) In addition to these problems our district managers, whom we must rely on to locate willing hospital coordinators, are presently away on vacation. (**10**) Until the time that they have returned to work, we will have to make arrangements for other ways to make contact with prospective participants who might take part in this evaluation.

(**11**) At the present time, we do not anticipate completion of the field trial evaluation until July 8th. (**12**) A preliminary report, however, will be submitted on June 15th and it will explain the current status of the report at that time.

The memo consists of twelve sentences that describe how the evaluation of a medical product has been delayed. The utility of each grammar checker was tested by having each analyze the memo according to the most "rigid rules" the checker provides.

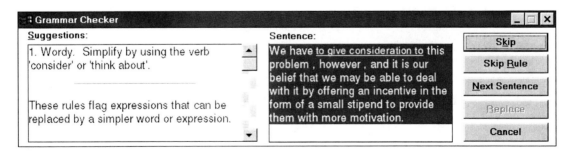

> **¾ Grammar Checker** _ □ ✕
>
> **Suggestions:**
>
> 1. This main clause may contain a verb in the passive voice.
>
> These rules flag usage of the passive voice.
>
> **Sentence:**
>
> To date , only seven hospitals have now made the decision to perform an evaluation of this product and approximately nine or ten evaluation hospitals **are required** in order to make an assessment of the new plastic slide clamp.
>
> Skip
> Skip Rule
> Next Sentence
> Replace
> Cancel

FIGURE 13.3

CorrecText Grammar Correction System

The first checker to be tested was Houghton Mifflin's CorrecText Grammar Correction System, which is offered as an integrated option, along with a spelling checker and thesaurus, in both Ami Pro 3.1 and WordPerfect for Windows 95.[33]

CorrecText analysis of this memo revealed very few problems under the "grammar rules option." The most common "problem" noted was use of the passive voice (see Figure 13.3), which CorrecText found in sentences (1) "are required"; (3) "are required"; (4) "is attributed"; and (12) "will be submitted." The next most common "problem" flagged was nominalization (verbs converted to nouns) (see Figure 13.4), though CorrecText does not refer to it in this way. CorrecText identified two nominalizations, in sentence (5) "given consideration to," for which CorrecText suggests "consider" or "think about"; and in sentence (7) "are of the opinion," for which CorrecText suggests "think" or "believe." The next problem noted is redundancy or dilution, in several forms; for example, CorrecText suggested changing the prepositional chain "In addition to these problems," in sentence (9) to "besides these problems"; in sentence (10), it suggested changing the redundancy "Until the time that they have returned" to "Until they have returned"; and in sentence (11), CorrecText suggested changing another redundancy, "At the present time," to "Right now."

> **¾ Grammar Checker** _ □ ✕
>
> **Suggestions:**
>
> 1. Wordy. Simplify by using the verb 'consider' or 'think about'.
>
> These rules flag expressions that can be replaced by a simpler word or expression.
>
> **Sentence:**
>
> We have to give consideration to this problem , however , and it is our belief that we may be able to deal with it by offering an incentive in the form of a small stipend to provide them with more motivation.
>
> Skip
> Skip Rule
> Next Sentence
> Replace
> Cancel

FIGURE 13.4

Under the "Style rules" option, CorrecText found only one instance of sentence level problems in addition to those found under the "Grammar rules" option. In sentence (4), it suggested that the writer might rephrase "on the part of" with "a more precise preposition," though it did not indicate which preposition might be more precise. Finally, with the "Word order rules" option selected, CorrecText found only one apparent problem, though in another category of editing, in word *choice*. In sentence (10), CorrecText questioned whether the word "prospective" was used correctly in the following phrase "to make contact with prospective participants." It offered "perspective" as a possibility and then directed the writer to check the definition. Having now completed the analysis, CorrecText produces for the writer a four-part review of readability statistics (see Figure 13.5)

WordPerfect and Grammatik

Just as Lotus's Ami Pro and Microsoft's Word for Windows rely on CorrecText for their parsing power, so Novell's WordPerfect for Windows relies on Grammatik for its text-management technology. First glance reveals few differences between CorrecText and Grammatik. Both offer the user a definable set of "rules" that determine the standards of textual analysis. In CorrecText, the most demanding standard is called "formal"; in Grammatik, it is called "very strict." Both flag problem expressions and offer explanations. And both provide the user with suggestions for revision and statistics that manufacturers claim express levels of reading ease.[34] However, Grammatik relies less on pattern matching, in which sentences are recognized primarily as groupings of vocabulary words, and more on parsing, in which the sentences are analyzed as structural units and grammatical patterns. This is evident from the "parsing tree," an element that

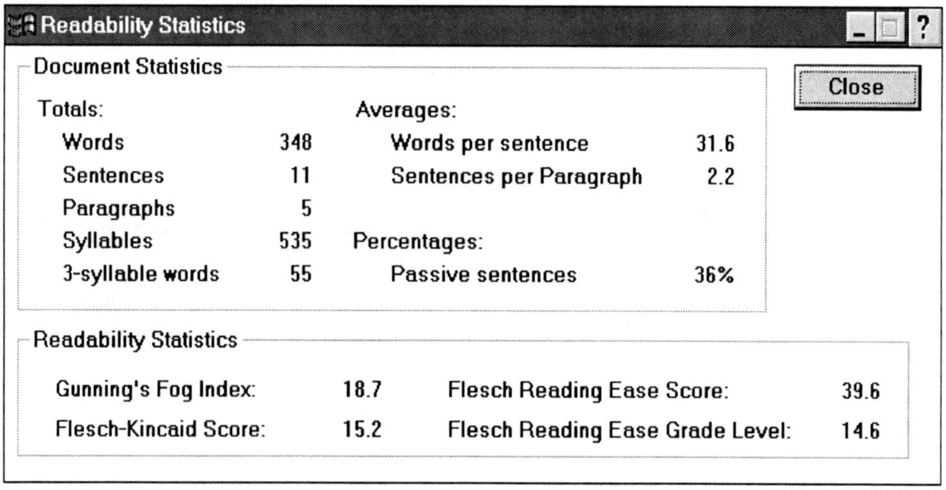

Readability Statistics

Document Statistics

Totals:		Averages:	
Words	348	Words per sentence	31.6
Sentences	11	Sentences per Paragraph	2.2
Paragraphs	5		
Syllables	535	Percentages:	
3-syllable words	55	Passive sentences	36%

Readability Statistics

Gunning's Fog Index:	18.7	Flesch Reading Ease Score:	39.6
Flesch-Kincaid Score:	15.2	Flesch Reading Ease Grade Level:	14.6

Close

FIGURE 13.5

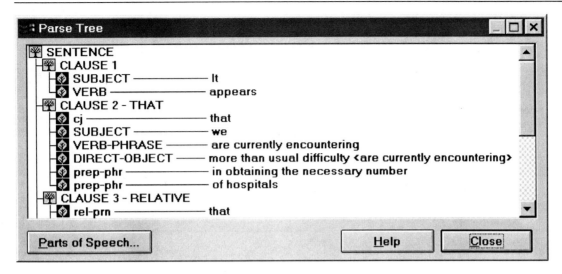

FIGURE 13.6

is available only in Grammatik. Grammatik's parsing tree offers the user a way of understanding the grammatical structure of the sentences it analyzes, either in the tree's basic form (see Figure 13.6), or through its hypertext linked extensions, which allow the user to review not just the parts of speech within the sentence but also their definitions. Grammatik thus provides the user with a means of identifying sentence elements as well as a handbook for refreshing one's understanding of those elements.

Grammatik also provides a much more thorough analysis of the text, in part because of its heavy reliance on parsing. Operating under the "very strict" option, Grammatik was able to identify the same types of problems as CorrecText did but went beyond it to flag the following instances CorrecText did not mark. It caught in sentence (1) the commonplace redundancy "current status" and recommended that the writer omit "current." It marked in sentence (3) the nominalization "made the decision" and appropriately suggested "decided" as a more concise replacement. Also in sentence (3), it marked the prepositional chain "in order to" and recommended reducing the expression to "to." In sentences (4) and (5), it marked similar prepositional chains, first "on the part of" and suggested "by" as a more concise replacement; second, "in the form of," for which it offered a choice of "as" or "in." In sentence (6), it marked the nominalization "are currently making use of" and suggested "are currently using" as a replacement, and it marked the hidden adverb "on a satisfactory basis" but surprisingly offered the writer only a general principle for revision instead of suggesting either the specific adjective "satisfactory" or the adverb "satisfactorily." In sentence (7), Grammatik caught the nominalization "are of the opinion" and suggested "think" or "believe" as more concise replacements. In sentence (10), it caught two similar nominalizations in "make arrangements," for which it offered the verb "arrange," and in "make contact with," for which it offered a range of choices in

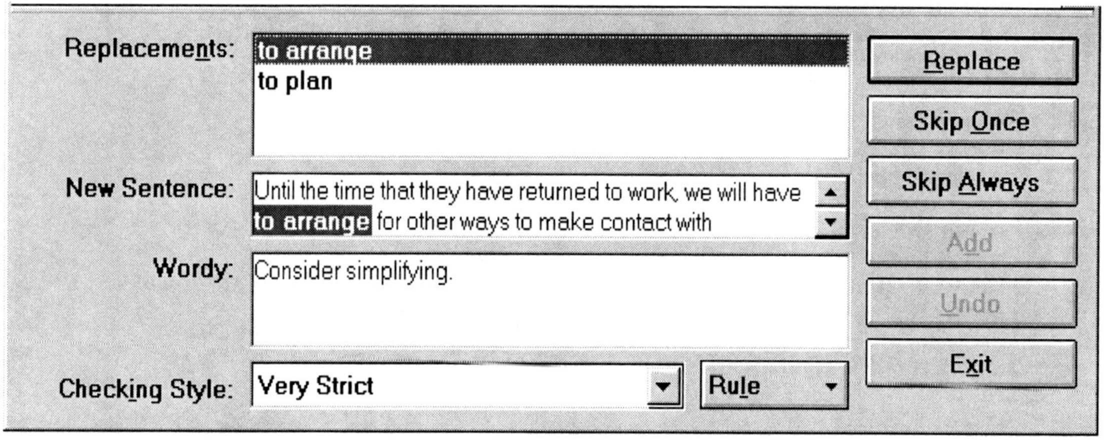

| Replacements: | to arrange | | Replace |
| to plan | | Skip Once |

New Sentence: Until the time that they have returned to work, we will have ▲
to arrange for other ways to make contact with ▼

Wordy: Consider simplifying.

Checking Style: Very Strict ▼ Rule ▼

Skip Always
Add
Undo
Exit

FIGURE 13.7

"meet," "reach," and "contact" (see Figure 13.7). Also worth note is Grammatik's ability to mark several expletive expressions (instances of "there is"), though it did not offer the writer much direction in revision. Finally, Grammatik provides readability scales much like those offered in CorrecText.

Grammatik thus produces a much more thorough analysis than CorrecText does, though the quality of analysis is different in degree and not kind. Grammatik does a more complete analysis of redundancies, nominalizations, and other verbose expressions, but it does essentially the same kind of analysis CorrecText does. It does, in short, the kind of analysis that might be expected from a computer program. As such, one would not expect it to compete well with a person who has an understanding of editorial technique and some experience in practice.

■ For Comparison: Enter the MBA

Determining how Grammatik and CorrecText would fare against their human counterparts required a comparison using the same sample memo introduced earlier. Twenty-five working professionals, who were enrolled in a first-quarter management communications course as part of their Executive MBA program of study, were given approximately six hours of instruction on techniques of revision, which included a review of five categories of editing: conciseness, usage, syntax, grammar, and punctuation. These students were then given thirty minutes to revise the sample memorandum. The same document had already been analyzed by CorrecText and Grammatik.[35]

As expected, the grammar checkers did not perform well against their MBA competitors, who were on average able to reduce the memo by 50 percent and revise for matters that require a greater understanding of context as well as editorial principle. Since the students were aware of the rhetorical relationship between the writer and reader, as they would be when editing at the workplace, they were able to revise according to information available only outside the text proper. For example, many decided that most of sentence (2) would not be necessary to a marketing manager who was primarily interested in the specifics contained in sentence (3), which explains how many hospitals have participated and how many remain for participation. Such a reading, which depends on extratextual understandings, is not possible with a program that is confined literally to text management.

At the paragraph level, students were able to delete entire sentences because of redundancies they identified elsewhere in the memo, an action which is simply not within the computer program's scope of operation. All other matters of editing that concerned evaluation of intersentence relationships, such as the use of transitions or the reference of pronouns, were similarly available to the students but not to CorrecText and Grammatik. The computer programs were much more competitive in analyzing intrasentence relationships, but the students were able to catch most of the nominalizations, while the grammar checkers caught only a few. In some cases, the grammar checker caught the nominalization, but simply recommended another way of expressing it. Instead of saying "perform an evaluation," the grammar checker suggested "do an evaluation." The students substituted the more concise "evaluate."

On matters of syntax, most students were able to distinguish between strategic use of passive constructions and poor uses that begged for an active revision. For example, half of the students converted sentence (4) "Delay on this project is attributed to the apathy and lack of interest on the part of the hospitals" to some version of "Hospital apathy has delayed this project" because they wished to place emphasis on the hospitals' role in delaying the project. Both CorrecText and Grammatik did an excellent job of identifying passive constructions but only as a mechanical pattern of expression; neither program was able to distinguish between effective and ineffective uses of the passive voice. Finally, the students identified and corrected most matters of punctuation, including placing commas in compound sentences and at the end of introductory clauses. All matters of punctuation went unnoticed by the grammar checkers.

Nevertheless, the grammar checkers were considerably faster, and they caught some of the errors. Grammatik, in particular, identified several expressions that might be made more concise and offered both explanations and a diagram of a given sentence's structure, complete with links to definitions of parts of speech and sentence-level components. Of the two programs, Grammatik appeared to offer a more comprehensive analysis as well as a greater ability to provide on-line examples and explanation. It also delivered on the letter of its manufacturer's claim that it is "the first grammar checker to actually rewrite sentences." It alone was able to offer the user suggestions for revision in the form of a rewritten sentence.

■ Some Observations

Several observations might be made about both the "new wave" of desktop grammar checkers and the claims their manufacturers make about them. The first is that they appear more like their predecessors, in both mainframe and personal computing environments, in the *quality of the analysis produced*, than their manufacturers—Microsoft, Lotus, and Novell—might have their customers suppose. True, a parsing tree is now available for viewing and grammatical diagnosis of sentence elements. One will also find that the explanations of "rules" are more immediately accessible and complete in these programs than they were in their predecessors. Also, the underlying technology has been improved and optimized for Microsoft Windows, an operating system that most industry analysts agree has become the standard for ease of use in personal computing. As a consequence, some operations, such as moving from an indicated correction to actually making the change in the document, can be performed more seamlessly. Still, in all respects related to text management, these integrated programs differ little from those that preceded them. And most significantly telling, the results of an analysis performed using Rightwriter 3.1 and the version of Grammatik embedded in WordPerfect for Windows show a negligible gain in the number of problem areas identified.[36]

The second observation contains problematic implications for manufacturers and users alike, since it raises a question of relevance: grammar checkers will provide the greatest benefit to those who are familiar with the basic mechanics of English grammar and syntax. Such a conclusion recognizes an essential feature of the grammar checker, which is that it *generally* provides the user with a range of choices, among expressions. Choosing wisely requires an ability to weigh the choices, and that requires a knowledge of language and a clarity of intention. For example, choosing between an active and passive construction involves knowing that both are options for expression—something that neither CorrecText nor Grammatik appears to honor—and an awareness of the emphasis one wishes to achieve within the sentence. The user who is unaware of these matters is left, in the best cases, to choose by chance; in the worst cases, the user will simply follow the advice of the program, e.g., "rewrite in the active," regardless of how much sense the advice may make. In short, CorrecText and Grammatik, and other similar programs reviewed here, work well for those who know enough to choose well from the options they provide and are informed enough to be suspicious of their more groundless directions.[37] Although such a conclusion would probably not surprise those who teach or study composition, it runs counter to many of the claims that the manufacturers of these programs have made. For example, one of the claims made for Lifetree's Correct Grammar contradicts any notion that the writer must have some level of knowledge to use the program wisely: "Correct Grammar is the grammar expert . . . so you don't have to be."[38]

The third observation is related to the second: grammar checkers appear to provide the greatest potential benefit to those who are familiar enough with the basic mechanics of English grammar and syntax to take advantage of the programs' configurable features. For example, writers who know they have problems with nominalizations or have difficulty spotting strings of prepositions may find that configuring the program for these matters will provide them with a dedicated if limited reader. Similarly, writers who know enough about the difference between rules of usage and principles of effectiveness will also be skeptical of the programs' default bias against passive constructions. These writers are thus in a position to switch the passive voice toggle off entirely or leave it on if they wish to review instances of the passive in their writing. Unfortunately, user configuration is limited to selecting from a predetermined number of choices. Although a program that allowed the user to write rules for analysis once existed, it apparently did not have a broad enough appeal to remain on the market.[39]

The fourth observation is more positive, and like the second generation review of Rightwriter, more optimistic: careful use of computer-assisted grammar checkers will introduce into a writer's material a critical element not available elsewhere in language software. One could argue that the mere presence of a critical review, even a mechanical one, can assist the writer in improving writing because such a presence helps to simulate some of the responses a commenting reader might make.[40] One might also argue that it is a level of criticism that meets or exceeds what is available to most writers through readings they may request from their coworkers. In many cases, the computer programs give reasons, or something like reasons, for the revisions they suggest. Because of this, they can offer more to the workplace writer than the coworker who says "it sounds better" as the basis for a proposed change or the supervisor who may be inclined not to provide a reason in defense of a particular expression. They also offer the curious writer a path for increasing awareness of both the reasons for making changes and the names and definitions of some sentence elements that are involved in revision.

Finally, many of the changes these programs propose are *good* changes, particularly by the standards of writing in business, where conciseness is probably more highly prized than it is elsewhere. Most current studies of management would support the changes suggested by Grammatik in its analysis of the sample memo, particularly those changes that reduce the number of words without a loss in meaning. However, such support would be offered with skepticism, about both the capabilities of the programs as replacements for competent editors as well as the promise implied by the claims their manufacturers have made.

RELATED READINGS

Any list of works on computers and the process of revision should be viewed with skepticism simply because of the speed with which this field is developing. Because of that, the brief list below emphasizes principles of application instead of actual software programs. In addition to works on this list are several major studies listed in the notes to this chapter.

Kiefer, Kathleen E., and Smith, Charles R. "Textual Analysis with Computers: Test of Bell Laboratories' Computer Software." *Research in the Teaching of English* 17 (1983): 127–143.

Kiefer, Kathleen E., and Smith, Charles R. "Improving Students' Revising and Editing: "The Writer's Workbench System" in *The Computer in Composition Instruction*, 1973, 231–242.

Montague, M. *Computers, Cognition, and Writing Instruction*. New York: SUNY Press, 1990.

Sharples, M. *Cognition, Computers, and Creative Writing*. Chicester, England: Ellis Horwood Limited, 1985.

NOTES

1. Reviewed here are the programs that the industry has come to regard as the "major three" of personal and business computing. The first according to share of the market is Microsoft's Word for Windows 6.0, which ships with a built-in version of Houghton Mifflin's CorrectText Grammar Correction System, with underlying technology by Language Systems, Inc. The second in market share is Novell Corporation's Wordperfect 6.1 for Windows, which incorporates a technology developed by Reference Software, the company that pioneered Grammatik. And finally in market share is Lotus Corporation's Ami Pro 3.1, which relies on the same grammar-checking technology found in Microsoft's offering.

2. S. C. Hooper, *Using Word Processors in High School and College Writing Instruction: A Critical Review of Current Literature* (1987) (ERIC Document Reproduction Service No. ED 286–203). T. A. Maik, "Word Processing in the Business Writing Classroom: Applications and Reactions," *The Bulletin of the Association for Business Communication* (1987) 50(4): 46. B. Tone & Winchester, "Computer-Assisted Writing Instruction," *ERIC DIGEST: Clearinghouse on Reading and Communication Skills* (1988, Report No. 2) (ERIC Document Reproduction Service No. ED 293130). For those who have come to the opposite or to considerably more mixed conclusions, see Glenn Pearce and Randolph Barker, "A Comparison of Business Communication Quality between Computer Written and Handwritten Samples," *Journal of Business Communication* (Spring 1991): 141–50; C. Daiute, "Physical and Cognitive Factors in Revising: Insights from Studies with Computers," *Research in the Teaching of English* 20(2): 141–59; C. Etchison, "A Comparative Study of the Quality and Syntax of Compositions by First-Year College Students Using Handwriting and Word Processing," Glenville, WV: Glenville State College, 1985 (ERIC Document Reproduction Service No. ED 282215).

3. Gerrard, L. (1981). "Using a Computerized Text-Editor in Freshman Composition" (ERIC Document Retrieval Service No. ED 227512).

4. Bean, J. C. (1983). "Computerized Word-Processing as an Aid to Revision," *College Composition and Communication* 34 (2): 146–48.

5. Several concerns should probably be raised here. Although one might well claim that good things may come from making writing easier and faster, such a statement does not make the case for the result of *better* writing; it makes a case, and a circular one at that, for ease and speed. In fact, one might argue the opposite, that ease and speed result in hasty and ultimately poor writing. The same is true of revision, which will not improve writing simply because one has the incentive to make changes. Unless the changes are good ones, revision *of itself* will have little value.

6. A review of product literature since July 1994 will show that Microsoft Corporation, Novell, and Lotus Development have all extended claims for the ability of their word processors to improve readability. In 1995, Novell introduced "PerfectSense" and Lotus followed with "SmartSense," both terms coined to indicate the technology responsible for this increased ability. With the release of Word 6.0 in 1994, Microsoft introduced "IntelliSense," its label for a similar and competing technology.

7. On the predominance of word processing and how easily one can forget that it is the predominant business software application, see Al Williams, *Communication and Technology, Today and Tomorrow*, a publication of the Association for Business Communication, 1995.

Of the four commonly recognized major applications—spreadsheet, telecommunications, database, and word processing—word processing is by far the most heavily employed.

8. On the importance of writing in business, many studies exist. One that is infrequently cited but is both recent and comprehensive is Dan B. Curtis, Jerry L. Winsor, and Ronald D. Stephens, "National Preferences in Business and Communication Education, *Communication Education* 38, no. 1 (January 1989): 6–13. See also James A. Belohov, Paul O. Popp, and Michael S. Porte, "Communication: A View from the Inside of Business," *The Journal of Business Communication* 11 (1979): 53–59; Garda W. Bowman, "What Helps or Harms Promotability?" *Harvard Business Review* 42 (January–February 1964): 6–26; Francis J. Connelly, ed. "Accreditation Research Project Report of Phase 1," *AACSB Bulletin* 14 (Winter 1980): 2–15; S. Divita, "The Business School Graduate—Does the Product Fit the Need?" L. Preston, ed., *Business Environment/Public Policy 1979 Conference Papers.* AACSB, St. Louis (1979): 167–68; Alfred G. Edge and Ronald Greenwood, "How Managers Rank Knowledge, Skills and Attributes Possessed by Business Administration Graduates," *AACSB Bulletin* 11 (October 1974): 30–34; J. W. Hildebrandt, F. A. Bond, E. L. Miller, and W. W. Swinyard, "An Executive Appraisal of Courses Which Best Prepare One for General Management," *The Journal of Business Communication* 19 (Winter 1982): 5–15.

9. See Lorinda L. Cherry and W. Vesterman, "Writing Tools: The STYLE and DICTION Programs," *Computer Science Technical Report,* No. 91 (Murray Hill, NJ: Bell Laboratories, 1981); Lorinda L. Cherry, "Computer Aids for Writers," *ACM Sigplan Notices* 16 (no. 6, June 1981): 6267. For more on the early development of computer-assisted error detection, see Smith, Kiefer, and Gingrich, "Computers Come of Age in Writing Instruction," *Computers and the Humanities* 18 (1984): 215–24.

10. Nina H. McDonald et al., "The Writer's Workbench: Computer Aids for Text Analysis," *IEEE Transactions in Communication,* 30 (No. 1, January 1982): 105–110.

11. See Lance A. Miller et al., "Text Critiquing with the Epistle System: An Author's Aid to Better Syntax," National Computer Conference, May 4–7, 1981, *Proceedings* (Arlington, VA: AFIPS Press, 1981): 649–55; George E. Heidorn et al., "The Epistle Text-Critiquing System," *IBM Systems Journal,* 21 (1982): 305–26.

12. Heidorn et al., "Epistle," 305.

13. For more on NLP and NLP rules for parsing, see George E. Heidorn, "Augmented Phrase Structure Grammars," in *Theoretical Issues in Natural Language Processing,* ed. B. L. Nash-Webber and R. C. Schank, (Menlo Park, CA: Association for Computational Linguistics, 1975).

14. Although such an interface, which even took advantage of multiple colors to communicate functional distinctions, was considered quite advanced at the time of the Epistle experiment, it would be regarded as awkward, at least in the *degree* of the application, by today's standards. Still, no contemporary program has in *kind* moved beyond the concept of a windowed interface.

15. W. Strunk, Jr., and E. B. White, *The Elements of Style*, third edition, (New York: Macmillan, 1979). J. E. Warriner and F. Griffith, *English Grammar and Composition*, (New York: Harcourt, 1963).

16. Charles Smith, Kathleen Kiefer, and Patricia Gingrich, "Computers Come of Age in Writing Instruction," *Computers and the Humanities* 18 (1984): 215.

17. On *Wandah,* see Ruth Von Blum and Michael E. Cohen, "WANDAH: Writing Aid and Author's Helper," in *The Computer in Composition Instruction: A Writer's Tool,* ed. William Wresch (Urbana, IL: NCTE, 1984), 154–73. On *Homer,* see Michael E. Cohen and Richard A. Lanham, "Homer: Teaching Style with a Microcomputer" in *The Computer in Composition Instruction. A Writer's Tool,* ed. William Wresch (Urbana, IL: NCTE, 1984), 83–90.

18. For more on WANDAH, HOMER, and other less well-established programs used to

teach composition in college and university classrooms, see Marjorie Montague, *Computers, Cognition, and Writing Instruction* (Ithaca: State University of New York Press, 1990), 53–60. WANDAH is now distributed by Harcourt Brace Jovanovich, 7555 Caldwell Avenue, Chicago, IL 60648.

19. Charles R. Smith and Kathleen Kiefer, "Using the Writer's Workbench Programs at Colorado State University." *Sixth International Conference on Computers and the Humanities*, ed. Sarah K. Burton and Douglas D. Short, (Rockville, MD: Computer Science Press, 1983), 672–84.

20. Kathleen E. Kiefer and Charles R. Smith, "Textual Analysis with Computers: Test of Bell Laboratories' Computer Software," *Research in the Teaching of English* 17 (1983): 201–214.

21. Charles Smith, Kathleen Kiefer, and Patricia Gingrich, "Computers Come of Age in Writing Instruction," *Computers and the Humanities* 18 (1984): 222.

22. However, these can be distinguished from the next generation of "grammar checkers" because they were not really integrated but worked instead from a host program's macro. For example, a macro that *was accessed from within* in an early version of Wordperfect would exit the user from the word processor and enter text into the Grammatik, the grammar checker. Grammatik's operations would then take place outside the word processor. When Grammatik was finished, it would return the user to WordPerfect.

23. Other programs were released during this time, but they were not very competitive and enjoyed only a short life on the market. Among them: Scandanavian Systems' Readability Plus, the Modern Language Association's Editor, and Softkey Corporation's Key Grammar Checker.

24. *Poweredit,* version 1.0, Artificial Linguistics, Inc, 2301 North Akard, Suite 200, Dallas TX 75201 (214.880.9604); *Rightwriter*, version 1.0, Decisionware, Inc., 2033 Wood Street, Suite 218, Sarasota FL 33577 (813.923.0233); *Correct Grammar*, Lifetree Software Inc., 33 New Montgomery Street, Suite 1260, San Franciso CA 94105 (415.541.7864); *Grammatik II*, Reference Software International, 330 Townsend Street, Suite 119, San Francisco CA 94107 (415.541.0222).

25. Willis Buckingham, "Rightwriter," *Computers and the Humanities* 21 (1987): 69.

26. Buckingham, "Rightwriter," 70.

27. Michael Neuman, "Rightwriter 3.1," *Computers and the Humanities* 25 (1991): 57–58. Still, this optimism must be tempered with the same reviewer's assessment that "The potential is exciting but a review of one popular style-checking program—*RightWriter 3.1* by RightSoft Inc.—suggests that despite many technological and pedagogical strengths, the algorithms are not yet sufficiently adjustable or sophisticated to accommodate expository writing at the introductory level."

28. From Novell on-line product information. This document is available at the following web site: http://wp.novell.com/wp/wpwin61/prwp6toc.htm.

29. All screen captures for CorrecText and Grammatik were produced using Corel Corporation's Corel Capture 6.0 running under Microsoft Windows 95 operating system.

30. Ami Pro, Version 3.1, Lotus Development Corporation, on-line documentation, search string was "grammar checking."

31. From Novell on-line product information. This document is available at the following web site: http://wp.novell.com/wp/wpwin61/prwp6toc.htm.

32. Initial memo taken from Cutter Laboratories, Emeryville, California. The memo was then revised to include more sentence-level problems that are characteristic of business writing, as suggested by the following mainstream texts: Richard Lanham, *Revising Business Prose*, 3rd ed. (New York: Macmillan, 1992); Mary Munter, *Guide to Managerial Communication*,

2d ed. (Englewood Cliffs, NJ: Prentice-Hall, 1987); and Harriet Tichy, *Effective Writing for Engineers, Managers, Scientists* (New York: Wiley, 1986).

33. Toward the end of writing this chapter, the author received an examination copy of IBM's Word Pro for Windows 95. Unfortunately, rerunning the analysis on it produced no difference over Ami Pro. While Word Pro appears to offer many changes over Ami Pro, this test suggests that the grammar checker may have been carried over without revision.

34. Much has been written in general about the limits of statistical representations of readability and in particular about the problems of using scales based on sentence length. For a good review, see Gary A. Olson, James DeGeorge, and Richard Ray, *Style and Readability in Business Writing* (New York: Random House, 1985).

35. For more on the comparative analysis and experiment we conducted in the EMBA Program at Saint Mary's College of California, see Barry Eckhouse, "Grammar Checkers Promise Better Writing, Improved Readability" at http://www.zdnet.com/~pcweek/reviews/0807/tcheck.html, August 7, 1995.

36. This comparison revealed less difference in the quality of analysis than did the comparison between Grammatik and CorrecText covered here.

37. Probably the most glaring example of groundless direction comes in the form of the programs' default bias against passive constructions, a bias that is unshared by all but the most rudimentary handbooks.

38. From an advertisement quoted in Frank Madden, "Correct Grammar," *Computers and the Humanities* 25 (1991): 60.

39. This was a limited edition of Grammatik 6.0, which was published as a stand-alone program as part of WordPerfect Corporation's "Main Street." Of all grammar checkers issued to date, this one had the greatest potential for development since it offered the user a way of composing "rules" for text analysis. Sadly, WordPerfect discontinued this version just before the company was purchased by Novell in 1994.

40. This was the author's experience using Bell Laboratories Writer's Workbench in business composition courses at the Haas School of Business at the University of California, Berkeley, from 1982 to 1986. Students reported that the Workbench printout made them feel as if one of the teaching assistants had typed their comments on improving the students' writing.

Appendix

A

SAMPLE DOCUMENTS

Principled Organization

The documents in this section represent serious attempts at applying the principles explained in Chapter 2, Disposition and the Competitive Message. They are not offered as perfect examples to be imitated, but as realistic examples with very good features. As such, they should invite productive discussion. Although the documents in this section may also demonstrate principles covered elsewhere in this book, they are not offered specifically as an application of them.

In most cases, writers have agreed to the publication of their names, positions, and company affiliations. This information is offered to provide each writing sample with a context that includes information about the industry and the writer's place within the organization. In other cases, proprietary information has been deleted or replaced but not in a way that should interfere with the usefulness of the sample or with the reader's ability to understand it.

The beginning of each document identifies the writer, the writer's current company and position, and the solicitation that prompted the writing. Also preceding each document are several brief comments from the author of this book.

Informative Writing

Warehouse Club Project

Writer: Chuck Drake

Position: Manager, Marketing

Company: Clorox Company

Writer's Solicitation:

Oral request from a sales manager: "I want to know just what made the Warehouse Club project so successful."

Author's Comments: Drake has done a very good job here of adapting the concept of principled organization to his own uses. He has selected a form of organization ("planning," "execution," and "termination") that is not generic but is derived from the stages of the project he is discussing. Note also that he reviews his organization in his final paragraph.

TO: Sales Manager

FROM: Chuck Drake

SUBJECT: Success of the Warehouse Club Project

Here is the memo you requested on the success of the Warehouse Club project. Because the project occurred in three distinct phases, I have included in this memo a review of successes in the planning, execution, and termination stages of the project.

The Warehouse Club project achieved its first success in the planning phase. To begin with, a multidisciplinary project team was formed to quickly develop a project timeline and project management structure. In just two weeks after the first project team meeting, final packaging options were selected, and a project completion deadline and budget were established. As far as typical Clorox projects go, this rapid progress during the planning phase was by far the fastest Project start up ever.

Even though the planning phase of the Warehouse Club project got off to such a terrific start, many opportunities for things to go wrong still lay ahead. After planning, many successes were again achieved during this, the execution phase of the project. For example, the package design testing went as scheduled yielding successful qualification results. Purchasing of all packaging materials occurred two weeks early, which gave manufacturing ample time to qualify during pre-production trials. Finally, a smooth start up occurred at all three plants one month ahead of the start of ship target date.

Although the Warehouse Club project met its chief goal of supplying product on the target start of ship date, even more successes occurred during the final or termination phase of the project. For instance, many managers had heard about the successes of the project during the planning and execution phases and praised the project team for working well together. Most importantly, customers who received the new product were delighted with the package quality and quickness of delivery. Many customers commented that the Warehouse Club project was one of Clorox's most successful projects in years.

In short, the Warehouse Club project was successful throughout all three (planning, execution and termination) project phases. Already, many other project teams are incorporating key learnings from the Warehouse Club project into their time lines, activity lists, and project management structures.

Informative Writing

Facilities Status Plan

Writer: Jon Jardine

Position: Vice President

Company: Bank of America

Writer's Solicitation:

Sample Document 2

Request for information: "I would like a status update on the merger facilities plans."

Author's Comments: Jardine has used the principle of time productively here by adapting it to the temporal stages of his topic, the "facilities plans." The principle of time is a very good choice here and for other responses to requests for status reports.

TO: Anonymous

FROM: Jon Jardine

SUBJECT: Facilities Status Plan

Here is the information you requested regarding the facilities plan for the merger. Because the project involves multiple sites and several phases, I have included a review of pre-merger, day-one, and post-merger stages of the project.

The facilities plan was developed pre-merger by analyzing loan volumes, FTE, and workstation requirements in both organizations. During this stage, a capacity model was developed based on predetermined "sites of choice." The model included productivity increases by percentage in its formula and provided projected FTE, workstations, and square footage required to accommodate the merged organization. From the model, phased plans were developed based on day one and post merger requirements. Because most of the new loan volume is domiciled in the south and our existing plans to consolidate the XXXX function into SSSS center, SSSS center will need to expand by 350 workstations. The north NNNN center will need to expand by 300 workstations to accommodate XXXX functions and the new loan.

The pre-merger stage involves relocating two departments that are non CLD related in the SSSS center and one in the north NNNN center. Once these units are moved, the areas will be built out to accommodate two SSSS teams (55 workstations) and the new RIPPS LAN (30+ workstations) in the south; in the north, the LOC servicing department will be expanded (35 workstations), and the new RIPPS LAN will be installed as well (30 workstations).

Day-one will allow us to meet the minimal requirements for this stage. However, I have not received all data, voice, and hardware requirements which could affect day-one and post- merger activities. On day-one, the departments will have back filled into the new built-out areas and have the appropriate connectivity to begin processing the new loan volumes. At this time, the Phase II build out will begin. This includes moving the file and storage rooms to off-site facilities and converting the area to workstations. Initial estimates indicate we will be able to get 100 new workstations in the south and 30 in the north.

Post-merger activities include relocating the Servicing and LBP departments in the SSSS center to more strategic locations within the building, and relocating servicing and collections in the NNNN center to another building within the same complex. Based on the current schedule, this will be completed by the middle of the fourth quarter 1992. However, if the funding approval is delayed, this will seriously impede our ability to meet the day-one and post-merger requirements.

That is the status of the facilities plan for the merger. The plan is in line with the division's strategic goals to streamline the production process. In addition, the phase approach will allow us to meet the pre-merger, day-one, and post-merger capacity requirements.

Informative Writing

Expense Reimbursement Policies

Writer: Marian Kindblad

Position: Controller

Company: Harris & Associates

Writer's Solicitation:

Oral request: "The president of the company asked me to prepare a memo to all employees, informing them of the outcome of the Cal Trans State Audit and the resulting changes to employee reimbursement policies."

Author's Comments: Kindblad has made very good use of one version of the principle of inquiry, a combination of *which, why,* and *how.* Notice that each paragraph opens with a transition that has a clear reference to her preview in the first paragraph.

TO: All Employees

FROM: Accounting

SUBJECT: Revisions: Expense Reimbursement Policies

The State of California has completed the audit of the firm's overhead expenses for the fiscal years 1989 through 1991. The results of this audit were that significant amounts of employees' reimbursable expenses have been disallowed. Disallowed expenses mean that these expenses cannot be included in the firm's overhead rate, and therefore, not reimbursed by the State. Because the firm will not be reimbursed for specific types of expenses, we must revise some of our reimbursement policies to comply with the state. The policy revisions are effective immediately. This memo details which expenses were disallowed, why the expenses did not comply with the state, and how the reimbursement policies have changed.

Categories of expenses which were targeted by the state as non-allowable are business meals, some travel charges, and any charge with insufficient documentation. The charges most often disallowed by the auditors were business meals. The firm's definition of a business meal has been any meal where business was discussed, which is broad in scope. Travel charges were less often cited but were a significant percentage of the overhead. The travel charges denied were meals and lodging, while all other travel related charges were accepted. The charges least often rejected were business expenses with insufficient documentation. Documentation includes the date and location of the event, who attended, and the nature of the business discussion.

The auditors listed several reasons why employees' expenses were rejected. The most important was insufficient documentation of the business expense. If the firm does not comply with the state in our documentation procedures, then we are not complying with the IRS, and are facing potential tax fines. Next in importance were the large number of disallowed business meals which were attended by employees only, and not clients. These meals were rejected because our office has several conference rooms where business can be discussed rather than going to a restaurant. Finally, excessive travel charges were denied because they exceeded the daily maximum rates set by the state of $116.00 for food and lodging.

Despite the weeks spent reviewing hundreds of expense reports, the matter of how to correct these noncompliance issues is fairly simple. The easiest issue to resolve is that of "employee only" business meals. Business-meals where clients are not present will no longer be reimbursed and these meetings should be held in the office. Providing sufficient documentation will also be easy to correct because the firm will be providing "Expense Documentation" slips to be filled out and attached with the appropriate type of expenses. This slip requires the four categories of information mandated by the IRS, and expenses will not be reimbursed without it. The new "Expense Documentation" forms are available in Accounting. Last, and not as simple, are the travel expenses. Our firm uses corporate rates for lodging, and our research shows that locating adequate lodging in large cities below the state's requirements is difficult. Therefore, the firm will absorb charges above the state's maximum rates and will continue to negotiate with hotels for reduced rates.

Your cooperation in complying with the firm's revised policies in the areas of business meals, travel, and documentation will improve the firm's credibility with our governing agencies and will keep our overhead costs at a level which is competitive in the industry.

Informative Writing

Diced Tomatoes

Writer: Dick Robinson

Position: Sales Manager, IntraFoods Division

Company: Golden Technologies Company

Writer's Solicitation:

Oral request from supervisor: "I have a meeting with Ingomar next week and they would like to discuss the possibility of adding a diced tomato line to their existing tomato paste line. Please give me your opinion of such a move."

Author's Comments: Robinson has done a fine job here by using two familiar principles of organization. He has presented one as the primary structure (advantages and disadvantages) and one as the substructure (obvious, less obvious, and short-term and long-term).

TO: Sales Manager

FROM: Dick Robinson

SUBJECT: Diced Tomatoes

Here is the memo you requested on Ingomar adding diced tomato capacity to their existing tomato paste line. Without knowing any of the costs associated with the project, I cannot comment on its financial feasibility. I have, however, included in this memo some advantages, some disadvantages, and a brief conclusion of a diced tomato project from a sales viewpoint.

An obvious advantage of adding diced tomatoes is that most of our tomato paste customers also use diced. Adding a diced line would allow us to kill two birds with one stone by selling two products to the same customer. The customer relationships we have would make sales of diced a very easy and natural transition.

A less obvious advantage of adding a diced line is Ingomar's quality image. Ingomar's tomato paste quality is the industry standard; moreover, if Ingomar could offer diced customers the same high quality, selling diced would be easy. As we have found in selling Ingomar's paste, quality sells itself.

The short-term disadvantage to entering the diced market is the current excess supply. Record tomato crops coupled with ensuing competition have forced diced tomato prices to a seven year low and very near, if not below, total cost. Adding volume to this market will only make matters worse. If Ingomar enters this market now, we can expect even lower prices as the competition intensifies. We can also expect, at least initially, that we will have to discount to get orders.

A long-term disadvantage to entering the diced market is new technology. Within the next few years, equipment will be available that will allow diced tomatoes to be produced and packed antiseptically. In addition to the obvious advantages of a sterile package, the aseptic packing line produces a firmer diced and allows for a more precise cut, making it possible to meet the exact size specification of any customer. The new equipment for producing antiseptically packed diced could render current technology obsolete.

In conclusion, the addition of a diced line would complement Ingomar's current production. We could effect sales with a minimum investment. The timing of the project, however, is the critical factor.

Informative Writing

XYZ Project

Writer: Proprietary

Position: Proprietary

Company: Proprietary

Writer's Solicitation:

Voice-mail request from the division manager: "I understand that an audit of the XYZ Project was conducted. Any reason to be concerned? Please get back to me in a couple of days."

Author's Comments: This writer has used *process, major issues*, and *expected outcomes* as a three-part structure because they describe the major parts of an external audit. Notice the use of the substructure of time (*before*, *during*, and *after*) in paragraph three, and the review of the primary structure in the final paragraph.

TO: Division Manager

FROM: Proprietary

SUBJECT: XYZ Project

Here is the information you requested regarding the XYZ project audit. Because this audit was actually an internal review prior to an actual regulatory audit, I have described our process, major issues, and expected outcomes of an external audit in this memo.

The process of our internal audit was structured as much as possible to simulate an actual regulatory audit. We used a consultant who was very familiar with energy conservation work. He was asked to be very business like and to conduct the audit according to his schedule and technical judgment. In general, our auditor was to role play a very aggressive regulator. The auditor spent over two days checking this project. Most of the project personnel were interviewed, with much of the technical data intentionally challenged.

Several major issues were raised by this simulated audit. Much of the early planning information, which dates back three or four years ago, was not readily available. Hence, the original justification of the project was perceived as weak. During the project, the reporting mechanisms were changed frequently. While this can be explained because of what we learned during the course of the project, this gives the appearance of being unorganized and uncontrolled. Finally, future uses of the project and conclusions are still being developed. Technology and information transfer are still key outcomes of the project; however, we learned that the paperwork and data do not clearly reflect this. With this past, present, and future perspective on the project management issues, we can turn to expected outcomes of a "real" audit.

We expect a real audit to be very positive for the company. While the issues raised by the simulated audit are substantive, the issues are readily rebutted. The past planning information has already been collected and organized. The project reports are inconsistent in style and content; nevertheless, the reports are regular, and we can show that informed management actions, based on these reports, were taken. Regarding the information transfer aspect of the project, this evaluation has been underway for at least three months and will be concluded in two weeks. The cost effectiveness of the work and validity of all contracts and costs were substantiated in the preliminary audit, and are not expected to be an issue in the regulatory audit.

On the basis of our process, major issues raised, and expected outcome, I believe there are no major risks if we receive a formal regulatory audit of the XYZ project. The internal, simulated audit was a very worthwhile endeavor.

SAMPLE DOCUMENTS

Argumentation

The prooflines and documents in this section are attempts at applying the principles explained in Chapters 3, 4, and 5. They are not offered as perfect examples but as good examples that demonstrate the important features of a difficult type of writing. They should invite productive discussion. Although the papers in this section may also demonstrate principles covered elsewhere in this book, they are not offered specifically as an application of them.

In most cases, writers have agreed to publication of their names, positions, and company affiliations. This information is offered to provide each writing sample with a context that includes information about the industry and the writer's place within the organization. In some cases, proprietary information has been deleted but not in a way that should interfere with the usefulness of the sample or with the reader's ability to understand it.

The beginning of each document identifies the writer, and the writer's current company and position. Also preceding each document are several brief comments from the author of this book.

Sample
Document 1

Argumentative Writing

Reducing Refinery Turnaround Expenses

Writer: John Miller

Position: Manager, Engineering

Company: Tosco Oil

Author's Comments: Miller's introduction is particularly well constructed. In his first paragraph, he raises issues about continued increases in turnaround expenses and refers to other companies using managers with responsibilities for turnaround. As a consequence, he is able to raise the following question at issue in a way that should make especially good sense to his reader: "We need to determine if assigning a project manager with full responsibility and authority for the turnaround planning and execution will reduce future refinery turnaround expenses."

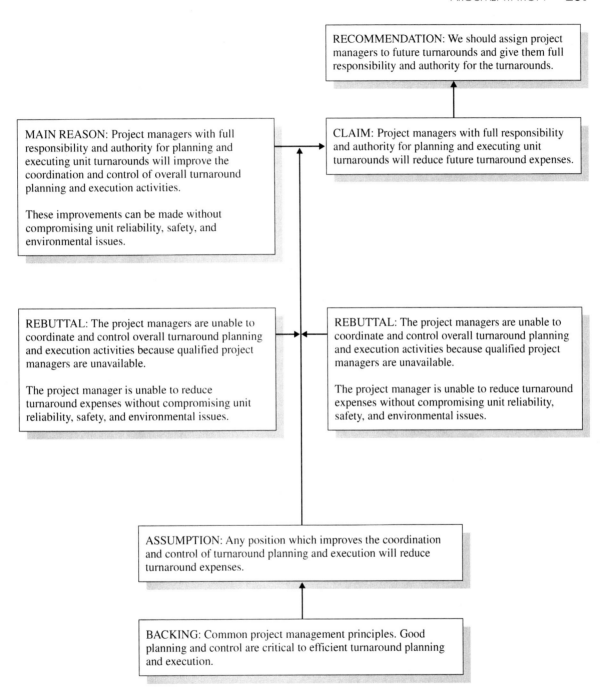

RECOMMENDATION: We should assign project managers to future turnarounds and give them full responsibility and authority for the turnarounds.

MAIN REASON: Project managers with full responsibility and authority for planning and executing unit turnarounds will improve the coordination and control of overall turnaround planning and execution activities.

These improvements can be made without compromising unit reliability, safety, and environmental issues.

CLAIM: Project managers with full responsibility and authority for planning and executing unit turnarounds will reduce future turnaround expenses.

REBUTTAL: The project managers are unable to coordinate and control overall turnaround planning and execution activities because qualified project managers are unavailable.

The project manager is unable to reduce turnaround expenses without compromising unit reliability, safety, and environmental issues.

REBUTTAL: The project managers are unable to coordinate and control overall turnaround planning and execution activities because qualified project managers are unavailable.

The project manager is unable to reduce turnaround expenses without compromising unit reliability, safety, and environmental issues.

ASSUMPTION: Any position which improves the coordination and control of turnaround planning and execution will reduce turnaround expenses.

BACKING: Common project management principles. Good planning and control are critical to efficient turnaround planning and execution.

FIGURE B.1

To: Refinery Manager

From: J. E. Miller

Subject: Reducing Refinery Turnaround Expenses

The Avon Refinery turnaround expenses continue to increase despite many organizational changes and improvements made in the last couple of years. We have created matrix turnaround project groups, TAC teams, made up of members from the different responsible departments. These multidisciplinary turnaround project groups normally contain all the personnel needed for developing, planning, and executing unit turnarounds efficiently. As a result, some improvements have been made in turnaround planning and execution. Unfortunately, our overall turnaround expenses continue to increase. Causes for continued increased turnaround expenses are partially due to increased safety and environmental restrictions. These factors, however, do not fully account for our inability to control and reduce turn around expenses. The problem appears to be caused by split responsibility and authority of the TAC team members. Many companies solve this problem by assigning a project manager overall responsibility for turnarounds. Our existing TAC teams do not have a single project manager with overall responsibility and authority to coordinate and control the turnaround planning and execution activities. We need to determine if assigning a project manager with full responsibility and authority for the turnaround planning and execution will reduce future refinery turnaround expenses.

Project managers are normally assigned to all major design and construction projects. The project manager's responsibility is to coordinate and control the many different tasks and disciplines required to develop and complete the project within budget and on schedule. Turnarounds are very similar to design and construction projects. They involve numerous different tasks and require the multidiscipline expertise of our TAC teams. The performance of our TAC teams can be increased by improving the coordination and control of the different tasks carried out by this group. Project managers with overall responsibility for planning and executing turnarounds, and given adequate authority to control overall required resources can solve the coordination and control problems of existing TAC teams. This will eliminate the delays or redundant efforts which lead to increased turnaround expenses.

The reason for the TAC teams' inability to reduce turnaround expenses may be the matrix organizational structure. No single group or person has overall responsibility and authority for the turnaround planning and execution. Most of the team members report to different departments that have different responsibilities and priorities. As a result, the responsibility and authority for different aspects of the turnaround are split among a number of individuals. Differences in personal opinions and priorities lead to coordination problems and delays. Teamwork, which is essential to the success of the TAC team matrix organization, breaks down because of different or conflicting member priorities. This leads to lower quality turnaround planning and reduced turnaround execution efficiency. Both of these problems prevent the TAC team from achieving its purpose, reducing turnaround expenses.

Project managers assigned overall responsibility for turnarounds can improve the coordination of TAC team member activities and eliminate the problem of different team member priorities. To accomplish these needed improvements, the TAC team and associated turnaround personnel should be assigned to report to the turnaround manager. The turnaround project team members' priorities and schedules must be set by the project manager. Our refinery management must fully support and give the turnaround project manager the authority to resolve and approve all final decisions required to plan and execute the turnaround efficiently. To control and reduce turnaround expenses the TAC teams need to make timely decisions and reach reasonable compromises on all issues related to the turnaround including work scope, repair methods, permitting, and schedules. Only by assigning a single project manager full responsibility for our major turnarounds and by empowering them with adequate authority to accomplish their jobs will we successfully reduce turnaround expenses. To insure individual member dedication to the team, their future appraisals and merit raises should be based largely on the turnaround manager's appraisal of their team and individual job performance.

Some managers believe that the existing TAC teams will be capable of reducing turnaround expenses without assigning an additional project manager. The TAC teams are relatively new to the refinery organization and need time to develop and perform efficiently. This should be true since the TAC teams are made up of some of our most experienced and capable personnel. The problems that face our TAC teams are increased turnaround execution regulatory demands and increased company priority to reduce turnaround expenses. It has been over two years since the TAC teams were first initiated. During this period, the TAC teams have developed and made definite improvements to our turnaround planning and execution. These improvements, unfortunately, have been offset by the increased demands of safety and environmental regulations. Despite the TAC teams' best efforts, our turnaround expenses continue to increase. Given sufficient time, of possibly another two or three years, the existing TAC team should be able to make the needed improvements for controlling and reducing turnaround expenses. If we are to control and reduce our turnaround expenses next year, the TAC team performances must increase at a greater rate than has been demonstrated to date. Because of the high company priority of reducing turnaround expenses in the short term, we need to accelerate the development of our TAC teams. Matrix organizations can work well if the team members are all equally motivated to achieve the same goals. Even much more experienced and well trained organizations than ours have difficulty managing matrix project teams to achieve consistent quality performance. To ensure and achieve greater project team performance, a single project manager is normally assigned the overall responsibility for the project. A project manager given adequate authority to fully control the TAC team and other resources necessary for completing the project within budget and schedule, will reduce turnaround expenses.

Choosing an ineffective project manager will not achieve the needed improvements in TAC team performance. A poor project manager could actually reduce the performance of our existing TAC teams. This is a potential problem that we must avoid in selecting a turnaround project manager. Selection of a turnaround project manager must be done carefully to ensure that necessary coordination and control improvements are made in planning and executing a turnaround. A number of very qualified and experienced individuals are on the present TAC teams. We should select the most qualified people and assign them full responsibility for the turnaround development through execution. A replacement for their responsibilities on the TAC team must also be assigned. Turnaround project management is a full-time job. They must be allowed to concentrate their full efforts to overall coordination and planning for the turnaround.

Some managers are concerned that too much priority will be put on turn around project expense and schedule management. Giving the turnaround project manager too much authority could lead to compromising safety and environmental issues during the turnaround, and unit reliability in the longer term. This is a potential problem if we do not carefully choose the proper person to manage the turnaround, and do not clearly communicate that the overall turnaround responsibility includes completing it efficiently without reducing unit reliability, safety, or environmental compliance. Compromising on work scope, safety, and environmental issues does not mean a reduction in performance or quality in any of these areas. Compromising means managing and balancing the costs and risks encountered during a turnaround. Differences of opinion by team members are settled by mutual concessions. One of the reasons our turnaround expenses are so high is that often we do not compromise on many issues due to split responsibilities and authority. The project manager's responsibility will be to facilitate compromise during turnaround planning and execution without significantly reducing reliability, safety, or environmental compliance. Turnaround expenses will be reduced by eliminating wasted resources which do not provide any significant benefits.

We can improve the planning and execution of turnarounds at the Avon Refinery by assigning project managers and making them responsible for the overall turnaround development and execution. Given adequate authority and support, turnaround managers will improve the coordination and control of our turnarounds. The TAC team and associated turnaround personnel should be assigned to report to the turnaround manager. Turnaround managers will allow us to make the needed improvements to reduce turnaround expenses. Reduced refinery turnaround expenses will help improve Tosco's future cash flows and ability to make large capital investments required for clean fuels and environmental compliance regulations. This will help us to remain competitive in the future refining market and will be critical to the long-term survival of the company.

Argumentative Writing

Laptop Computers

Writer: Richard Dorfman

Position: Senior Account Manager

Company: General Electric Information Services

Author's comments: Dorfman has approached developing his main reason in a creative and productive way: instead of using the journalistic questions directly, he has offered subordinate points that explain the three key terms of his main reason: *productivity*, *customer service*, and *company image*. These three subordinate points are then presented in separate paragraphs. Note also his strategic use of the backing. The magazine article he refers to was distributed for general reading by upper management.

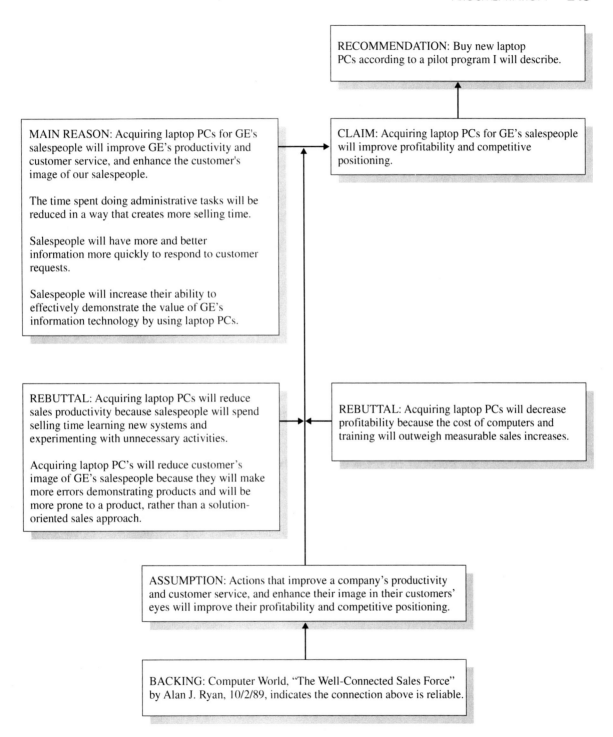

RECOMMENDATION: Buy new laptop PCs according to a pilot program I will describe.

MAIN REASON: Acquiring laptop PCs for GE's salespeople will improve GE's productivity and customer service, and enhance the customer's image of our salespeople.

The time spent doing administrative tasks will be reduced in a way that creates more selling time.

Salespeople will have more and better information more quickly to respond to customer requests.

Salespeople will increase their ability to effectively demonstrate the value of GE's information technology by using laptop PCs.

CLAIM: Acquiring laptop PCs for GE's salespeople will improve profitability and competitive positioning.

REBUTTAL: Acquiring laptop PCs will reduce sales productivity because salespeople will spend selling time learning new systems and experimenting with unnecessary activities.

Acquiring laptop PC's will reduce customer's image of GE's salespeople because they will make more errors demonstrating products and will be more prone to a product, rather than a solution-oriented sales approach.

REBUTTAL: Acquiring laptop PCs will decrease profitability because the cost of computers and training will outweigh measurable sales increases.

ASSUMPTION: Actions that improve a company's productivity and customer service, and enhance their image in their customers' eyes will improve their profitability and competitive positioning.

BACKING: Computer World, "The Well-Connected Sales Force" by Alan J. Ryan, 10/2/89, indicates the connection above is reliable.

FIGURE B.2

TO: Sales Manager

FROM: Richard Dorfman

SUBJECT: Laptop Computers

According to the October 2, 1989 *Computer World* article entitled "The Well-Connected Sales Force," companies such as Levi Strauss, Sterling Drugs, and Hanes Hosiery have improved their profitability and competitive positioning as a result of giving salespeople better information support systems, attributing much of their success to salespeople using laptop PCs. GE's salespeople refer to this magazine article when selling to vice presidents of sales and marketing, helping us demonstrate the potential for improved profitability through sales force automation using information technology.

Based on our sales experience, we are finding that companies having geographically disbursed sales forces, selling highly complex business solutions, operating worldwide will profit most from using laptop PCs. Certainly, GE's sales force fits this profile, since our mission is providing multinational clients better access to information for improved decision making, for competitive advantage, and to achieve higher profits. Given the success other companies have achieved, GE's business profile, and management's increasing attention to improving sales productivity, we need to determine if acquiring laptop PCs for GE's salespeople will improve GE's profitability and competitive positioning.

Much of our time is spent communicating information: demonstrating to prospective clients the value of information systems solutions; helping clients order new services, checking the status of shipments, resolving billing disputes; and internally communicating sales reports, forecasts, pricing proposal, and market data.

While many of these communication processes are automated, GE salespeople cannot take full advantage of them, since we are often away from our offices. Equipped with laptop PCs, we could better communicate timely information with clients, prospective clients, and colleagues, such as special pricing requests, proposal data, and problem status updates. Because virtually all GE sales and client support situations require team management, timely communication is critical to our success.

As we try to develop strong client relationships, our need increases for more immediate access to up-to-date customer, competitive, and market data. Acquiring laptop PCs for GE's salespeople will increase our productivity by reducing the time we spend doing administrative tasks resulting in more face-to-face selling time, and improve customer service by providing clients with more timely and accurate information. Using laptops could eliminate unnecessary trips into the office and reduce alternative, more costly means of communication.

When purchasing laptops has been discussed in the past, some felt it would reduce sales productivity because salespeople would waste selling time learning new systems and experimenting with unnecessary activities, arguing against automation on the grounds that the cost of computers and related training will outweigh potential sales gains. While this is a valid concern for many businesses, GE's ability to sell successfully depends upon how responsive we are to our clients and how well we demonstrate both our products and the value of automation.

Results from other companies implementing laptops for their sales force indicate that properly planned implementations can reduce the time salespeople spend doing administrative tasks and create more face to face selling time. If salespeople could use the time saved to increase their sales activity by even one more sales call per week, the resulting productivity improvement will more than justify the additional cost. Because sales communication systems are already being used, the usual training and startup costs other companies have should not apply.

Critics opposing automation may point toward increased problems resulting from errors demonstrating products. While it is true that salespeople will be more often tasked with showing customers our products, this additional practice time will improve the quality of demonstrations and better prepare us for unexpected problems.

Other opponents of issuing laptops to our salespeople fear we may develop tendencies toward a product, rather than a solution-oriented sales approach. While this may have happened to other companies, given that GE's clients and prospective customers are seeking strategic use of information support systems, they will question why we are not taking advantage of the very technology we are recommending. To be successful, GE salespeople need more and better information more quickly to respond to customer requests and marketplace demands.

Not only will buying laptop PCs for GE's salespeople improve productivity, customer service, and competitive positioning resulting in greater profitability, their purchase legitimizes what we sell, maximizing our chances of meeting our long range revenue objectives. If we do not automating our sales, I am concerned we may undercut the effectiveness of what we are selling as well as the message that automation is an enhancement to sales productivity. This would jeopardizing our reputation as an information technology leader. Given our immediate need to substantially improve productivity, my frequent use of PCs, and my experience using our products, I recommend GE provide me a laptop PC for six months, starting March 1, to market test its viability and to more precisely quantify the value GE can expect to receive from sales force automation.

Argumentative Writing

Automated Fax Response System

Writer: Robert Armijo

Position: General Manager

Company: Mobius Technologies

Author's comments: Armijo originally produced an argument in the form of a syllogism and counterstatements, and it was recast into the accompanying proofline. Because of that, backing is not provided. Particularly worth noticing in Bert's document is his use of the journalistic questions. The openings of paragraphs two three and five are clearly framed from the questions *what*, *who*, and *how*. Also worth noting is his rebuttal to the claim in paragraph six. It is clearly introduced as the concern of another. The basis of the rebuttal is indicated, and Armijo's response follows.

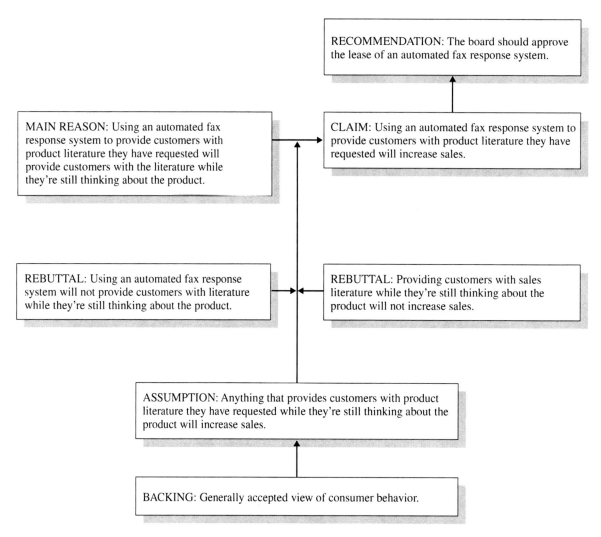

FIGURE B.3

To: Recipient

From: Bert Armijo

Subject: Automated Fax Response System

As the board requested, I have examined the possibility of using an automated fax response system at Mobius to fulfill customer requests for literature. Such systems are in wide use by other successful mail-order companies.
The manufacturers of the systems promise that their products will improve
customer service and thus increase sales. Therefore, we must determine if using an automated fax response system at Mobius will increase sales.

An automated fax response system is a computer phone system which allows customers to dial in and request information on Mobius products.
Customers enter our product codes on their touch-tone phone to specify
what information they want to receive and their fax phone number, and
then the system sends the requested literature to the customer's fax machine. Because the system is automated, it operates around the clock, and
allows customers to call when it is convenient for them. The system at-
taches to our existing phone switch, and will allow customers to access
the system at our existing phone numbers. Therefore, we would benefit
from the system almost immediately without having to change our existing advertisements or catalogs.

Using automated fax response system becomes more important if we consider who is using them. Our two largest competitors, Radius and Daystar,
have both implemented automated fax response systems during the last
year. Daystar no longer mails printed material; if a customer does not
have a fax machine, Daystar will fax it to a local Mail Boxes Etc. fran-
chise for the customer at Daystar's expense. MacWarehouse, our largest
retailer, has had an automated fax response system, which provides information on hundreds of products, for almost two years. All three companies promote their fax response systems heavily in advertisements and
brochures. Based solely on the rapid sales growth of these three companies during the last year, we can conclude that automated fax response
systems are an effective method to respond to customer's requests for
information.

To understand the effect the automated fax response system will have on sales, we need to examine how the system will operate in the sales cycle Our research shows that only thirty percent of prospective customers are ready to order from Mobius when they make their first call. Other customers call to request information which they will use to decide whether to buy. Further, almost forty percent of our sales come from first time customers making their second call. Therefore, our sales volume depends upon our ability to convert those informative calls into sales calls. Logically, these callers will never be more receptive to our message than when they place the call. So, if we can provide the literature immediately, we will convert more of these prospects to sales.

However, some board members believe that providing customers with sales literature while they're still thinking about the product will not increase sales. I can appreciate this concern, because it isn't obvious that if we provide prospective customers with literature quickly, we will affect sales closure. However, data we collect during follow-up calls reveal that more than twenty percent of prospective customers are no longer interested when they receive the literature one week later because they purchased another product, talked to someone who disapproved of the idea, or simply had time to reconsider the purchase. Another ten percent never received the literature, so we mail another package to the customer. Therefore, we currently lose one third of our sales prospects, and if we use the automated fax response system, we will eliminate both problems.

Because of our current cash flow problems, we can expect concerns about the cost of the fax response system. While this is reasonable, we must not forget that the financial effect of the system is far greater than the actual cost of the equipment. Mobius would lease the system, so the initial capital requirement will be only $4,000. Based on our current volume of inquiries, I project $3,000 per month in phone charges for the system, but we can offset this cost if we reduce the printing and mailroom labor costs. However, the increase in sales will make the return period for the system only two to three months.

Our sales people have also expressed concern that an automated fax response system won't provide customer information for sales follow up. Their concern is valid, because many systems don't provide follow-up customer information, and we currently call every prospective customer one week after we mail literature. However, the system we're considering has just been introduced, and has the capability to collect enough information for our sales people to make their follow-up calls. Therefore, the only effect of the system on follow-up calls will be allowing sales people to call customers the same day.

We can see that use of an automated fax response system will lead to increased sales. To ensure that Mobius takes advantage of this opportunity, I recommend that the board approve the lease of an automated fax response system.

Argumentative Writing

Standardized Interview Questions

Writer: Chuck Drake

Position: Associate Marketing Manager

Company: Clorox Company

Author's comments: Drake's use of the journalistic questions is evident in paragraphs three (*what*), four (*how*), five (*why*), and seven (*who*). In addition, he is able to use the question *when* in paragraph six to emphasize the urgency and timing of his eventual recommendation. Notice also his treatment of opposition in paragraphs eight, nine, and ten. In each case, he introduces the opposing point of view, offers some explanation for that view, and then responds to it.

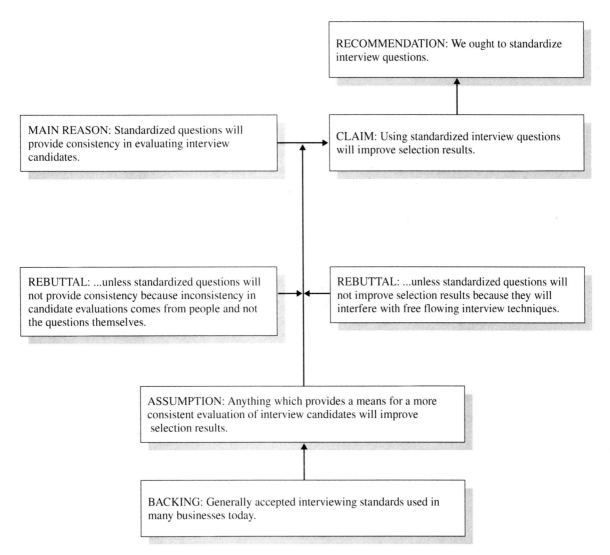

FIGURE B.4

TO: Sales Manager

FROM: Chuck Drake

SUBJECT: Standardized Interview Questions

For several years, we have involved many of our staff in the interview process as a way to improve the quality of selection decisions. Our "team" approach to conducting interviews is aimed at improving our chances at selecting the best candidates for very important assignments we have on our staff. In the past, our interview "process" has been judged to be successful as demonstrated by the many fine new employees which have been identified and hired into our staff group.

Despite these past positive results, we are finding that our interview process does not consistently yield qualified new hires who have the skills necessary to contribute quickly and effectively in staff assignments. In addition, some staff members feel that our interview process has inappropriately valued the skills of other candidates which were not selected by the interview teams. Even more disturbing, some of the staff members who are usually involved in the interview process have earned a reputation of being "easy," "picky," or "unprofessional" in their style of interviewing as perceived by their peers. As staff managers, we should be concerned about the inconsistent opinions and results of our selection process. Recently, a suggestion was made that perhaps use of standardized interview questions would improve the consistency and therefore results of the interview process. Given the importance of new employee selection, we must determine whether using standardized interview questions will improve our selection results.

First, we should understand what the typical standardized questions are that would be used in our existing interview process as well as how they would be developed. Standardized questions are those necessary for each focus area considered by the interview teams during the interview process. An example question for the area of Interpersonal skills would be: "Give an example of a situation in which you have had to mediate an argument at work or elsewhere and explain how you helped resolve this conflict." Another example question in the area of Technical skills might be: "Explain a situation where something broke down or began operating improperly either at work or elsewhere and you had to figure out what went wrong and effect repairs." All questions would be worded such that each addressed a key job skill requirement.

How the standardized questions would be developed is very important. All staff members involved in the selection process would be asked to write down questions each feels would be appropriate for each interview focus area. A smaller group of staff would consolidate these lists into five or six questions for each focus area and send this revised list back to the staff for further comment and review. Finally, to ensure that the questions are "fair and legal" to ask interview candidates, a draft of the staff's list of questions would be sent to Personnel for review and comment. Once Personnel has completed the review, a final draft version of these questions would route one last time to the staff involved in interviewing to ensure acceptance of these new standards. Once accepted, these standard questions in interviews would begin to be used immediately. As job skills change or as otherwise warranted, the standardized interview questions would be reviewed and would follow the same process of development as just outlined.

Why would the use of standardized interview questions improve the overall consistency and results of our selection process? First, using standardized questions would allow for easy and more consistent comparison of different candidate responses as well as remove any interviewer bias involved in the line of questioning. Second, by applying the same questions several times to different candidates, interviewers will be better able to calibrate differences in candidate skill levels. This will improve the selection team's overall ability to detect candidate skill strengths and weaknesses. Further, using standardized interview questions would remove most of the interviewer "style" concerns that some staff have developed about each other by ensuring that a consistent line of questioning will occur during the course of an interview. This should improve the overall credibility of our selection process to the staff members who actively interview.

Now is the time to consider using standardized interview questions in our selection process. Now that the busy summer transition period is complete, many new people are in the department and will be involved in the interview process. In addition, the experienced staff members (who have interviewed previously and are familiar with staff jobs) will continue to be actively involved in the selection process as well. By implementing standardized interview questions now, the experienced staff members can best transfer their own interview experience to the new people who will soon be conducting interviews themselves. Another important time related reason to avoid delaying implementing standardized interview questions is the fact that our most recent new hires have not met our performance expectations due in part to a poor assessment of their skills made during staff interviews. We need to correct our interview process immediately so that the two hiring decisions we must make by January can benefit from an improved selection process.

The benefits of using standardized interview questions become clear when we consider just who will benefit. First, all new hires will benefit because more consistency in skill assessment will have occurred during the interview process, thus improving their chances of having the necessary skills to be successful in their new assignments. Second, all current staff members will benefit because the standardized questions will help them evaluate candidates more objectively and eliminate decisions based mostly on "candidate personality or gut feeling." Finally, management will benefit because by developing and using standardized interview questions, important skill requirements of new hires would be defined and therefore more likely to be met by new hires. In addition, standardized questions will make it less likely for "good" candidates to be rejected in the interview process and therefore increase the quality of hiring decisions overall.

However, some staff members do not believe that implementing standardized interview questions will improve selection results. Instead, they believe that using standardized questions will impair their own ability to "free form or adapt" questions to each candidates background which is essential to developing an overall assessment of a person's skill level. I do agree it is important to develop individualized questioning in an interview because often times answers to these creative questions do yield valuable candidate information. However, using standardized questions will not eliminate the opportunity to pursue these creative lines of questioning. Instead, standardized questions provide the essential basis or platform from which further interview questions could and should develop. Asking only six to seven required questions in the 45 min. interview would allow ample time to explore other lines of questioning with candidates.

Most managers would agree that the concern for the creative line of questioning could be overcome by limiting the number of standardized questions asked and by managing interview time effectively. However, other managers believe that implementing standardized interview questions is too simple an approach to trying to improve selection results by increasing consistency. They point out that by involving unskilled interviewers in the selection process, even standardized questions would be misinterpreted or improperly "weighted" during interviews. Furthermore, they believe that fewer, more skilled senior staff/managers should conduct all interviews in order to improve consistency instead of using standardized interview questions.

In all fairness, I do believe that our senior staff/managers have better interviewing skills primarily because of experience than do most other staff members. However, I would expect that these "veteran" interviewers would contribute to the development of standardized questions which would incorporate their vast interviewing experience. In addition, involving the other staff members in the selection process ensures consideration of the current requirements of the job. By discussing the candidate's answers to standardized questions with the entire interview team, the effects of misinterpreting or improperly "weighting" candidate answers will be minimized. Using standardized questions is the best way of using the experience possessed by all interviewers while providing a way for current job requirements to be considered in the candidate evaluation.

In short, unless we improve our selection process, we will probably repeat the same poor selection results that our current interview process has delivered. With the addition of standardized interview questions to our selection process, we can improve the success rate of selecting new hires with the right skills for staff assignments. In sum, we need to begin to develop and implement the use of standardized interview questions in our interview process right away.

Argumentative Writing

Data Modeling Internship Program

Writer: Bette Smith

Position: Director

Company: Pacific Bell

Author's comments: Smith's proofline and document are extraordinary in their complexity of planning and presentation. They involve double claims, multiple points under the main reason, and multiple points of opposition. However, notice that the basic design of the presentation is the same. Only some parts, such as the question at issue, have been delayed because of the need to prepare the reader for both claims. Notice also the organizationally useful reference to company events and studies (e.g., the internal presentation in the backing) to support the idea contained in the assumption.

RECOMMENDATION: Increase the use of DMT in the SDLC.

MAIN REASONS: Use of Data Modeling Techniques in the SDLC will enhance the technical capability of our developers.

Use of Data Modeling Techniques in the SDLC will result in improved data accuracy and consistency, minimized redundancy, and identified data stewardship.

Use of Data Modeling Techniques in the SDLC will result in data sharing between business applications.

CLAIMS: Use of the DMT in the SDLC will reduce the company's system development costs.

Use of the DMT in the SDLC will increase productivity of the developers.

REBUTTALS: ...unless the use of Data Modeling Techniques in the SDLC will not enhance the developers' technical ability because project managers will not support a data driven approach to Systems Development.

...unless the use of Data Modeling Techniques in the SDLC will not result in improved data accuracy and consistency, minimized data redundancy, and identified data stewardship because every business application believes they control the ability to change, delete, and update information.

REBUTTALS: ...unless the use of Data Modeling Techniques in the SDLC will not increase developers' productivity because the internship program will keep employees off their normal job for six months.

...unless the use of Data Modeling Techniques in the SDLC will not reduce the cost of Systems Development because it takes longer to develop a business application using a data driven software approach.

ASSUMPTION: Any technique that enhances systems developers' technical capabilities will result in increased productivity. Any technique that results in improved data accuracy and consistency, minimized redundancy, identified data stewardship, and data sharing between business processes will reduce the cost of Systems Development.

BACKING: Richard Nolan presentation to Pacific Bell information Systems personnel, 1 1988. Pacific Bell studies show a 40% improvement in developers' productivity when repeatable software development processes are used. Carnegie Mellon's Software Engineering Institute studies show a 45-60% improvement in developers' productivity as a consequence of repeatable software development processes.

FIGURE B.5

TO: Anonymous

FROM: Bette Smith

SUBJECT: Data Modeling Internship Program

In the last three years, we have consolidated three organizations into the Systems Technology (ST) Department. As a result, we now have over 2000 software developers who support and maintain more than 400 business applications. Most of these applications were developed prior to divestiture, and they support a specific work operation in our Company. Consequently, our applications contain redundant information which cannot be shared with other applications because data is not consistently represented and data stewardship is not clearly understood.

To meet the needs of our new business units, our processes must become more integrated. Our developers must quickly provide our clients with new applications that can provide accurate, timely, and consistent information that can be shared by multiple work groups. At the same time, to maintain our competitive advantage, we must reduce the maintenance costs of our existing applications and minimize the development costs of our new ones. Some managers have great confidence in using data modeling in the SDLC; they think using the technique will increase productivity and reduce our development costs. Others are much more skeptical; they believe using data modeling in the SDLC will reduce productivity and increase costs. Therefore, we must determine whether using data modeling techniques in the SDLC will increase developers' productivity and reduce systems development costs for our Company.

Data modeling is an analysis technique that provides an unbiased understanding of how a business uses information, without consideration for specific processing alternatives. We teach the use and application of data modeling in the SDLC in our Data Modeling Internship Program, which is six months long. During the first three months, interns participate in five weeks of classroom training and fifteen subject area workshops. In addition, they are given presentations on related SDLC topics and they must complete a series of readings from experts in the data analysis field. During the last three months of the program, interns complete an on-the-job data modeling project, and they are assigned to an experienced data modeler who acts as their mentor. At the end of the program, interns return to their work groups and use the data modeling techniques on new and existing business applications.

Data modeling becomes important when we begin to appreciate exactly how this technique works. Developers who use data modeling techniques will enhance their technical capabilities by being able to build "data driven" applications. While traditional systems development techniques focused on building unique business processes, data driven applications work by creating common data stores which can be used by many integrated processes. Developers who use data modeling techniques can quickly create systems with accurate, shareable data because the data model helps them identify data uses, values, representations, and stewards (i.e. owners who control data changes, deletions, and updates). As a consequence, our clients require fewer systems, and our developers are more readily available for new, interesting assignments which require their enhanced technical capabilities.

As a consequence of the way DMT works, the use data modeling techniques in the SDLC will improve data accuracy and consistency, minimize redundancy, and identify data stewards. The data model is a graphic representation with accompanying documentation that specifies the things we keep information about and the way they interact. Characteristics of a data model include standard language/notation, unique data structures, and organized records of data element definitions, rules, stewardship, and business policies. Thus, the model enables communication among business users and systems developers because it captures agreed upon systems requirements and textual definitions of relevant information.

Understanding the further value of DMT depends in part on understanding where the data model information is stored. Data will be stored in our corporate repository, and will be available to other clients and systems developers who analyze the information as a guide for creating integrated business process specifications; hence, the model facilitates data sharing by more than one business application. The data model provides a context within which definition and organization of business objectives is possible; and organization charters and supporting goals can be combined by referencing to the corporate data resources portrayed in the data model. Because data modeling enables data sharing between business applications, business systems planning and prioritization can be optimized. The result will be fewer, more effective systems developed to meet unique business needs, with existing business processes providing essential, shareable data.

Unfortunately, some managers do not believe data modeling techniques will improve the technical capabilities of our developers. These managers do not believe in a data driven systems development approach, so their developers do not use data modeling techniques. However, Richard Nolan, a frequent contributor to the *Harvard Business Review*, stresses that data processing needs in the future will shift orientation from "process" to "data" as our need for information becomes more complex. We are already seeing this happen as our business units identify their diverse business application requirements. Data modeling is an effective technique that enables the transformation from process to data driven systems.

Planners in our new business units are also skeptical of data modeling techniques. They question whether we can improve data accuracy and consistency or control redundancy because every business application believes they can change, delete, and update information. We agree with the planners. We cannot insure data management and control without a clear understanding of who stewards specific data elements in our business. By using the data model as a focal point for capturing business information and rules, the data modeler acts as an unbiased facilitator who brings together business planners and resolves issues of ownership and control of information. As an added benefit, the data modeler can help business planners identify data elements no longer essential to our business.

Other managers do not believe productivity will increase by using data modeling techniques in the SDLC because the Data Modeling Internship Program keeps interns off their jobs for six months. While the start-up training time is extensive, studies have shown that the use of data modeling techniques in the SDLC results in improved system designs that optimize database performance. For example, studies in our own company as well as those conducted by Carnegie Mellon's Software Engineering Institute, show that developers' productivity is improved by at least 40% when repeatable software processes, like data modeling, are used in the SDLC. Hence, future application and database development will be streamlined when we use data modeling techniques.

Finally, many people believe the use of data modeling techniques in the SDLC will not reduce the cost of systems development. They cite recent examples of projects which have taken longer because developers used data modeling techniques. Whenever a new method or technique is introduced, projects often experience increased costs and time delays. However, as people become familiar with data modeling techniques as well as the benefits of sharing information, they quickly see the value these techniques have in eliminating nonessential business processes. By taking advantage of data sharing, developers can reduce programming time, stop redundant database development, and minimize data reconciliation efforts. As a result, our costs for systems development and maintenance will decrease.

Today, we find ourselves operating at a time of increasing competition and complexity. Fragmentation of corporate data resources prevents us from providing flexible, timely systems which can support new business needs and opportunities. Our future success hinges on the quality and availability of information for all levels of management. By using data modeling techniques in our SDLC, we can increase our developers' productivity which will help them create timely, efficient business applications. Development costs will decrease because these new applications will enable data sharing and consistency across integrated business processes.

If we don't use data modeling techniques in our SDLC, we must continue on our present path of developing an ever increasing number of work group specific applications. In addition, eighty percent of our current developers work on maintaining existing applications. This percentage has been increasing steadily in the last ten years. If we do not introduce new techniques that improve our developers' productivity, our maintenance costs will continually increase.

With the introduction of data modeling in our SDLC, we can improve the productivity of our developers and thereby create effective, easily maintained systems and reduce our overall systems development costs. Because such results are so important, I recommend we begin the technology transfer of data modeling techniques to our developers by implementing the Data Modeling Internship Program, effective April 1, 1999.

SAMPLE DOCUMENTS

Revision

The documents in this section consist of five writers' attempts at applying the material covered in the last five chapters of this book. Each writer has provided an original document, a revision, and a list of reasons for the revision. Sentences in the original document are numbered, and the writer's reasons for the revision include numbers that match those in the original.

These papers are not offered as perfect examples but as good examples of a particular approach to revision, one that emphasizes conciseness, word choice, word order, punctuation, and grammar. They should invite productive discussion. Although the papers in this section may also demonstrate principles covered elsewhere in this book, they are not offered specifically as an application of them.

In most cases, writers have agreed to publication of their names, positions, and company affiliations. This information is offered to provide each writing sample with a context that includes information about the industry and the writer's place within the organization.

The beginning of each document identifies the writer, and the writer's current company and position. It also provides information about the number of words in the original document and the number of words in the revision. These numbers should not be taken too seriously. They are offered only as general indicators of changes in conciseness.

Revision

Borland Mailing List

Writer: Kenneth Donnelly

Position: Senior Management Engineer

Company: Bay Area Rapid Transit District

Total Number of Words in the Original: 206
Total Number of Words in the Revision: 107

ORIGINAL MEMORANDUM

B O R L A N D
1850 Green Hills Road
Santa Cruz, CA
RE: (1) Borland Strategic Direction Presentation

Ladies & Gentlemen:

(2) One of our Computer Coordinators, Jane Jones, recently received an invitation for a preview of your firm's upcoming Windows products, as well as ObjectVision 2.0. (3) BART has recently added several additional people to its Information Systems' staff that would have liked to have participated in this presentation; specifically John Smith and myself.

(4) Our Information Systems' staff is currently evaluating Windows 3.0, ObjectVision, and several other software packages for BART's future needs/direction and would benefit from this type of preview. (5) We have been very impressed with the performance offered by the ObjectVision product and are excited about the upcoming release of version 2.0.

(6) Please add John Smith and myself, Kenneth Donnelly, to your mailing list so we can participate in upcoming presentations. (7) The following address should be used:

John Smith
BAY AREA RAPID TRANSIT
800 Madison Street, IBB5
Oakland, CA 94607

Kenneth Donnelly
BAY AREA RAPID TRANSIT
800 Madison Street, IBB5
Oakland, CA 94607

(8) If possible, we would like to preview a copy of ObjectVision 2.0 when it is available. (9) Please feel free to contact myself at (510) 464-7508, or John at (510) 464-6314, to arrange a preview.

Sincerely,

Kenneth P. Donnelly
Senior Management Engineer

REVISED MEMORANDUM

B O R L A N D
1850 Green Hills Road
Santa Cruz, CA 95060
RE: Borland Mailing List

Ladies/Gentlemen:

Please add John Smith and me to Borland's mailing list. We want to be included in presentations and product previews. This will help the BART Information Systems department better plan its direction.

We would like to preview a copy of ObjectVision 2.0. John or I can be contacted at (510) 464-7508 to arrange the preview. We are impressed with ObjectVision 1.0 and are excited about version 2.0.

Use the following address for John and me:

BAY AREA RAPID TRANSIT
800 Madison Street, IBB5
Oakland, CA 94607

Sincerely,

Kenneth P. Donnelly
Senior Management Engineer

REASONS FOR REVISING THE MEMORANDUM

1. Change this reference. The reference is misleading. The memo does not deal with the presentation, but with adding John Smith and Ken Donnelly to Borland's mailing list. The reference should be "Borland Mailing List."

2. Delete this sentence. The subject of this letter is adding names to Borland's mailing list. Sentence (6) should be used as the opening sentence, with corrections. By deleting this sentence, the writer can avoid the use of "recently" as the reader should know when the invitation was sent.

3. Delete this sentence. This sentence is not a part of the letter's subject. By deleting this sentence, the writer can avoid the unnecessary use of the word "recent" and the redundant use of "additional."

4. The content of this sentence should be changed and made a part of a sentence following the subject. A reference can be made to "presentations." The technical jargon phrases, "evaluating" and "software packages," should be removed. The redundant use of "currently" and "several" should be omitted. Delete the incorrect use of the slash, "/", and the redundant "direction." "Type of preview" is abstract; change to "preview."

5. Change this sentence. Eliminate the technical jargon "product." This sentence is longer than necessary to convey the subject. It should be reduced and follow sentence (8).

6. Delete the writer's name and change "myself" to "me." Move this sentence to the opening paragraph. Use the compound subject "so we can participate in upcoming presentations" as a subject of the following sentence.

7. Delete the redundant addresses. Identify the address once. (It is different from the one included on the letterhead).

8. Move this sentence to the second paragraph. Delete the prepositional chain "If possible." Omit the redundant phrase "when it is available." ("Preview" is a term used by Borland.)

9. Delete the prepositional chain "feel free to."

Singular Achievement Award

Writer: Crystal Elledge

Position: Program Manager

Company: Pacific Bell

Total Number of Words in the Original: 225
Total Number of Words in the Revision: 189

ORIGINAL MEMORANDUM

TO: Executive Director

FROM: Director

SUBJECT: SINGULAR ACHIEVEMENT AWARD

(1) I recommend that my team of Technical Directors receive a Singular Achievement Award in the amount of $500 each. (2) Team members are: Laura Doe, Ed Smith, Jane Roe, Jack Sprat, Mike Mighty, Pauline Peril, and Sue Moe.

(3) This award is in acknowledgment of the team's focus on process improvement as the road to cost containment. (4) As a team, they decided that the most appropriate approach to meeting budget constraints was to reduce the district administrative overhead. (5) They analyzed the structure and function of the district and recommended that technical teams be reorganized in a way that reduced Technical Director positions from eight to four. (6) This reduced the salary requirements by approximately $250,000. (7) This recommendation has been implemented.

(8) This team has role modeled the type of leadership and risk taking that Pacific Bell should nurture. (9) They took the risk of eliminating four of their own jobs because it was the best solution for the business. (10) Those positions remaining have greater complexity and large spans of control, increasing their personal risk. (11) Despite this increased load, this team has volunteered to be self managed for a period of time following my retirement.

(12) This team has earned recognition for their leadership in process improvement, despite personal risk.

REVISED MEMORANDUM

TO: Executive Director

FROM: Director

SUBJECT: SINGULAR ACHIEVEMENT AWARD

I recommend my Technical Directors for a Singular Achievement Award of $500 each. Team members are Laura Doe, Ed Smith, Jane Roe, Jack Sprat, Mike Mighty, Pauline Peril, and Sue Moe.

This award would acknowledge the team's focus on containing costs by improving processes. As a team, they decided the most appropriate expense to reduce was the district administrative overhead. After analyzing the structure and function of the district, they recommended reorganizing technical teams, reducing Technical Director positions from eight to four. This recommendation has been implemented, saving approximately $250,000.

Pacific Bell should nurture the type of leadership and risk taking exemplified by this team. They risked elimination of four of their jobs because it was the best solution for the business. The remaining Technical Directors face greater personal risk from increased job complexity and spans of control. Despite this increased load, this team has volunteered to manage themselves for a time following my retirement.

This team has earned recognition for their leadership in process improvement, despite personal risk.

REASONS FOR REVISING THE MEMORANDUM

1. "Team of Technical Directors" is redundant. Replace with "Technical Directors." Delete the prepositional chain "in the amount of."
2. No change.
3. The phrase "is in acknowledgment of" is a hidden verb. Replace it with "would acknowledge." "Process improvement" is a jargon term and a hid-

den verb. Replace this with "improving processes." The phrase "the road to" is a cliché. Delete it. "Cost containment" is both jargon and hidden verb. Replace it with "containing costs" and reorder the sentence for clarity.

4. The "that" is unnecessary. Delete it. "Approach to meeting budget constraints" is jargon and a very wordy way of saying "reduce expenses."

5. "In a way that" is a prepositional chain. Delete it.

6. "This" vaguely refers to the recommendation, which is the subject of the following sentence. Combine this and the following sentence, reversing order to clarify the cause and effect relationship. "Reduced the salary requirements by" can be replaced by the clearer "saving."

7. Combine this sentence with the previous one. See notes for sentence 6.

8. "Role modeled" is jargon. Replace it with "exemplified." Then reorder the sentence to place emphasis on the subject, Pacific Bell.

9. "Took the risk of" is a hidden verb; change it to "risked." Changing the object from "risk" to "elimination" gives the "it" in the subordinate clause a stronger reference. The best solution for the business was the elimination of the jobs, not the risk. "Their" and "own" are redundant.

10. "Increasing their personal risk" is a dangling modifier that appears to modify "the positions." Reword the sentence to establish the Technical Directors as the ones facing increased risk.

11. "Self managed" is jargon. Replace this "with manage themselves." "A period of time" is redundant. Use "time."

12. "Process improvement," as noted above, is jargon.

Foodmaker Steak Fajita Seasoning

Writer: Teresa Supnet-Rosa

Position: Account Manager

Company: McCormick & Co., Inc.

Total Number of Words in the Original: 344
Total Number of Words in the Revision: 245

ORIGINAL MEMORANDUM

TO: Customer Service & Material Control

FROM: Teresa Supnet-Rosa

RE: Foodmaker Steak Fajita Seasoning, F39259

(1) Foodmaker, Inc. (FMI) has informed me that they will be expanding the testing of their Steak Fajita melt to 16 stores, commencing in mid October. (2) This, in turn, necessitates production of seasoning, F39259, for their use.

(3) An initial batch of marinated meat will be produced the week of August 20th which will require approximately 200 pounds of seasoning. (4) A second production on the week of September 3rd will require 250 pounds of product. (5) Their estimated weekly seasoning usage will be 125 pounds (for the actual market expansion) beginning in early October.

(6) I have checked the inventory for unique raw materials used in this seasoning and have found that we have an adequate amount to produce seasoning for their August 20th and September 3rd needs. (7) These raw materials are F&C items which have been brought in within the past three months. (8) The R#, Lot#, and location of these items are on the attached sheet. (9) Please check to assure these raw materials are in fact still in inventory. (10) Albeit we apparently have these same ingredients with different lot numbers in inventory, they are at least a year old. (11) FMI requires us to use "fresh" flavors in our upcoming production. (12) The old items will be worked off at a later date.

(13) At this time, I believe that we should bring in enough of the F&C flavors to cover us for the months of October and November. (14) As the lead time for these ingredients can be quite lengthy, it is necessary to order these items ASAP.

(15) FMI has told me that Choice Meat Company (CMC) will be placing the orders for the seasoning. (16) Since CMC has a tendency to order product at the last minute, Tom Smith and I will work together to minimize this occurrence.

(17) I will keep you updated with any additional information as it becomes available to me.

(18) If you have any questions, please see me.

REVISED MEMORANDUM

TO: Customer Service & Material Control

FROM: Teresa Supnet-Rosa

RE: Foodmaker Steak Fajita Seasoning, F39259

Foodmaker, Inc. (FMI) informed me that the test market of its Steak Fajita Melt will expand to 16 stores beginning in mid October. To help FMI prepare for market expansion, we need to supply their processor, Choice Meat Company (CMC), with 200 pounds of Steak Fajita Marinade Seasoning #F39259 by August 20th. An additional 250 pounds of product is required by September 3rd. By early October, CMC's estimated weekly seasoning use increases to 125 pounds. Since CMC often requires us to deliver products within 24 to 48 hours of its order, Tom Smith and I will work with CMC to prevent this occurrence.

I checked inventory for the unique raw materials used in the seasoning and found an adequate amount for the August 20th and September 3rd production. The items' R numbers, lot numbers, and location are provided on the attached sheet. Please confirm the material amounts correspond with the lot numbers since computer inventory variances are common. These items are F&C ingredients purchased within the last three months. Although the same items delivered approximately one year ago are available, FMI requires us to use three to six-month old ingredients. We will determine the disposition of the old material later. To meet October and November production needs, please order the appropriate amount of F&C flavors this week.

I will inform you of additional information as the project progresses.

REASONS FOR REVISING THE MEMORANDUM

1. "Testing" is jargon for "test market"; omit it and replace with the common form.

2. Delete this sentence because of redundancy. See (3).

3. This wordy sentence implies FMI's preparation for the expanded test market and my company's involvement. The sentence is too vague. Move information about processor in (15) into this sentence, since it is a part of the preparation process.

4. "A second production" is too wordy; change to "an additional." Prepositional chain "on the week of" change to "by September 3rd."

5. Word choice: "usage" is incorrect; replace with "use." "Will be" contains a hidden verb; replace with "is." The phrase in parentheses is redundant; omit it. Move sentence (16) after (5) for continuity of thought. Correct (16) by removing dilute verb "has a tendency" and replacing with "often requires." Complete corrections by omitting "together," which is redundant, and "minimize," which is an incorrect use of the word in this phrase; replace with "prevent."

6. Move sentence (8) after (6) for continuity. Sentence (9) follows (6) and (8) also for continuity. Since "inventory" indicates the <u>current</u> list of items, (9) contradicts this definition. Correct the sentence to inform reader of the variance problem, and justify the need to confirm information.

7. Change "raw materials" to "items" for brevity. Replace "past" with "last" for correct usage.

8. 8. & 9. See (6).

10. Omit "apparently have" because it is nonsense; you either have or you don't have something. Also ingredients that are "at least one year old" will obviously carry a "different lot number." The phrase "in our upcoming production" is unnecessary, since this is what ingredients are used for.

11. See (10).

12. Correct the sentence by replacing jargon "will be worked off" with "disposition."

13. "At this time" is nonsense; omit it. Omit "I believe at this time we should order"; the phrase is wordy, and an indirect way to ask the reader to do something. (14) & (15) See (3). (16) See (5). (17) The sentence is corrected for clarity. (18) Omit. If the readers question anything, they will call me.

Employee Liaison Coordinators

Writer: Pam Harris

Position: Employer Liaison

Company: Kaiser Permanente

Total Number of Words in the Original: 613
Total Number of Words in the Revision: 346

ORIGINAL MEMORANDUM

TO: Chiefs of Psychiatry

FROM: Signature

SUBJECT: Employee Liaison Coordinators (1)

(2) The purpose of this memo is to outline a proposed way in which the employee liaison coordinator can be useful to the Mental Health and ADAP departments throughout the Region. (3) As this is a new position, there is hopefully still some flexibility in defining their duties and responsibilities.

(4) For the employee liaison coordinator to truly be the most helpful to our department, they must be perceived as, and in some way in reality be a part of the department. (5) To this end, a certain percentage, i.e., half-time, of the position should be allocated specifically to the Mental Health and ADAP departments, and for this period of time they should answer to the Chiefs of Psychiatry and ADAP, much as they now do to the PIC for other responsibilities at the medical center. (6) It would be extremely desirable for them to attend the staff meetings of the Mental Health and/or ADAP departments, so that they can be intimately connected with the everyday workings of the departments as well as know the individual department members. (7) This more intimate relationship would help them in interpreting contractual language, in a way that is consistent with the understanding of Mental Health and ADAP departments, to employers as problems were presented to them. (8) It would be desirable, if feasible, for the coordinators to actually have an office, at least part-time, within these departments. (9) At staff meetings, they could act as a conduit to express to staff members general and specific concerns of employers around access to services.

(10) The employer liaison coordinator can also be helpful as far as tracking patients is concerned. (11) This could include calling specific patients that miss ADAP groups, specifically those that are management referrals. (12) It could also include keeping departmental statistics on individual patients for EAP's around physician management referrals, and more general statistics that could be funneled through the Chiefs of ADAP to provide to employers on a regional basis. (13) I think overall one of the more important roles of employer liaison coordinator would be to track management referrals and make sure that the "ball isn't dropped" on these patients and that employers are continuing to receive information they need as those patients progress through our program, and make sure that they not disappear from treatment or get lost in a way that gives the employers the impression that we are not responsive to their needs.

(14) The employer liaison coordinator's part of the work with EAP's and employers would be helping clarify policy issues and what is available to people around specific patients, as long as it can be done in a way that does not directly involve clinical material about the patient. They may clarify what sort of clinical information is appropriate for Kaiser to share with employers, and clarify how this information will be communicated to employers. (15) The employer liaison coordinator could act as an ombudsman for concerns that can be addressed and enlisting the assistance of the Chief of Psychiatry and ADAP as needed, much as Patient Assistance does with specific patient concerns.

(16) In general, the employer liaison coordinator could act as an interface between employers and EAP's in our department in a way that will give them a specific person to contact, hopefully a friendly voice and maybe a face they know, and that gives a sense of Kaiser as a large, rich program but with a more personal face on it. If done correctly, this will allow providers to spend more of their time providing clinical care and communicating clinical information in a more efficient manner to employers, and yet remain attuned to EAP and employers' concerns.

REVISED MEMORANDUM

TO: Chiefs of Psychiatry

FROM: For Signature

SUBJECT: Proposed Role of Employer Liaison in Mental Health and
              ADAP Departments

For the employer liaison to help our department, this person becomes, in some way, a part of the department. A given percentage of the position, i.e. half-time, should be allocated to the Mental Health and ADAP departments, and for this allocated period, the liaison should answer to the Chiefs of Mental Health and ADAP instead of the PIC.

To become an intimate part of the daily work and staff of the department, this person should attend staff meetings. This intimate relationship will help them interpret our contract to employers and allow them to present to staff general and specific employer concerns. And, if feasible, the liaison should have an office, at least part time, in the department.

The employer liaison can help us track patients by calling management referrals who miss ADAP groups. The liaison can also keep department statistics for EAP's on individual physician management referrals, and general statistics, at the discretion of the Chiefs of ADAP, for employers throughout the region. This is an important role. It would help us assure that employers receive all of the information they need, and that our patients do not disappear from treatment. The liaison can clarify policy issues and available services for specific patients for EAP's and employers, as long as it does not directly involve clinical material about the patient. The liaison may clarify what clinical information is appropriate to share with employers and how this information is communicated. Overall, the liaison would act as an ombudsman to our employers, responding to concerns as much as Patient Relations does with specific patients.

The employer liaison would be a single contact, a friendly voice, and a familiar face between our department and employers and EAP's. The liaison would present Kaiser as a large, rich program with a personal face. If done correctly, this will allow providers more time to provide clinical care and communicate clinical information and still be aware of EAP and employer concerns.

REASONS FOR REVISING THE MEMORANDUM

1. Incorrect and redundant title: the position is a liaison, not a coordinator of liaisons. Omit sentence (2) and add to the subject line of memo.

2. & 3. Omit line (2) since it has now been added to subject and does not need to be repeated in the opening paragraph of text, and (3) now seems redundant and not needed for the meaning of the text. The subject states new position and proposed role, and this suggests that the position is still flexible.

3. Hidden verb: change "to truly be the most helpful" hidden verb to "to help." Drop "be perceived as" because that is not being proposed in the following text. Drop "in reality" because it's redundant. You can't "be" without being in reality.

4. Drop "to this end" because it's assumed and a cliché.

5. "It would be desirable" is an expletive and hidden verb.

6. Drop "more." Hidden verb: change "in interpreting contractual language" to "interpret our contract."

7. & 9. Change order of sentences to connect (9) with previous discussion of attendance at staff meetings, and then structure as part of sentence (7).

8. Hidden verb: "be helpful as far as tracking patients is concerned" is changed to "help us track."

9. Combine with sentence (10) for conciseness.

10. Hidden verb and expletive: change "It could also include keeping departmental statistics" to "keep department statistics."

11. Cliché: "ball isn't dropped." This is redundant to repeat track management referrals, etc. The writer has just discussed referrals, so say "this is an important role."

Kalok 3200 Address Mark System

Writer: Michael Hassel

Position: Project Director

Company: Kalok Corporation

Total Number of Words in the Original: 941
Total Number of Words in the Revision: 746

Note: This sample consists of only the opening section (the first four paragraphs) of the original and longer technical document.

ORIGINAL SPECIFICATION

(1) The Kalok 3200 drive uses a 1,7 data code and a split sector servo scheme. (2) To implement this scheme with a minimum of hardware and micro code overhead the drive uses a soft sector data format. (3) The decoder has the intelligence to find a sector when address mark enable is asserted. (4) It can correctly sync itself to the data after read gate is asserted. (5) It can also write an address mark if address mark enable is asserted during a write. 6) This spec describes the algorithms used to implement the Address Mark detect, Bit sync, encode and decode functions.

(7) When the controller is neither reading from nor writing to the disk it does not keep track of where the sectors are on the disk. (8) Before the controller either reads or writes it must first find the proper sector. (9) To do this the controller starts by looking for an Address Mark.(10) Address Mark is a unique pattern written on the disk that violates the code's rules, in this case the pattern violates the bandwidth of the code by writing two 7 "O's" patterns followed by two 11 "O's" patterns. (11) The controller asserts Address Mark Enable asynchronously with the disk and the Address Mark Detect circuitry (AMD) must find an Address Mark by searching the incoming data the AM pattern. (12) The algorithm to do the detection is shown in figure 1.

(13) The AMD circuit is reset by the Address Mark Enable signal (AMEN). (14) When the controller asserts AMEN the circuit begins to look for the 7 "O's" pattern. (15) A counter counts Reference clocks and looks for 6 or more "O's" in a row. (16) When it sees the 6 "O's" pattern it begins

the AM Detect sequence. (17) The same counter that counted 6 "O's" now looks for 9 or more "O's" in a row. (18) If it sees the 9 "O's" pattern AMD is set and will stay set until AMEN is asserted. (19) A watch-dog counter counts data bits and will reset the sequence if the 9 "O's" pattern is not seen before the sixth data bit.

(20) 1,7 code uses both phase and frequency to encode data. (21) The code converts three possible code positions into two data bits. (22) The same patterns will decode differently if the bits are grouped differently. (23) Therefore we need to synchronize the data at the code bit level. (24) This is done by writing a pattern that would be ambiguous if the phase were unknown, but because we know the pattern that was written we can block the data to be correctly decoded. (25) This same field is used to sync the PLL for the Data Separator.

REVISED SPECIFICATION

The Kalok 3200 drive uses a 1,7 code and a split sector servo. The drive uses a soft sector data format to implement the servo with a minimum of hardware and micro code. The decoder finds sectors when address mark enable is asserted and correctly synchronizes the data after read gate is asserted. The encoder can write address marks. This spec describes the algorithms that detect Address Mark, synchronize bits, and encode and decode data.

When the controller is neither reading nor writing, it does not know where the sectors are. Therefore, it must find the proper sector. First, the controller looks for an Address Mark, a unique pattern written on the disk. It violates the code's rules by violating the bandwidth of the code by writing two seven "O's" patterns followed by two eleven "O's" patterns. The controller asserts Address Mark Enable asynchronously, and the Address Mark Detect circuitry (AMD) searches for the AM pattern. Figure 1 shows the detection algorithm.

The Address Mark Enable signal (AMEN) resets the AMD circuit. When the controller asserts AMEN, the circuit looks for the 7 "O's" pattern. A counter looks for six or more reference clocks without a "1," and it then begins the AM Detect sequence. The same counter now looks for nine or more "O's" in a row and then sets AMD. A watch-dog counter will reset the sequence if the nine "O's" pattern is not seen before the sixth data bit.

1,7 code converts three possible code positions into two data bits using both phase and frequency to encode data. The same patterns will decode differently if the bits are grouped differently. Therefore, we need to synchronize the data at the code bit level. By writing a pattern that would be ambiguous if the phrase were unknown, we can block the data correctly. This same field is used to sync the PLL for the Data Separator.

REASONS FOR REVISING THE SPECIFICATION

1. Omit title, since it is included in the opening sentence. The word "data" is redundant and "scheme" is imprecise.

2. This is a periodic sentence; change the clauses. The scheme is talking about the servo, so this should say "servo." "Overhead" says nothing; delete it.

3. Hidden verb in "has the intelligence to find." Make this "finds."

5. "It" is the encoder, so this should say "encoder." "During a Write" is redundant.

7. "From . . . to the disk" is redundant because it can read or write no where else. Hidden verb in "keep track of," can be changed to "Know." Insert a comma for the introductory clause.

8. "Before" makes "first" redundant.

9. "To do this," is also redundant.

10. "In this case" can be replaced by "this." **(11).** "With the disk" is redundant. "Must find an Address mark by searching" hides the verb "searches."

12. Make "is shown" active so that figure 1 clearly shows it.

13. Make "reset" active to show that the AMEN is acting on the AMD.

14. "Begins to look" can be shortened to "looks."

15. "A counter counts" is redundant. Sentence 16 can become a clause, and this allows "when it sees . . ." to become "then."

17. "That counted 6 "0's" is not necessary to identify the counter. **(19).** "Counts data bits" is redundant. Write out numbers to avoid confusion with "0."

20. Was combined with 21.

23. Insert a comma for the introductory "therefore."

24. "But because we know the pattern . . ." is redundant.

INDEX

CPSIA information can be obtained at www.ICGtesting.com
Printed in the USA
266867BV00004B/9-86/P